Also Available from Routledge
Eye On Education
(www.routledge.com/eyeoneducation)

Reinvigorating Classroom Climate: Everyday Strategies to Inspire Teachers and Students
Maurice J. Elias

The Playbook for Self-Directed Learning: A Leader's Guide to School Transformation and Student Agency
Tyler S. Thigpen, Caleb Collier, Amber Bryant and Brittney Toles

Harnessing Formative Data for K-12 Leaders: Real-time Approaches to School Improvement
Stepan Mekhitarian

Radical Principals: A Blueprint for Long-Term Equity and Stability at School
Michael S. Gaskell

Abolitionist Leadership in Schools: Undoing Systemic Injustice Through Communally Conscious Education
Robert Harvey

Leading the Next Era of Public Education

A Roadmap for Personalized, Student-Centered, and Equitable Schools

Taylor P. Wrye

NEW YORK AND LONDON

Designed cover image: Getty Images

First published 2026
by Routledge
605 Third Avenue, New York, NY 10158

and by Routledge
4 Park Square, Milton Park, Abingdon, Oxon, OX14 4RN

Routledge is an imprint of the Taylor & Francis Group, an informa business

© 2026 Taylor P. Wrye

The right of Taylor P. Wrye to be identified as author of this work has been asserted in accordance with sections 77 and 78 of the Copyright, Designs and Patents Act 1988.

All rights reserved. No part of this book may be reprinted or reproduced or utilised in any form or by any electronic, mechanical, or other means, now known or hereafter invented, including photocopying and recording, or in any information storage or retrieval system, without permission in writing from the publishers.

For Product Safety Concerns and Information please contact our EU representative GPSR@taylorandfrancis.com. Taylor & Francis Verlag GmbH, Kaufingerstraße 24, 80331 München, Germany.

Trademark notice: Product or corporate names may be trademarks or registered trademarks, and are used only for identification and explanation without intent to infringe.

ISBN: 978-1-041-23912-3 (hbk)
ISBN: 978-1-041-23911-6 (pbk)
ISBN: 978-1-003-73905-0 (ebk)

DOI: 10.4324/9781003739050

Typeset in Palatino
by Deanta Global Publishing Services, Chennai, India

Leading the Next Era of Public Education

Leading the Next Era of Public Education presents a comprehensive framework for transforming any school or district in our rapidly evolving, technology-rich world. Cognitive bias, institutional routines, and compliance cultures keep schools tied to what is familiar over what is effective. Are these legacy structures effectively serving teachers and students in the age of artificial intelligence (AI) and extended reality (XR)? This book offers a practical roadmap for executive leaders, governing bodies, and school-level teams seeking to transition from incremental fixes to system redesign. The book aligns strategy, operations, and instruction to support districts in delivering equitable, student-centered outcomes.

Chapters include a wealth of fresh ideas in the following areas:

- **Leadership and governance**: mission clarity, transparent communication, adaptive scheduling, strategic planning, and community engagement
- **System architecture**: integrated technology ecosystems, interoperability, cybersecurity, data quality, and sustainable budgeting
- **Teaching and learning**: asset-based pedagogy, competency-based progression, Universal Design for Learning, and responsible AI integration
- **Equity and accountability**: inclusive design routines, digital equity benchmarks, ethics-centered feedback, and public reporting tied to student impact
- And much more!

Readers will leave with a coherent, implementable vision for an adaptive, equitable, student-centered public education system that replaces legacy structures that no longer serve all learners and prioritizes mastery, agency, and well-being.

Taylor P. Wrye, Ed.D., is Director of Technology and Innovation for Nauset Public Schools, MA, and a National Certified Educational Technology Leader. He earned his doctorate from Drexel University, where his research focused on equity in digital learning. A former middle-school principal, Dr Wrye applies restorative principles of trust and equity to guide systems-level change in education. His work focuses on AI and XR integration, digital equity, and student data privacy. He serves on national committees like the Consortium for School Networking Innovative Technology Committee and advises policymakers on the future of K–12 educational technology.

To my family. Your brilliance, curiosity, and unwavering support inspired this work and the belief that something better is possible.

Contents

Introduction: It Begins Here   xi

SECTION 1
The Need for Change 1

  1 Legacy without Progress: The Weight of Yesterday on
    Today's Schools 3

  2 Familiarity over Function: How Inertia
    Undermines Innovation 25

  3 The Great Pivot: Rethinking Education after COVID-19 ... 33

SECTION 2
**Equity by Design: Building Personalized Pathways
for All Learners** 55

  4 Defining Personalized Learning:
    Foundations for the Future 57

  5 Beyond Smart: How AI and XR Are Reshaping the
    Architecture of Learning 74

  6 From Instructor to Architect: Transforming the Role
    of Educators... 101

SECTION 3
**The Architecture of Resistance: Systems, Structures,
and the Challenge of Reform** 119

  7 From Instructor to Architect: Transforming the Role
    of Educators... 121

  8 Modernizing Infrastructure and Governance 131

  9 Advancing Equity in the Age of AI 140

SECTION 4
Redrawing the Boundaries: The Evolving Institutional Function of Public Schools 163

10 The Institutional Anchor: Rethinking the Purpose of Public Schools. 165

11 Overextended: The Operational Burden of Dual Mandates in Education 188

12 Reimagining Support Systems through Innovation and Partnership. 207

SECTION 5
The Screen-Time Paradox: Public Anxiety and Pedagogical Potential. 213

13 The Anti-Screen Narrative. 215

14 Prioritizing Relationships in the Digital Age 229

15 Technology That Listens 236

SECTION 6
A Roadmap for Transformation: From Vision to Systemic Change. 249

16 Beyond Readiness: Designing the Foundations of Transformational Education 255

17 Transformation by Design: Rethinking How Change Begins 264

18 Embedding Innovation: From Initial Change to Systemwide Transformation 287

19 A New Policy Blueprint: Creating Conditions for Scalable Transformation. 299

    The Vision for the Future. 309
    Appendix 319

Introduction

It Begins Here

This book has been a long time coming. For years, I have held the conviction that something essential is missing from the way we talk about, design, and deliver public education in the United States. My motivation is not rooted in dissatisfaction, but in a growing awareness of what education could become. I recognize that many educators, schools, and districts are engaged in remarkable work, and that meaningful efforts to innovate are underway. Yet these efforts are often isolated, inconsistent, and lacking in the broad systemic support necessary to transform the broader structure of American public education. It is increasingly clear that the current model of teaching and learning does not adequately meet the needs of today's students and is too slow to anticipate the demands of a rapidly changing world. This realization compelled me to ask more difficult questions, challenge entrenched assumptions, and begin writing. I believe many share this sense of urgency and commitment to change but remain uncertain about where to begin or how to bring that change to life.

I initially titled this project *A Failure to Launch*, echoing the working title of my doctoral dissertation. Like many early-stage doctoral students, I believed I was on the verge of uncovering a transformative breakthrough in digital learning, one that would fundamentally reshape the US education system and then the world. Instead, I was rightfully humbled. Rather than identifying the golden ticket or a singular solution, I encountered a landscape defined by complexity, contradiction, and constraint. Yet within that complexity, I also glimpsed the immense potential of what education could become. During my dissertation proposal, one committee member offered advice that has stayed with me. After I presented the bold and transformative title *A Failure to Launch*, he responded, "Save that title, not for the dissertation, but for your first keynote or better yet, your first book. That is a title that will surely get everyone's attention." That moment resonated not only because it was memorable but also because it revealed a deeper truth. The barriers to innovation in public education are not primarily technical or legislative. They are human. They are rooted in tradition, misaligned incentives, untapped potential, and the fear of the unknown.

As this book took shape, I realized *A Failure to Launch* no longer reflected the message I wanted to share. While the system has produced missteps and misguided reforms, what administrators, educators, and students accomplish every day is far from failure. This book is not focused on shortcomings. It invites readers to reimagine what public education can become. We have the capacity to grow, think differently, and reimagine public education on our terms. The title *Leading the Next Era of Public Education: A Roadmap for Personalized, Student-Centered, and Equitable Schools* reflects this evolution. It marks a shift from critique to possibility, from inertia to action, and from resignation to redesign.

What might that redesign look like? Picture an education system fully redesigned for the mid-21st century, where learning environments are structured to meet the needs of all learners by default, eliminating the need for individual accommodations. In this model, students explore ancient Rome through virtual reality, dissect a heart through immersive simulation, and collaborate globally on projects or research. Real-time translation and captioning ensure that the language barrier is a thing of the past, enabling seamless communication across auditory and visual platforms. The system adapts to each student's needs, interests, and pace. Artificial intelligence (AI) supports differentiated instruction, creativity is intentionally nurtured, and learning is no longer confined by outdated curricula, rigid schedules, or unequal access to resources. Education is organized around mastery, relevance, and flexibility, rather than the time-bound models of another era.

This is not a futuristic fantasy. It is the real and tangible promise of personalized learning powered by modern technology. In an era defined by exponential technological advancement and a rapidly evolving global economy, this vision is not optional; it is essential.

Yet the US public education system remains tied to outdated models of schooling, leaving too many students unprepared for the complexities and uncertainties of the middle 21st century.

This book argues that personalized, interdisciplinary learning that is equipped with thoughtful, equitable applications of technology is no longer a pedagogical preference. It is a systemic necessity. The growing gap between what schools teach and the competencies students need for the future workforce demands a bold reimagining of public education (Brynjolfsson & McAfee, 2014; Levy & Murnane, 2013). As Hatch et al. (2021) asserted, "We are preparing students for an unpredictable future with an educational system that was designed for a world that no longer exists."

Calls for educational reform are not new. For decades, education scholars and practitioners have urged a move away from industrial-era models toward systems that foster creativity, adaptability, and lifelong learning. As early as 2005, Friedman stated in his book *The World Is Flat 2.0* that students were being trained for jobs that had not yet been invented, using tools that had not yet been developed. Nearly two decades later, we remain mired in the same debates yet face even greater urgency at a more accelerated pace.

One of the most persistent obstacles to educational change originates not in policy chambers, but at the family dinner table. It is our collective cultural nostalgia for the so-called "good old days" of schooling. As Lehmann and Chase (2015) observed, education must be designed for the world as it could be, not recreated as it once was. Public discourse remains anchored to outdated sentiments such as, "Students today should learn cursive, just like we did," despite the increasing relevance of digital literacy, computational thinking, and AI fluency as foundational competencies (Selwyn, 2019; Wing, 2017). In an era where digital signatures have largely replaced handwritten ones, clinging to cursive as an essential skill underscores the widening gap between tradition and the realities of the digitally mediated world.

This book challenges that nostalgia. It offers a framework for moving forward, beyond the current educational landscape and toward an educational system designed for the world today's students will inherit. Children entering kindergarten today will spend their lives in the middle to late 21st century, not the 20th century, and our schools must reflect that future rather than replicate the past.

This generational divide is not abstract. I have seen it firsthand. As an elder Millennial, I often remind students, half-jokingly, that I am older than Google. They laugh in disbelief. When I hold up a floppy disk, their amusement shifts to confusion until they realize it is the "save" icon on their screens. I tell them stories about connecting to the internet through a phone line, using AOL, and waiting while the modem screeched and buzzed, only to be disconnected when someone picked up the landline phone in another room. We did not have the entire knowledge base of humanity at our fingertips. We had Ask Jeeves or, if we were lucky, Clippy, the animated paperclip when we needed help writing a paper. These anecdotes spark laughter, but they also highlight a deeper truth. Our education system continues to apply analog solutions to digital-era challenges.

Today's students are immersed in an AI-powered, interactive world beyond school walls. Yet within schools, they too often encounter static instruction, rigid compliance measures, and increasingly popular, but counterproductive, technology bans. If we fail to evolve our classrooms to reflect the world students already live in, we risk making learning feel irrelevant and forfeiting the opportunity to ignite their curiosity, creativity, and potential.

My professional journey in education began with a fascination for how technology could transform learning. As an elementary student, I eagerly anticipated time in the school's new computer lab. We would rush to claim one of the coveted Macintosh Classics with color screens, hoping to avoid the green monochrome monitors. The game Oregon Trail offered the same gameplay either way, but something about seeing the brown wagon and blue river made the experience feel realistic. Oregon Trail seamlessly blended history, geography, math, and decision-making. For many of my classmates, time in the lab felt like a reward. For me, it was something more. It was an invitation to explore, to inquire, and to learn with excitement. That feeling has remained with me ever since and has served as my leadership compass throughout my career. I have often said that school should rival Disneyland, a place where curiosity drives learning and discovery feels exciting.

As I transitioned from student to educator, I carried with me that same sense of curiosity and possibility. I embraced the early tools of what would become Web 2.0. This was a time of interactive simulations, multimedia archives, and collaborative platforms not as novelties, but as catalysts for creating more engaging, student-centered learning environments (Redecker & Punie, 2017; Gay, 2018; Mayer, 2019). One early teaching experience stands out as it conveyed the impact of Web 2.0 in the classroom. On a cold New England winter day in the middle of the school year, we were about to start a new unit of study in my 8th grade Ancient Civilizations class. In preparation for this lesson, I began to curate a slideshow of twenty photographs scavenged from the internet and displayed them in my classroom using a multimedia projector I had purchased myself, since this was well before such technology became standard in classrooms. The images I collected featured bustling cities, quiet farms, dense jungles, arid deserts, snowcapped mountains, and even some penguins. I asked my students to guess where each photo had been taken. Responses varied widely: South America, Asia, even Antarctica! Despite the photos of cities and jungles, the "Antarctica" response would constitute a classic middle-school teaching moment. When I revealed that every image depicted a different region of Africa, the room fell into thoughtful silence. For many students, it was the first time they realized that Africa is not a single, uniform landscape. That moment marked a shift in their understanding and set the stage for our unit on African civilizations. It was a small but powerful example of how technology can challenge assumptions, spark critical thinking, and foster deeper learning.

Today's students inhabit a vastly different digital landscape. They are digital natives immersed in hyper-personalized content through AI-powered platforms such as YouTube, TikTok, and Discord. Their experiences are immediate, adaptive, and deeply engaging, shaped by algorithms that anticipate their interests. Fitzpatrick et al. (2023), in *The AI Classroom,* imagine a future in which educators can "outsource the doing and focus on the thinking." Yet many schools, despite the growing presence of AI in widely used educational tools, continue to rely on rigid instructional models. Rather than using new innovative tools to ignite curiosity and deepen understanding, as the now outdated slideshow once did in my own classroom, technology is often limited to content delivery and compliance within the constraints of a legacy system. The result is a widening gap between how students learn outside of school and the experiences they encounter within it.

Recent evidence reinforces this divide. By July 2025, ChatGPT had more than 700 million weekly active users, generating 18 billion weekly messages each week. Notably, about 10 percent of interactions involved tutoring or teaching, with writing tasks dominating workplace use (Chatterji et al., 2025). Students are already integrating AI tools into their learning lives, often to seek guidance, feedback, or creative support. When schools restrict or ignore these practices, they deepen the disconnect between how students experience learning outside of school and what they encounter in classrooms.

This whole topic reflects a broader challenge. The issue is not the absence of innovation, but the inability to integrate and scale existing tools in coherent and systemic ways. As Ding (2024) explains, nations rise to power not by inventing new technologies, but by integrating them effectively. The challenge for education is not a lack of innovation, but the inability to scale it in meaningful and consistent ways. History offers powerful examples of successful integration. During the Industrial Revolution, the United States did not invent the textile loom, but places like Lowell, Massachusetts became national leaders by designing entire systems, factories, labor models, transportation networks, and capital structures around its use. Similarly, in education, the tools already exist for personalized learning platforms, adaptive assessments, and immersive technologies. Yet their effective and consistent use remains fragmented, adopted in isolated classrooms rather than embedded system wide.

Bridging this gap requires more than access to tools. It demands a reimagining of teaching and learning that aligns with how students actually engage with the world. The divide between vibrant, personalized digital experiences and static, industrial-era models underscores the urgency of change. Fullan et al. (2018) call for a shift "from sorting talent to developing the talent of all learners," a vision that redefines the role of educators as facilitators, mentors, and designers of authentic learning experiences (Darling-Hammond et al., 2020).

This transformation, however, must be guided with care. AI is not without its limitations. While these tools offer immense potential, they also present serious risks: algorithmic bias, data privacy concerns, and the commodification of learning (Mamlok, 2021). If left unexamined, these risks will exacerbate the very inequities we seek to solve. These concerns mirror broader public sentiment. A 2025 cross-national survey of 10,000 adults found that half perceive AI as a major societal problem, while fewer than one in three express optimism about its potential (Seismic, 2025). Parents, in particular, voiced concerns about AI weakening relationships and limiting opportunities for their children. For school leaders, this means that adopting AI is not just a technical challenge but also a social one. Building trust and addressing these fears is essential if AI is to be positioned as a tool for equity and learning rather than as a source of anxiety. With thoughtful implementation and a firm commitment to student-centered pedagogy, technology can serve as a force for equity and innovation. It is not a replacement for educators, but a tool that can amplify their impact.

Understanding how to implement this transformation responsibly requires more than theory. It demands leadership grounded in practice. In my roles as a middle-school principal in Massachusetts and Connecticut, and now as Director of Technology and Innovation, I have worked to push the needle of progress while confronting persistent barriers. I have seen firsthand how outdated policies, limited professional development, and inconsistent access to digital tools continue to hinder innovation (Hatch et al., 2021; Picciano et al., 2012). Throughout my career, I have advocated for modernized systems, equitable infrastructure, and scalable technology integration. My doctoral research during the COVID-19 pandemic further illuminated how these structural challenges impacted schools in real time. While some districts adapted swiftly to pandemic distance learning, others struggled to maintain even the most basic instructional continuity (OECD, 2020). These disparities are not coincidental. They are systemic. Addressing them requires solutions that are equally systemic, guided by a willingness to rethink the foundations of what public education truly means.

Leading the Next Era of Public Education seeks to illuminate a path forward, one grounded in equity, adaptability, and a commitment to student-centered innovation. It is born out of both personal conviction and professional experience. The question is no longer whether AI will change education. It already has. The real question is whether public schools as a whole will rise to the challenge or remain anchored to past practices. My hope is that this book serves as a catalyst for courageous conversations, bold action, and a step forward for a public education system worthy of the students it serves.

References

Brynjolfsson, E., & McAfee, A. (2014). *The second machine age: Work, progress, and prosperity in a time of brilliant technologies.* W. W. Norton & Company.

Chatterji, A., Cunningham, T., Deming, D. J., Hitzig, Z., Ong, C., Shan, C. Y., & Wadman, K. (2025). *How people use ChatGPT* (Working Paper No. 34255). National Bureau of Economic Research. https://doi.org/10.3386/w34255

Darling-Hammond, L., Flook, L., Cook-Harvey, C., Barron, B., & Osher, D. (2020). Implications for educational practice of the science of learning and development. *Applied Developmental Science, 24*(2), 97–140. https://doi.org/10.1080/10888691.2018.1537791

Ding, J. (2024). *Technology and the rise of great powers.* Princeton University Press.

Fitzpatrick, D., Fox, A., & Weinstein, B. (2023). *The AI classroom: The ultimate guide to artificial intelligence in education.* TeacherGoals Publishing.

Friedman, T. L. (2006). *The world is flat [Release 2.0]: A brief history of the twenty-first century.* Farrar, Straus and Giroux.

Fullan, M., Quinn, J., & McEachen, J. (2018). *Deep learning: Engage the world change the world.* Corwin.

Gay, G. (2018). *Culturally responsive teaching: Theory, research, and practice* (3rd ed.). Teachers College Press.

Hatch, T., Corson, J., & Gerth van den Berg, S. (2021). *The education we need for a future we cannot predict.* Corwin.

Lehmann, C., & Chase, Z. (2015). *Building school 2.0: How to create the schools we need.* Jossey-Bass.

Levy, F., & Murnane, R. J. (2013). *Dancing with robots: Human skills for computerized work*. Third Way.

Mamlok, D. (2021). Algorithmic bias and the challenge of governing artificial intelligence. *AI & Society, 36*, 931–940. https://doi.org/10.1007/s00146-020-01081-4

Mayer, R. E. (2019). Thirty years of research on online learning. *Applied Cognitive Psychology, 33*(2), 152–159. https://doi.org/10.1002/acp.3482

OECD. (2020). *Education responses to COVID-19: Embracing digital learning and online collaboration*. OECD Publishing. https://doi.org/10.1787/d75eb0e8-en

Picciano, A. G., Seaman, J., Shea, P., & Swan, K. (2012). Examining the extent and nature of online learning in American K–12 education: The research initiatives of the Alfred P. Sloan Foundation. *The Internet and Higher Education, 15*(2), 127–135. https://doi.org/10.1016/j.iheduc.2011.07.004

Redecker, C., & Punie, Y. (2017). *European framework for the digital competence of educators: DigCompEdu*. Publications Office of the European Union. https://doi.org/10.2760/159770

Seismic. (2025). *On the razor's edge: Public attitudes toward AI in 2025*. Seismic. https://report2025.seismic.org/media/documents/On_the_Razors_Edge_Seismic_Report_2025.pdf

Selwyn, N. (2019). *Should robots replace teachers? AI and the future of education*. Polity Press.

Wing, J. M. (2017). Computational thinking's influence on research and education for all. *Italian Journal of Educational Technology, 25*(3), 7–14. https://doi.org/10.17471/2499-4324/922

Section 1
The Need for Change

The first step toward educational transformation is acknowledging the systemic limitations that have long constrained public schooling in the United States. As Emler et al. (2024) argues, a modern system must prioritize innovation, problem-solving, and collaboration rather than passive knowledge consumption. Despite decades of policy reform and technological advancement, the foundational structures of K–12 education continue to reflect industrial-era priorities such as standardization, uniform pacing, and hierarchical instruction. These paradigms, once viewed as pedagogically innovative, have not evolved in response to developments in cognitive science, shifting workforce demands, or the realities of a digitally mediated world. We will begin by examining the persistence of outdated models and outline the consequences of remaining stagnant, including widening opportunity gaps, declining student engagement, and the entrenchment of inequities shaped by geography, race, and socioeconomic status.

It is essential to understand the historical foundations and current constraints of today's educational landscape, as well as how the overreliance on standardized assessments and seat time requirements has undermined educational equity and relevance. We will then begin to examine the psychological and systemic inertia that inhibits reform, including cognitive biases, bureaucratic resistance, and cultural nostalgia for familiar yet ineffective practices. Next, we will analyze the disruption caused by the COVID-19 pandemic, offering a comparative look at how some states and districts have leveraged the crisis to reimagine education, while others have struggled to maintain continuity.

Together, these points argue that transformation requires more than isolated and temporary innovation. It demands a coordinated, systemic response grounded in equity, adaptability, and pedagogical integrity. The analysis outlined in this part provides the intellectual and empirical rationale for rethinking the very purpose, structure, and delivery of public education.

Reference

Emler, T. E., Lai, C., & Lei, J. (2024). Yong Zhao: Leading the paradigm shift. In B. A. Geier (Ed.) *The Palgrave handbook of educational thinkers*. Palgrave Macmillan. https://doi.org/10.1007/978-3-031-25134-4_199

1

Legacy without Progress

The Weight of Yesterday on Today's Schools

A fifth-grade student engages with an adaptive learning system from a local learning hub, a community space for collaboration, creativity, and connection. Progress is based on demonstrated mastery, not seat time. The student explores ecosystems through extended reality, completes applied learning challenges with global peers using instant translation, and receives real-time feedback from AI tools calibrated to the student's strengths, needs, and pace. Learning is interdisciplinary, personalized, and available anytime. It is not limited by bells, calendars, resources, subject-matter experts, or physical classrooms.

The next morning, the same student returns to a traditional school building that starts at 7:15 a.m. Learning is segmented by age, divided into fixed subjects and time blocks, and success is defined by a test administered on a single day but written months earlier. Innovation must operate inside a structure built for standardization rather than growth.

This is not a technology problem. It is a systems problem. These models do not integrate. Under pressure, they separate. One prepares students for the future. The other reproduces familiar, outdated patterns. Education has largely remained unchanged despite a fundamentally different world for today's children, so schools must move beyond an industrial-era model toward creativity, adaptability, and lifelong learning.

(Wagner, 2012)

Public education in the United States is at a critical crossroads. Despite growing recognition that the world has changed, the system designed to prepare young people for it has not. While other sectors have adapted to the demands of the middle 21st century, embracing flexibility, personalization, and innovation, American schools continue to operate primarily within a framework built for the industrial age.

This chapter provides a foundational critique of the framework. It begins by tracing the historical roots of public education in the United States, explaining how the original democratic and humanistic purposes of schooling have been gradually eroded by standardization, bureaucratization, and systemic inequity. It then examines the structural features of the current system, including time-based instruction, testing regimes, outdated technology integration, and inequitable funding, which collectively prevent meaningful innovation. Finally, it introduces the role of technology and the potential of competency-based learning as key levers for transformation, while cautioning against shallow or misaligned implementation.

Let me be very clear: The purpose is not to assign blame but to clarify what the system is and what it needs. Before redesigning the system, we must understand how and why this system no longer serves the students it was meant to uplift. I have structured it so that each section that follows dissects a core component of the current education model and shows how it contributes to a growing disconnect between school and the world beyond it.

How an Industrial Blueprint Still Shapes Our Schools

Education forms the foundation of a thriving society, and yet the prevailing structure of public education in the United States remains deeply rooted in an outdated, industrial-era model (Wagner, 2012). At the time of its inception, this model was a groundbreaking innovation that dramatically expanded access to education and opportunity for millions of Americans who might otherwise have been excluded. It laid the groundwork for widespread literacy, civic participation, and social mobility. However, it was designed primarily to prepare students for a workforce that no longer exists. Today, public education often emphasizes standardization, rote memorization, and compliance over the development of critical thinking, creativity, and adaptability. As we know, the world is evolving rapidly, shaped by technological innovation and shifting workforce demands. As Friedman (2006) observes in *The World Is Flat 2.0*, "The playing field is being leveled," underscoring how digital connectivity has reshaped economic and social expectations. For far too long, the education system has remained out of step with these changes, resulting in widening inequities, growing student disengagement, and a deep misalignment between what schools teach and what students need to succeed.

This challenge cannot be solved through superficial reform or isolated programmatic tweaks. Initiatives such as No Child Left Behind (2002), Race to the Top (2009), the Every Student Succeeds Act (2015), and Future Ready Schools were all well-intentioned. However, each initiative or educational reform largely reinforced compliance-based accountability structures without addressing the root causes of educational inequity or systemic inertia that it was claiming to address. The root of this problem is deeply embedded and multidimensional. It affects every facet of public education, including curriculum, assessment, funding, professional learning, leadership, and equity. Before meaningful solutions can be designed, we must recognize the scope and interdependence of the challenges we face. Only through a comprehensive and systemic approach can we begin to reimagine a public education system that reflects the realities of a changing world and the diverse needs of all learners.

Civic Ideals and Structural Inertia: The Historical Roots of Educational Inequity

To understand how we arrived at this point, it is essential to revisit both the aspirations and contradictions of early American public education. The ideals of civic literacy, social mobility, and democratic participation were embedded in the early design of the system, but they were never fully realized. The necessity to transform public education is not a recent development but one rooted in the foundational principles of American schooling. From the earliest days of the republic, public education was envisioned as a mechanism to promote universal literacy, civic engagement, and social mobility. Nowhere were these ideals more actively pursued than in New England, particularly in Massachusetts and Connecticut. I have spent my professional career in these states and observed both the enduring legacy and the implications of past reforms. Horace Mann, as the first secretary of the Massachusetts Board of Education, articulated a vision of public, nonsectarian education as essential to sustaining democracy (Cremin, 1957; Sunker, 2022; Stitzlein, 2021). Massachusetts led the nation in establishing compulsory schooling laws in 1852 (Reese, 2005), while Connecticut founded the first public teacher training institution in 1839 (Fraser, 2007), setting early precedents for rigorous educator preparation.

New York also played a foundational role in shaping the national education landscape. The New York Common School Act of 1812 established a statewide framework for organizing and funding public education, introducing the position of Superintendent of Common Schools to oversee the system (Gutek, 2011). This legislation marked one of the earliest state-level efforts to institutionalize public schooling in a coherent and scalable manner. Although my professional work has centered on Massachusetts and Connecticut, I spent my formative years in Lake George, New York, where I experienced both the strengths and limitations of rural public education. I completed my undergraduate studies in Utica, New York, located in what historians call the "Burned-Over District," a hotbed of 19th-century religious revivalism and reform movements (Cross, 1950). Perhaps it is one of the few places where the crowds for the Second Great Awakening rivaled those of Game 7 of the 2004 American League Championship Series between the Boston Red Sox and the New York Yankees. But that is a story for another book.

Baseball loyalties aside, I recognize that innovation in public education was never confined to New England. New York played a pivotal role, as did states such as Pennsylvania and Ohio, which enacted transformative reforms during the 19th century. These efforts expanded access, professionalized teaching, and formalized governance. Together, they represented a broader national commitment to the idea of education as a public good. Yet these civic goals were never applied equitably. Early federal policies often advanced exclusionary or assimilationist practices. The Civilization Fund Act of 1819, for example, funded missionary-led schools that sought to assimilate Indigenous populations by erasing Native languages and cultural traditions (Lomawaima & McCarty, 2006). African American students were systematically excluded from equal access to quality education, both in the North and South, where segregated and underfunded schools reinforced racial inequities (Anderson, 1988; Watkins, 2001). Women and immigrant communities also encountered barriers to equitable education, ranging from limited access to outright segregation (Rury, 2005; Tyack & Hansot, 1992). Modern scholarship underscores that these inequities were not only historical but remain deeply embedded in contemporary structures. Research on racial inequality in education demonstrates that patterns of exclusion continue to shape opportunity and achievement today (Education Week, 2023; Diem & Welton, 2020).

Throughout the 19th and early 20th centuries, public education emerged as a transformative societal force, offering access to literacy and civic participation, particularly for immigrants and working-class communities. More than a system of economic preparation, it served as a tool of nation-building, intended to cultivate a shared civic identity and social cohesion. Over time, however, this mission became constrained by bureaucratization and increasing stratification. Political, economic, and cultural forces reshaped the system, gradually replacing its humanistic and democratic foundations with a technocratic emphasis on standardization (Tyack & Cuban, 1995; Green, 2020). These structural inequities are mirrored today in how accountability-driven policy environments disproportionately impact marginalized students. As Nasir and Darling-Hammond (2025) argue, equity gaps persist not because of individual failings but because systemic reforms have often reinforced rather than dismantled historical hierarchies.

As the nation industrialized and urbanized, education systems expanded rapidly but unevenly, often perpetuating inequities rather than resolving them. By the late 20th century, reform discourse was dominated by themes of efficiency, accountability, and quantifiable outcomes, which frequently came at the expense of whole-child development and teacher autonomy. Although equity and opportunity remained prominent in policy rhetoric, their translation into practice was inconsistent and insufficient. Modern studies reinforce this trajectory. Research on teacher diversity shows that exclusionary histories continue to manifest in underrepresentation of educators of color, with measurable consequences for student achievement and belonging (Gershenson et al., 2021). Similarly, the enduring role of Historically Black Colleges and Universities reflects how institutions created in response to exclusion remain vital sites of equity and justice today (Gasman, 2025).

The foundational ideals of public education are increasingly overshadowed by policy environments that emphasize compliance, prioritize test scores, and sustain inequitable funding structures. These pressures by default often reward conformity over curiosity and operational efficiency over educational purpose, undermining the transformative vision articulated by early reformers. Recognizing this historical trajectory is essential for guiding future reform. It affirms that public education has always been a mirror of broader societal values and that meaningful transformation will require not only structural change but also a renewed commitment to the public purposes that once defined American schooling.

Time, Testing, and the Tyranny of Standardization

While the roots of public education were grounded in democratic ideals, the modern system is shaped by structural features that often undermine those values. Among the most persistent are outdated approaches to time, assessment, and instructional design. Public education in the United States continues to rely extensively on standardized assessments as the dominant indicators of student achievement. While these assessments provide a uniform metric for system-level accountability, they offer limited insight into the depth, complexity, and variability of student learning. Rather than promoting holistic development, standardized tests tend to narrow the curriculum to what is most easily measured, suppress inquiry-based approaches, and marginalize essential competencies such as collaboration, creativity, problem-solving, and communication (Fullan et al., 2018; Lehmann & Chase, 2015). The result is a system that privileges procedural compliance over intellectual curiosity, particularly disadvantaged students from historically underserved communities.

This same logic of standardization extends beyond assessment and into the daily structure of schooling. In most systems, students are expected to engage with specific subjects at fixed times. Science during second period, English after lunch, and similar patterns are common. Although models such as block or waterfall scheduling offer minor variations, the school day remains segmented into rigid intervals governed by bells rather than by students' developmental rhythms or cognitive readiness. This approach assumes that learning can be compartmentalized into neatly bounded time slots, independent of subject integration or learner variability.

Such compartmentalization distorts the nature of knowledge. Scientific inquiry requires mathematical reasoning. Historical understanding benefits from literary analysis. Artistic expression can deepen engagement with civic and cultural issues. Yet the prevailing schedule enforces an artificial separation of disciplines, marginalizing interdisciplinary thinking and innovative learning experiences. Even more critically, it disregards the neurodiversity of learners. Not every student is cognitively prepared to engage with complex material at 7:45 a.m. or capable of creative output just before dismissal. The inflexibility of time-bound instruction reinforces a one-size-fits-all model that is misaligned with the realities of how learning occurs.

Addressing these structural shortcomings requires more than isolated reforms. Competency-based education (CBE) offers a more equitable and responsive alternative by shifting the focus from time spent to learning demonstrated. Originating in teacher education and workforce training programs in the 1960s and 1970s, early CBE models emphasized observable skill mastery over time-based progression (Gervais, 2016). In the early 2000s, CBE reemerged as a reform movement in K–12 and higher education, driven by advances in technology, concerns about equity, and dissatisfaction with traditional assessment models. In a CBE framework, students' progress is based on mastery of clearly defined competencies rather than the accumulation of instructional minutes. This model prioritizes authentic assessment, emphasizes formative feedback, and fosters learner agency (Hatch et al., 2021). Mastery is demonstrated through meaningful performance aligned to rigorous academic and cognitive standards, not inferred from seat time or age.

Emerging technologies, including adaptive learning platforms and artificial intelligence (AI)-driven assessment tools, further enhance the potential of competency-based models. These tools enable real-time data collection, individualized diagnostics, and targeted instructional support. When implemented within a coherent pedagogical framework, technology can increase personalization, promote equity, and improve learning outcomes without compromising academic rigor (Fullan et al., 2018).

Yet the adoption of technology alone does not constitute transformation. Too often, digital tools are layered onto outdated instructional models, primarily used to automate grading, digitize worksheets, or enforce rigid pacing. In these instances, technology perpetuates the very limitations that CBE seeks to address. The result is a superficial form of innovation where tools are misaligned with purpose, and pedagogy remains unchanged.

What is needed is not a refinement of existing tools or schedules but a comprehensive redefinition of how learning is structured, measured, and supported. A systemic shift toward competency requires coherence across policy, pedagogy, and professional learning. It demands a departure from the industrial logic of time-based efficiency in favor of learner-centered flexibility, depth, and purpose. Without such transformation, public education will continue to reflect the priorities of the past rather than the potential of the future.

Trapped in the Past: Why EdTech Fails without Pedagogical Reform

One of the most visible signs of attempted reform is the use of educational technology. Despite decades of new tools, most schools did not or were unable to rethink the underlying pedagogy or purpose that should guide their use. The trajectory of educational technology reflects the broader shifts in pedagogical thought and technological capability. It has evolved through a series of overlapping paradigms, each shaped by societal needs and advancements in communication tools. Education 1.0, rooted in industrial-age schooling, typifies a teacher-centered, passive model of instruction focused on rote memorization, standardization, and unidirectional knowledge transfer. In this phase, technology played a minimal role, often limited to chalkboards and textbooks, reinforcing a top-down structure of authority in the classroom.

Education 2.0 emerged alongside Web 2.0 technologies, introducing interactivity, collaboration, and content creation. Platforms such as blogs, wikis, and learning management systems encouraged students to become contributors rather than mere consumers of information. The model was more participatory but often still teacher-guided, with limited transformation of the underlying instructional architecture.

Education 3.0 reflected a more profound pedagogical shift, integrating constructivist and connectivism principles that emphasized personalized, inquiry-based learning in networked environments. Students were encouraged to explore, create, and collaborate across global platforms, blurring the boundaries between formal and informal learning (Gerstein, 2013). This model aligned more closely with 21st-century competencies, empowering learners to take ownership of their educational journeys.

Building upon this foundation, Education 4.0 and its emerging extension, Education 4.5, as I affectionately refer to it, marks the integration of artificial intelligence, immersive technologies, and advanced data analytics into the learning ecosystem. These stages emphasize real-time personalization, predictive analytics, and virtual or augmented environments that can simulate authentic learning contexts. However, they also introduce new ethical dilemmas and equity concerns, such as surveillance, algorithmic bias, and digital access gaps (Redecker & Punie, 2017). The promise of these technologies is substantial, but so are the risks if implementation fails to prioritize transparency, inclusivity, and student agency.

Despite the evolution of these paradigms, many educational institutions remain constrained in these outdated models. They implement technology with good intentions but without reimagining pedagogy, resulting in digital worksheets instead of dynamic learning environments. Often, the barriers are not technical but cultural: Insufficient vision, inadequate infrastructure, lack of professional development, and policy constraints hinder transformation. In these settings, technology reinforces rather than disrupts entrenched structures.

Educational technology should not be used to digitize traditional practices. It should enable richer forms of inquiry, interdisciplinary connection, and learner-driven exploration. True innovation requires more than devices and bandwidth; it demands a pedagogical shift that centers on purpose, equity, and student empowerment. As we move deeper into the age of AI and automation, the imperative is clear: Modern tools must be harnessed not to replicate the past but to shape a more just, inclusive, and future-ready system of education.

Algorithmic Efficiency or Authentic Learning? AI, Ethics, and the Future of Instruction

As AI enters the classroom, its promise must be balanced against the professional knowledge of educators and the rights of learners. Technology alone cannot drive transformation; people must. Educators fear a future in which their expertise is devalued and their autonomy replaced by algorithmically driven pacing. These concerns echo long-standing frustrations with mandated instructional scripts. Pacing guides, while intended to ensure curricular alignment, often function as rigid directives that overlook student readiness and curiosity. When adherence to the guide takes priority over responsiveness to learners, instruction becomes a race through content instead of a journey toward meaningful understanding. AI-driven systems risk replicating this pattern by emphasizing efficiency over depth and coverage over comprehension. Whether delivered through analog systems or digital platforms, the outcome is the same. Teachers are positioned as implementers rather than as instructional leaders.

To counter this risk, AI must be embedded within pedagogical frameworks that preserve professional judgment and center learner agency. Competency-based approaches, when grounded in authentic assessment and ethical implementation, can help achieve this balance. These models enable students to progress based on demonstrated understanding and allow educators to tailor supports in ways that reflect individual needs and context. In this application, AI does not dictate instruction; instead, it supports deeper learning, more equitable access, and richer opportunities for critical thinking and self-direction.

The task ahead is not to reject AI. If that were the goal, this book would not exist. The challenge is to ensure that AI's integration into education reflects core public values. These include equity, transparency, and the right of every learner to be recognized, supported, and challenged. Meeting this challenge will require principled leadership, human-centered design, and a steadfast commitment to empowering educators as professionals rather than as passive operators of algorithmic systems.

How Outdated Funding Structures Perpetuate Inequality

Structural inequity is not limited to pedagogy and policy. It is deeply entrenched in the ways schools are financed, sustaining vast opportunity gaps across communities and generations. One of the most deeply entrenched challenges in US education is the inequitable distribution of resources. Unlike countries that fund education through centralized or needs-based mechanisms, the United States relies heavily on local property taxes to finance public schools. This structure ensures that wealthier communities, which have high property values and robust local tax bases, consistently provide their schools with superior resources, facilities, and staffing. In contrast, districts that serve low-income communities must contend with chronic underfunding, aging infrastructure, limited access to advanced coursework and extracurricular opportunities, and higher rates of teacher turnover. This systematic disparity undermines the principle of equal educational opportunity and perpetuates generational cycles of disadvantage (Fitch, 2023; Urban Institute, 2023).

States often praised for high educational performance, including Connecticut and Massachusetts, still exhibit significant disparities in per-pupil spending, student support services, and academic outcomes. In Massachusetts, Proposition 2½ imposes a rigid cap on the amount municipalities can raise through property taxes, limiting annual increases to 2.5 percent unless voters approve an override. Although this policy was intended to control tax burdens, it often restricts local investment in education, particularly in communities with limited economic growth or constrained tax bases. As a result, districts may face structural deficits that make it difficult to maintain programs, update facilities, or invest in staffing, even as student needs grow (Massachusetts Department of Revenue, n.d.).

In Quincy, Massachusetts, the implementation of Proposition 2½ in the early 1980s led to significant budget cuts across the Commonwealth. The city was required to reduce municipal spending by $18.7 million in the first year, with $8.2 million of that coming from the school budget. Despite a $11 million allocation from the state to offset the loss of property tax revenues, the schools did not receive any of that money. This case illustrates the challenges of relying on promised aid to compensate for local funding limitations (Education Week, 1983).

Connecticut presents a parallel scenario, where reliance on local property taxes for school funding has led to stark disparities between affluent and low-income districts. For instance, Bridgeport, a city with a predominantly Black, Indigenous, and People of Color (BIPOC) student population, spends approximately $4,182 less per student than the state average for majority-white districts. This funding gap translates into fewer instructional resources, larger class sizes, and limited access to enrichment opportunities. In contrast, neighboring towns such as Greenwich and Westport invest significantly more in their schools due to their substantial tax revenue, resulting in enhanced educational opportunities for their students (Center for Children's Advocacy, 2023).

These disparities scratch the surface and reflect a deeper issue of equity, not just differences in resource allocation. Where a child lives continues to determine the quality of education they receive, which contradicts the promise of a free and equal public education.

Some states have taken meaningful steps toward funding reform. New Jersey's School Funding Reform Act and California's Local Control Funding Formula (LCFF) are often cited as models of more equitable, needs-based funding systems. These efforts shift funding to account for student poverty, English-language learner status, and other indicators of need, rather than relying solely on local tax revenues. In New Jersey, the implementation of funding reforms was associated with a 10 percent increase in graduation rates among low-income students and measurable gains in academic achievement (Jackson et al., 2016). While these reforms have demonstrated positive impacts, they remain exceptions rather than standard practice. Many states lack the political will, fiscal flexibility, or constitutional mandates to enact similar policies. Legal challenges, local resistance in wealthier districts, and competing budgetary priorities often delay or dilute reform efforts.

The persistence of these funding inequities reflects broader issues in public policy that are unable to address systemic injustice in education. Despite decades of litigation and research, a stark mismatch persists between the needs of students and the resources allocated to meet them. Federal funding, while helpful in some contexts, is insufficient to overcome the vast disparities created by local financing models. Without comprehensive, equity-centered reform at both the state and federal levels, opportunity gaps will continue to widen, disproportionately impacting students of color, students with disabilities, and those from economically disadvantaged backgrounds.

Addressing these inequities requires more than marginal increases in funding. It demands a redefinition of adequacy, a more precise measurement of student need, and a shift in how education is prioritized in public budgeting. Until then, the United States will continue to operate a system in which access to quality education is not a guaranteed right but a reflection of geographic and economic privilege.

Underequipped and Undervalued: The Erosion of Professional Capacity

No reform can succeed without strong teachers. Yet, in too many districts, educators are underprepared, undersupported, and unequally distributed. This is particularly harmful when navigating new technologies and instructional demands. Among the most significant in-school predictors of student achievement is teacher quality. Effective teachers foster engagement, personalize instruction, and help close persistent opportunity gaps. However, access to high-quality educators remains uneven. Schools that serve low-income communities experience higher rates of teacher turnover and are more frequently staffed by early-career or uncertified educators (Goldhaber et al., 2022). These structural inequities become even more pronounced in digital learning environments when educators lack the necessary skills, confidence, or support to utilize technology in instruction effectively.

Digital fluency, defined as the ability to integrate technology purposefully to support learning outcomes, is now a core component of instructional effectiveness. Many teachers continue to enter the profession without adequate preparation in educational technology. Some teacher preparation programs provide a basic exposure to these tools, and many current educators completed their degrees long before current platforms existed. During my tenure as a middle school principal, this gap became especially evident at the onset of the COVID-19 pandemic. As instruction transitioned online, several veteran teachers who were considered highly effective based on student performance continued to rely on the big green overhead projectors. I am talking about the green machines that emitted so much heat that sitting nearby became hot, sticky, and uncomfortable. If you looked into the lens of the projector, the light was brighter than the sun. Of course, middle school students would be caught trying to see who could stare at the light the longest. That being said, imagine that these classrooms were arranged in static rows of desks, and their instructional methods had changed little since the early 2000s. The sudden shift to distance learning exposed the unpreparedness of many educators, not due to resistance to change, but rather a systemic lack of preparation and ongoing support.

This disconnect is rarely about unwillingness. More often, it is the result of chronic underinvestment in professional learning. School districts frequently allocate substantial funding for platforms, devices, and software, but invest far less in the professional development needed to use these tools for instructional purposes. In many cases, training is treated as a procedural requirement, completed once to satisfy implementation guidelines. One-time sessions without follow-up do little to build the confidence or capacity that educators need to integrate technology meaningfully. This approach overlooks the complexity of instructional practice and fails to address the diverse needs of educators working in various classroom contexts.

Even when professional development is available, it often focuses narrowly on how to operate a tool rather than on how technology can support deeper learning and learning outcomes. Teachers benefit most from professional learning that provides time for exploration, access to coaching, and opportunities for collaboration and reflection. They require support that extends beyond technical guidance and addresses how digital tools can facilitate culturally responsive pedagogy, formative assessment, and inquiry-based instruction (Darling-Hammond et al., 2020).

Integrating students' cultural identities, lived experiences, and perspectives into instruction is crucial for fostering engagement and a sense of belonging. Technology, when used intentionally, can support this objective. Tools such as virtual and augmented reality, student media creation platforms, and interactive simulations enable educators to move beyond static, standardized content. These resources expose students to diverse narratives, histories, and real-world problem-solving experiences. Their impact is most substantial when used to support culturally responsive teaching practices, ensuring that learning is both personalized and representative of the communities from which students come.

The effective use of educational technology depends on educators who are confident, professionally supported, and empowered to make instructional decisions. Teachers must be treated as designers of learning, not as passive implementers of external mandates. When provided with the knowledge, time, and collaborative structures needed to integrate technology with purpose, classrooms become more inclusive, adaptable, and responsive to the diverse needs of all students.

As education systems continue to modernize, it is crucial that all educators, not just those in well-resourced districts, have access to sustained and meaningful professional development. Technology on its own does not improve instruction. It is the professional capacity of teachers to use digital tools in ways that enhance learning and improve outcomes that ultimately determines whether technology leads to lasting educational progress.

Beyond Access: Rethinking Equity in a Digitally Divided World

Equitable access to devices and the internet is essential, but it is also insufficient. The digital divide is also pedagogical, cultural, and linguistic, and closing it requires more than broadband. In the 21st century, digital access is not a luxury. It is a prerequisite for full participation in public education, civic life, and the workforce. The COVID-19 pandemic exposed and amplified long-standing inequities in connectivity, device access, and digital literacy. Students in rural and low-income communities were disproportionately affected, as many lacked reliable broadband at home, sufficient devices for each learner, or adult support in navigating digital tools. These disparities disrupted learning, widened opportunity gaps, and made clear that access to technology is now inseparable from access to educational opportunity (Sieck et al., 2021; Wrye, 2022).

Although federal programs such as E-Rate and the Emergency Connectivity Fund have provided essential support to districts working to expand internet access, gaps persist. Infrastructure alone does not ensure equity. Households in underresourced areas frequently face challenges beyond bandwidth. These include limited access to translated materials, difficulty affording service once subsidies expire, and a lack of digital literacy among parents and caregivers. Additionally, many school systems lack the internal capacity to sustain maintenance, training, and adaptation once initial funding is exhausted.

Efforts to bridge the digital divide must be grounded in local context and shaped by community partnerships. The Cape Cod Commission's broadband initiative offers a compelling example. In response to regional disparities, the Commission collaborated with local governments, libraries, and school districts to assess infrastructure needs and implement targeted solutions. In a public school system on Cape Cod, this work resulted in a cross-agency strategy in which the school district and public libraries collaborated to increase hotspot availability. The school district had unused hotspots in storage, while libraries faced community demand without adequate supply. By coordinating efforts, the initiative improved access without requiring additional funding. This case illustrates the value of collaboration across sectors and responsiveness to local needs.

Equitable digital access must also address the quality of student experience, including digital fluency, culturally relevant content, and inclusive instructional design. Devices and broadband are only as useful as the practices and environments they support. Digital fluency should be developed and assessed as a core skill, alongside reading and mathematics. Students must learn not only to consume information, but also to create, communicate, and think critically in digital spaces. The tools and content used in classrooms should reflect students' identities, languages, and lived experiences. Instructional materials that ignore cultural context or assume uniform background knowledge risk alienating students and reinforcing exclusion.

Districts must be deliberate in adopting practices that support universal design and accessibility. This includes selecting platforms that comply with the Web Content Accessibility Guidelines, ensuring compatibility with screen readers, enabling captioning for video content, facilitating keyboard navigation, and integrating with translation tools. Providing content in alternative formats such as transcripts, image descriptions, and simplified layouts is necessary for students with disabilities. These actions are not optional.

They are legal requirements under the Americans with Disabilities Act (ADA) and Section 504 of the Rehabilitation Act of 1973. Title II of the ADA obligates public entities, including school districts, to ensure equal access to all programs and services, including digital instruction. When content is inaccessible, students with disabilities face systemic barriers to participation and learning. Without proactive measures, digital education may replicate or intensify the inequities it is intended to reduce.

Closing the digital divide in the 21st century requires more than distributing devices or expanding internet service. It demands a coordinated and sustained effort to align infrastructure, instructional practices, and community engagement. Only through this systems-level approach can every student, regardless of location or background, gain access to the tools and support needed to succeed in a connected world.

Redesigning, Not Repairing: The Case for Systemic Educational Transformation

Incremental reform is no longer enough. The time has come for a deliberate, systemic redesign of public education to reflect the needs of the present and the potential of the future. This is a call for equity, agency, and purpose, not as aspirational goals, but as the foundation of learning environments for the middle 21st century. Incremental reform is insufficient. The future of education must be designed with intention to meet the needs of the present and the demands of an uncertain future. This requires moving beyond time-based advancement, standardized assessments, and compliance-oriented accountability systems. It calls for a new vision of learning grounded in equity, flexibility, and student agency.

This transformation cannot be reduced to a single policy shift, digital tool, or instructional model. Many interdependent components must evolve in concert, including funding structures, teacher preparation, digital infrastructure, curriculum design, community partnerships, and student voice. Each of these areas must change in tandem. This is a systems-level challenge that requires a systems-level response. What follows in this book is not a narrow prescription but a comprehensive framework for reimagining learning environments that are inclusive, resilient, and prepared for the future.

The lessons of the pandemic make clear that layering technology onto outdated systems is insufficient. The same is true for AI. Public opinion remains fragile and divided, with strong calls for regulation, accountability, and transparency (Seismic Foundation, 2025). At the same time, evidence shows that learners are already relying on AI at scale, often for tutoring, problem-solving, and writing support (Chatterji et al., 2025). The future of education depends on bridging these two realities: addressing public fears while leveraging the ways students are actively using AI to support their learning. Without this alignment, schools risk becoming further disconnected from the world their students already inhabit.

Policy must prioritize funding equity, support innovation at scale, and eliminate outdated structures that maintain educational inequality. Technology must serve to enhance human potential, not replace it. Educators must be empowered as designers of transformative learning experiences, rather than being treated as passive implementers of top-down directives.

What lies ahead is an urgent invitation to rethink public education at every level. This moment demands more than marginal improvements. It requires a coordinated, courageous, and purpose-driven effort to move from inertia to innovation. Transformation begins not with perfection, but with the willingness to question long-standing assumptions and the determination to build something better.

References

Anderson, J. D. (1988). *The education of Blacks in the South, 1860–1935*. University of North Carolina Press.

Center for Children's Advocacy. (2023). *Racial disparities in Connecticut education funding*. https://schoolstatefinance.org/resource-assets/Racial-Disparities-in-CT-Education-Funding.pdf

Chatterji, A., Cunningham, T., Deming, D. J., Hitzig, Z., Ong, C., Shan, C. Y., & Wadman, K. (2025). How people use ChatGPT (NBER Working Paper No. w34255). National Bureau of Economic Research. https://doi.org/10.3386/w34255 SSRN

Cremin, L. A. (1957). *The republic and the school: Horace Mann on the education of free men.* Teachers College Press.

Cross, W. R. (1950). *The burned-over district: The social and intellectual history of enthusiastic religion in western New York, 1800–1850.* Cornell University Press.

Darling-Hammond, L., Zielezinski, M. B., & Goldman, S. (2020). *Using technology to support at-risk students' learning.* Alliance for Excellent Education. https://all4ed.org/wp-content/uploads/2014/09/UsingTechnology.pdf

Diem, S., & Welton, A. D. (2020). *Anti-racist educational leadership and policy: Addressing racism in public education.* Harvard Education Press.

Education Week. (1983, March 16). *Tax-limitation law seen as cause of financial squeeze in Massachusetts.* https://www.edweek.org/policy-politics/tax-limitation-law-seen-as-cause-of-financial-squeeze-in-massachusetts/1983/03

Education Week. (2023, March 20). *The origins of racial inequality in education.* https://www.edweek.org/policy-politics/the-origins-of-racial-inequality-in-education/2023/03

Fitch, M. (2023, June 16). *Connecticut school finance: Challenges and solutions.* Yankee Institute for Public Policy. https://yankeeinstitute.org/2023/06/16/education-study-finds-minimal-correlation-between-state-education-spending-and-academic-outcomes/

Fraser, J. W. (2007). *Preparing America's teachers: A history.* Teachers College Press.

Friedman, T. L. (2006). *The world is flat 2.0: A brief history of the twenty-first century.* Farrar, Straus and Giroux.

Fullan, M., Quinn, J., & McEachen, J. (2018). *Deep learning: Engage the world, change the world.* Corwin.

Gasman, M. (2025). *HBCUs: The affirmation of Blackness and the spirit of excellence.* Harvard Education Press.

Gershenson, S., Hansen, M., Hart, C. M. D., & Lindsay, C. A. (2021). *Teacher diversity and student success* (Rev. ed.). Harvard Education Press.

Gerstein, J. (2013, May 13). *Education 3.0 and the pedagogy (andragogy, heutagogy) of mobile learning.* User Generated Education. https://usergeneratededucation.wordpress.com/2013/05/13/education-3-0-and-the-pedagogy-andragogy-heutagogy-of-mobile-learning/

Gervais, J. (2016). The operational definition of competency-based education. *The Journal of Competency-Based Education, 1*(2), 98–106. https://doi.org/10.1002/cbe2.1011

Goldhaber, D., Quince, V., & Theobald, R. (2022). Teacher quality gaps in US public schools. *Educational Researcher, 51*(1), 17–30. https://doi.org/10.3102/0013189X211068987

Green, J. (2020). *Education and state formation: Europe, East Asia, and the Americas.* Palgrave Macmillan.

Gutek, G. L. (2011). *Historical and philosophical foundations of education: A biographical introduction* (5th ed.). Pearson.

Hatch, T., Corson, D., & Gerth van den Berg, J. (2021). *The education we need for a future we cannot predict.* Corwin.

Jackson, C. K., Johnson, R. C., & Persico, C. (2016). The effects of school spending on educational and economic outcomes: Evidence from school finance reforms. *The Quarterly Journal of Economics, 131*(1), 157–218. https://doi.org/10.1093/qje/qjv036

Nasir, N. S., & Darling-Hammond, L. (Eds.). (2025). *Equity and education since Brown v. Board: Where do we go from here?* Teachers College Press.

Lehmann, C., & Chase, Z. (2015). *Building school 2.0: How to create the schools we need.* Jossey-Bass.

Lomawaima, K. T., & McCarty, T. L. (2006). *To remain an Indian: Lessons in democracy from a century of Native American education.* Teachers College Press.

Massachusetts Department of Revenue. (n.d.). *Proposition 2½ overview.* https://www.mass.gov/info-details/proposition-2-1-2-overview

No Child Left Behind Act of 2001, Pub. L. No. 107–110, 115 Stat. 1425 (2002). https://www.congress.gov/bill/107th-congress/house-bill/1

Race to the Top Program: Executive summary. (2009). US Department of Education. https://files.eric.ed.gov/fulltext/ED557422.pdf

Redecker, C., & Punie, Y. (2017). *European framework for the digital competence of educators: DigCompEdu.* Publications Office of the European Union. https://doi.org/10.2760/159770

Reese, W. J. (2005). *America's public schools: From the common school to "No Child Left Behind."* Johns Hopkins University Press.

Rury, J. L. (2005). *Education and social change: Contours in the history of American schooling* (3rd ed.). Routledge.

Section 504 of the Rehabilitation Act of 1973, 34 C.F.R. pt. 104.

Seismic Foundation. (2025). On the razor's edge: AI vs. everything we care about (Seismic Report 2025). Seismic Foundation. https://report2025.seismic.org/media/documents/On_the_Razors_Edge_Seismic_Report_2025.pdf

Sieck, C. J., Sheon, A., Ancker, J. S., Castek, J., Callahan, B., & Siefer, A. (2021). Digital inclusion as a social determinant of health. *npj Digital Medicine*, 4(1), 52. https://doi.org/10.1038/s41746-021-00413-8

Stitzlein, S. M. (2021). *Learning how to hope: Revitalizing democracy through our schools and civil society*. Oxford University Press.

Sunker, H. (2022). Public education and democracy: Lessons from Horace Mann. *Journal of Educational Change, 23*(1), 1–19. https://doi.org/10.1007/s10833-021-09432-3

Tyack, D., & Cuban, L. (1995). *Tinkering toward utopia: A century of public school reform*. Harvard University Press.

Tyack, D., & Hansot, E. (1992). *Learning together: A history of coeducation in American public schools*. Yale University Press.

Urban Institute. (2023). *Which states prioritize equity in school renovation funding?* https://www.urban.org/urban-wire/which-states-prioritize-equity-school-renovation-funding

US Department of Education. (2015). *Every student succeeds act*, Pub. L. No. 114–95, 129 Stat. 1802. https://www.congress.gov/114/plaws/publ95/PLAW-114publ95.pdf

Wagner, T. (2012). *Creating innovators: The making of young people who will change the world*. Scribner.

Watkins, W. H. (2001). *The white architects of Black education: Ideology and power in America, 1865–1954*. Teachers College Press.

Wrye, T. P. (2022). *The great equalizer: Distance learning and its impact on education equity* (Doctoral dissertation), Drexel University. https://doi.org/10.17918/00001294

2

Familiarity over Function

How Inertia Undermines Innovation

> "The most dangerous phrase in the English language is, 'We've always done it this way.'"
>
> Attributed to Rear Admiral Grace Hopper

Education plays a central role in advancing society, yet schools often remain bound to outdated instructional models. Advances in cognitive science, technology, and pedagogy exist alongside classrooms shaped by routines from a different era. This persistence is not the result of individual reluctance but a convergence of psychological, cultural, and institutional forces that sustain inertia. Tyack and Cuban (1995) refer to these enduring patterns as the "grammar of schooling," emphasizing their deep roots in organizational history.

Cognitive biases encourage educators and leaders to favor the familiar even when evidence suggests better alternatives. Kahneman (2011) shows how anchoring and confirmation bias lead individuals to privilege existing practices and dismiss contradictory evidence. Professional norms and policy constraints reinforce this preference, creating environments where innovation feels risky. Governance structures and accountability systems entrench these patterns further, rewarding compliance more than adaptation. Cultural narratives and community expectations amplify these pressures, framing change as disruption rather than progress (McDermott & Varenne, 1995).

Understanding these forces clarifies why innovation struggles to take hold in schools. The persistence of familiar routines is not accidental. It is embedded in individual psychology, institutional design, and societal expectations. Recognizing these roots of inertia is essential for building systems that adapt to new knowledge and respond to the evolving needs of learners.

Psychological Barriers

Familiarity offers comfort in uncertain environments, but it also creates resistance to innovation. In schools, this resistance often stems from cognitive biases that favor the known over the unknown. Educators and leaders may default to existing routines because those practices feel safe, even when research or new tools suggest more effective approaches. Kahneman (2011) explains that anchoring and confirmation bias drive individuals to rely on familiar reference points and to seek evidence that reinforces existing beliefs. These patterns make it easier to justify incremental adjustments than to engage in meaningful transformation.

Risk aversion compounds these effects. Argyris (1990) observed that organizational actors often rely on defensive reasoning strategies that protect established routines but hinder learning. In education, this is intensified by the perception that test scores, funding, and community trust are fragile resources that cannot be risked. March and Olsen (2011) argue that institutions are particularly prone to risk avoidance when accountability pressures are high, reinforcing the appeal of stability over experimentation. In such environments, even promising innovations are dismissed as disruptive or impractical.

Recognizing these psychological patterns is critical to overcoming inertia. Comfort with the familiar does not equal effectiveness. Breaking this cycle requires deliberate efforts to confront bias, design safe spaces for experimentation, and reward adaptive thinking. When schools normalize reflection and risk-taking, they create the conditions for innovation to emerge and take root.

Structural Barriers

Beyond individual psychology, the design of educational systems embeds resistance to change. Governance models, accountability structures, and policy frameworks often reward compliance rather than adaptation, leaving limited room for innovation. Tyack and Cuban (1995) argue that these institutional designs are historically built to preserve stability rather than foster experimentation.

Standardized testing remains one of the strongest anchors of this inertia. Narrow definitions of success tie student performance to test outcomes, which in turn drive instructional time, curriculum design, and resource allocation. Au (2011) demonstrates that high-stakes testing narrows curriculum and reduces the space for innovative instruction. Teachers and administrators, under pressure to meet performance targets, are compelled to prioritize short-term metrics over deeper learning opportunities.

Efforts at flexibility, such as competency-based education, are frequently undermined by legacy systems. Seat time regulations, graduation requirements, and rigid accountability structures limit the ability of schools to adopt models that emphasize mastery and personalization. Even when districts attempt alternatives, state and federal policies often force them back into compliance with traditional benchmarks (Patrick & Sturgis, 2015).

Bureaucratic structures add another layer of resistance. Decision-making authority is fragmented across multiple boards, agencies, and departments, complicating coherent reform. Policies designed to ensure stability can inadvertently stifle adaptation, as administrators navigate overlapping regulations and conflicting mandates. Ravitch (2010) notes that centralized accountability often creates rigidity that undermines the very improvements it seeks to ensure. The result is a system that prioritizes predictability and order over responsiveness and growth.

Structural barriers turn inertia into a self-reinforcing cycle. Educators may want to innovate, but systemic constraints limit their ability to act. Breaking this cycle requires rethinking accountability, loosening rigid requirements, and designing governance systems that measure success through learning outcomes rather than procedural compliance.

Cultural and Social Narratives

Resistance to innovation in education extends beyond schools. Cultural expectations and social narratives shape how communities interpret reform and influence how leaders respond.

The grammar of schooling, including traditions such as age-based grades, bell schedules, and homework, defines what many people believe school should look like. Tyack and Tobin (1994) describe these structures as deeply ingrained cultural patterns that persist even in the face of reform. Parents and communities often equate such routines with legitimacy, viewing alternatives as risky. Concerns about student performance reinforce this conservatism, as families fear that unfamiliar practices may jeopardize college admission or career prospects.

Media coverage amplifies these perceptions. Reports that frame reforms as failures before results are available erode confidence in change. Political polarization intensifies the problem by turning curricular choices and technology adoption into cultural disputes. Ruha Benjamin (2019) warns that public narratives about technology often reproduce existing inequities, which can frame innovation as a threat rather than an opportunity. Under these conditions, even modest shifts are misrepresented as attacks on tradition or values.

These narratives shape educational policy as much as evidence does. McDermott and Varenne (1995) emphasize that culture not only defines what is possible but also limits what is imagined as legitimate schooling. Leaders who pursue reform must contend with public opinion, which often carries more weight than research. Innovation gains credibility when schools communicate clearly, demonstrate transparency, and explain how changes serve students. Without trust and shared understanding, reforms are unlikely to take root.

Building Trust and a New Social Contract

Innovation in education requires more than new structures or policies; it depends on trust. Communities are unlikely to support reforms if leaders fail to demonstrate openness and clarity. Bryk and Schneider (2002) found that relational trust among educators, families, and communities is a central factor in sustaining school improvement. Without this foundation, even well-designed reforms collapse under suspicion and resistance.

Trust grows when communication is transparent, consistent, and responsive. Families and educators want to know not only what changes are happening but also why they matter. When leaders articulate purpose and connect reform to shared values, they build legitimacy. Fullan (2021) argues that meaningful change emerges when schools pursue both improvement and moral purpose, aligning reforms with the broader aim of advancing equity and student success.

Reimagining the social contract of schooling requires reframing the relationship between schools and the public. Education has traditionally been defined by compliance with standardized expectations. A renewed contract must emphasize adaptability, shared responsibility, and collective investment in innovation. As Mehta and Fine (2019) suggest, schools need to create cultures that prioritize deep learning and civic engagement, signaling to communities that reform is not disruption but an opportunity to strengthen democratic life.

When schools embed communication, trust, and shared values into reform efforts, they build the social foundation necessary for transformation. Without this, innovation risks being dismissed as a passing initiative rather than a durable shift in how education serves society.

Stakeholder Roles

The persistence of educational inertia is reinforced by the actions and constraints of those who operate within the system.

Educators, administrators, and policymakers each shape the conditions under which reform is either embraced or resisted.

Teachers often navigate a tension between professional judgment and institutional expectations. Research shows that educators value autonomy but frequently operate within environments that restrict risk-taking (Ingersoll, 2003). When pressured by accountability systems or community expectations, teachers default to established routines that feel safe and legitimate.

Administrators face similar dilemmas. They are tasked with balancing stability and innovation while responding to external scrutiny. Spillane (1996) found that district leaders often interpret reform mandates through the lens of existing practices, effectively narrowing their scope. In this way, leadership structures that aim to coordinate change frequently reinforce continuity instead.

Policymakers, while positioned to create enabling conditions for reform, often introduce constraints that unintentionally stifle innovation. Levin (2001) argues that policies designed to ensure accountability can create rigid compliance cultures that discourage experimentation. When regulations prioritize measurable outcomes over adaptive learning, reform efforts are reduced to procedural alignment rather than systemic transformation.

Each group operates with different pressures, yet their actions converge to reinforce inertia. Teachers protect students from the risks of untested practices, administrators preserve organizational stability, and policymakers seek predictability through regulation. Breaking this cycle requires collaborative approaches that align professional practice, leadership vision, and policy frameworks toward adaptability and equity.

Toward Innovation

Breaking free from educational inertia requires intentional design that moves beyond incremental adjustments. Innovation becomes possible when schools confront entrenched patterns, align structures with learning goals, and cultivate cultures that support adaptation.

Bridging divides among stakeholders is central to this process. Bryk et al. (2015) emphasize that sustainable improvement emerges from collaborative networks rather than isolated initiatives. When educators, administrators, and policymakers share responsibility for reform, they create conditions where innovation can be tested, evaluated, and refined.

Designing for change also requires schools to embed flexibility into their systems. Fullan and Quinn (2016) argue that coherence in reform is achieved not by uniformity but by aligning diverse practices around a shared moral purpose. This means building accountability systems that reward learning and adaptation rather than compliance. Schools that prioritize experimentation, reflection, and collective problem-solving are better positioned to respond to evolving needs.

Educational inertia is not inevitable. It is the product of choices, structures, and narratives that can be reimagined. By breaking cycles of resistance and designing systems that value adaptability, schools can move from familiarity toward transformation. Innovation takes hold when reform is not an external mandate but an internal capacity, sustained through trust, collaboration, and a shared vision of equity.

References

Argyris, C. (1990). *Overcoming organizational defenses: Facilitating organizational learning*. Allyn and Bacon.

Au, W. (2011). Teaching under the new Taylorism: High-stakes testing and the standardization of the 21st-century curriculum. *Journal of Curriculum Studies, 43*(1), 25–45. https://doi.org/10.1080/00220272.2010.521261

Benjamin, R. (2019). *Race after technology: Abolitionist tools for the new Jim Code*. Polity.

Bryk, A. S., Gomez, L. M., Grunow, A., & LeMahieu, P. G. (2015). *Learning to improve: How America's schools can get better at getting better*. Harvard Education Press.

Bryk, A. S., & Schneider, B. (2002). *Trust in schools: A core resource for improvement*. Russell Sage Foundation.

Fullan, M. (2021). *The right drivers for whole system success.* Centre for Strategic Education.

Fullan, M., & Quinn, J. (2016). *Coherence: The right drivers in action for schools, districts, and systems.* Corwin.

Ingersoll, R. M. (2003). *Who controls teachers' work? Power and accountability in America's schools.* Harvard University Press.

Kahneman, D. (2011). *Thinking, fast and slow.* Farrar, Straus and Giroux.

Levin, B. (2001). Conceptualizing the process of education reform from an international perspective. *Education Policy Analysis Archives, 9*(14). https://digitalcommons.usf.edu/usf_EPAA/388/

March, J. G., & Olsen, J. P. (2011). The logic of appropriateness. In R. E. Goodin (Ed.), *The Oxford handbook of political science.* Oxford University Press.

McDermott, R., & Varenne, H. (1995). Culture as disability. *Anthropology & Education Quarterly, 26*(3), 324–348. https://doi.org/10.1525/aeq.1995.26.3.05x0936z

Mehta, J., & Fine, S. (2019). *In search of deeper learning: The quest to remake the American high school.* Harvard University Press.

Patrick, S., & Sturgis, C. (2015). *Maximizing competency education and blended learning: Insights from experts.* International Association for K–12 Online Learning (iNACOL).

Ravitch, D. (2010). *The death and life of the great American school system: How testing and choice are undermining education.* Basic Books.

Spillane, J. P. (1996). Districts matter: Local educational authorities and state instructional policy. *Educational Policy, 10*(1), 63–87. https://doi.org/10.1177/0895904896010001004

Tyack, D., & Cuban, L. (1995). *Tinkering toward utopia: A century of public school reform.* Harvard University Press.

Tyack, D., & Tobin, W. (1994). The "grammar" of schooling: Why has it been so hard to change? *American Educational Research Journal, 31*(3), 453–479. https://doi.org/10.3102/00028312031003453

3

The Great Pivot

Rethinking Education after COVID-19

> "The pandemic didn't break the education system; it revealed it was already wbroken in ways we had chosen to ignore."
>
> Attributed to Arne Duncan, former
> US Secretary of Education

The onset of COVID-19 created an unprecedented disruption in public education. Schools across the United States were compelled to abandon long-standing practices and adopt emergency distance learning. Within days, fixed schedules, synchronous instruction, and seat time requirements gave way to digital platforms and asynchronous models. This was not a simple logistical shift but an unplanned assessment of institutional adaptability, instructional flexibility, and systemic equity.

Long-standing inequities, including unequal digital access, outdated pedagogical practices, and insufficient infrastructure, could no longer be ignored. The pandemic forced a public reckoning with assumptions about how schools operate and whom they serve. For many students and families, the shift brought instability and uncertainty. Emergency distance learning was a reactive measure, not the result of intentional design, and public perception of digital instruction remains shaped by these crisis-driven origins.

Despite the challenges, the disruption also created space for reimagining education. Traditional boundaries of time and space dissolved, allowing educators to experiment with new approaches to collaboration, feedback, and student autonomy. Some students, particularly those who had struggled in conventional classrooms, experienced new opportunities for success. Others faced greater difficulties without consistent in-person support.

Before 2020, distance learning was often dismissed as supplemental or fringe in public education. COVID-19 forced districts to treat it as a central instructional mode. The abrupt upheaval revealed both the brittleness and adaptability of schools. These divergent experiences raised a critical question: if education can change so dramatically in a crisis, why has it resisted transformation for so long?

If anything, the pandemic illuminated long-overlooked possibilities. It demonstrated that new models of learning are both feasible and necessary. Rather than minimize the hardships of the transition, educators and policymakers must examine what was revealed, what failed, and what succeeded to design a more equitable, flexible, and resilient system.

How Pandemic Distance Learning Redefined Time, Autonomy, and Engagement

The COVID-19 pandemic catalyzed a profound shift in educational delivery, compelling schools to implement remote learning models at an unprecedented scale. This transition revealed the transformative potential of flexibility in fostering student agency. In contrast to traditional models characterized by fixed schedules, synchronous instruction, and uniform expectations, remote environments afforded students greater autonomy over when, where, and how they engaged with content.

Emerging research suggests that this flexibility was particularly advantageous for students experiencing social anxiety, attention-related challenges, or complex family responsibilities. These learners reported increased engagement when permitted to shape their educational routines (Borup et al., 2020a). Virtual tools such as chat functions and asynchronous discussion boards provided alternative avenues for communication, enabling students to participate without the immediacy pressures of face-to-face interactions. These features not only expanded access but also supported inclusive learning by accommodating diverse communication preferences and mitigating social barriers.

The asynchronous structure of many remote learning programs empowered students to learn at their own pace, select project formats aligned with their strengths, and revisit materials as needed. This autonomy fostered a sense of ownership and intrinsic motivation, which are key components of deeper learning and academic persistence (Zhang et al., 2021). For students who had previously felt constrained by conventional classroom models, remote learning offered a context in which they could thrive.

Before examining the theoretical foundations of these outcomes, it is essential to distinguish between pandemic distance learning and formal distance learning. Pandemic distance learning refers to the reactive, improvised instructional models implemented during COVID-19–related school closures. These approaches were marked by urgency, limited preparation, inconsistent access to technology, and a lack of cohesive instructional design. In contrast, distance learning when planned intentionally is characterized by strategic alignment of pedagogy, technology, and learner support systems. It leverages asynchronous and synchronous modalities to promote access, flexibility, and engagement through a coherent instructional framework. The distinction is not merely semantic; it is foundational to understanding the challenges and opportunities that emerged during the pandemic (Hodges et al., 2020).

Importantly, these outcomes are grounded in long-standing educational theory. The shift to remote instruction was not merely logistical; it prompted a reevaluation of core assumptions about learner engagement and autonomy. Central to this reconsideration is the concept of student agency, deeply rooted in constructivist theory, which posits that learners actively construct meaning through interaction with content, context, and community (Vygotsky, 1978). Remote and asynchronous modalities, by design, support this kind of learner-directed exploration and promote active engagement.

Self-determination theory (SDT) provides an additional framework for understanding the motivational benefits of flexible learning environments. According to Deci and Ryan (2000), autonomy, competence, and relatedness are essential psychological needs that drive motivation. Online learning structures that enabled students to determine the timing, pace, and format of their work addressed the need for autonomy in ways that traditional brick-and-mortar classrooms often could not. As reported in multiple studies, including my own research (Wrye, 2022), students who exercised control over their learning schedules demonstrated increased agency and stronger investment in academic outcomes (Zhang et al., 2021).

The benefits of flexibility were not universally accessible. The abrupt transition to distance learning exposed the persistent and often overlooked digital divide. This divide includes disparities in access to devices, reliable internet, and supportive home learning environments. Students from economically disadvantaged backgrounds frequently lacked the tools necessary to benefit from the affordances of remote learning (Katz et al., 2025). These inequities were further exacerbated by uneven resource distribution across states, districts, and individual schools. While affluent districts rapidly implemented one-to-one device programs, under-resourced systems struggled to establish basic infrastructure (Li et al., 2022; Wrye, 2022).

The pandemic underscored a critical truth: flexibility in education cannot exist independently of equity. Autonomy without access is an illusion. For flexible learning to function as a catalyst for student agency rather than a mechanism for widening disparities, schools must provide all students with the tools, training, and support required to succeed. As districts design post-pandemic instructional models, a comprehensive approach that integrates pedagogical innovation with systemic support is imperative. Ensuring that flexibility is not reserved for the privileged few but extended to all learners is essential to building a more equitable and resilient education system.

While the shift to flexible, student-directed learning revealed new opportunities, it also exposed significant challenges in engagement, instructional quality, and systemic readiness. For many students and educators, the realities of pandemic learning were marked not by autonomy and agency but by disruption, disconnection, and uncertainty.

The Limits of Flexibility: Engagement, Readiness, and Professional Strain

While flexibility and student autonomy offered significant benefits during remote learning, they were accompanied by serious challenges that tested the capacity of students, educators, and families alike. The abrupt shift to digital instruction created barriers for learners requiring consistent structure and support. Asynchronous models, though empowering for some, often failed to meet the developmental or logistical needs of many students. Simultaneously, educators frequently under-resourced and unprepared, faced the dual burden of adapting to unfamiliar technologies while attempting to sustain instructional continuity.

Although remote learning created opportunities for innovation, it has been widely remembered for its engagement challenges and instructional disruptions. These difficulties were especially pronounced among younger learners and students lacking robust adult support at home, populations for whom independent learning is often developmentally inappropriate or logistically unfeasible. Educators received minimal preparation, and curricula designed for in-person delivery were hastily adapted to online formats that often fell short of pedagogical best practices.

Traditional student engagement strategies such as eye contact, proximity, and spontaneous formative feedback became ineffective in virtual environments. Teachers who had limited experience with educational technology prior to the pandemic were particularly disadvantaged. Many struggled with learning management systems, collaborative platforms, and video conferencing tools. As one educator shared in my own research, "I didn't just have to teach, I had to learn how to teach all over again, but online and through a tiny screen" (Wrye, 2022).

Even the act of turning on a webcam became a novel and often uncomfortable experience. Both educators and students grappled with privacy concerns, screen fatigue, and the psychological dissonance of school taking place in home environments. Over time, educators demonstrated notable resilience and growth, developing new digital competencies and rethinking their instructional identities. However, this adaptation was uneven. A national survey by Trust and Whalen (2021) found that only 14% of teachers received adequate professional development for online instruction prior to or during the transition.

Empirical studies highlight the emotional and instructional toll of this period. Educators reported declining student participation, limited synchronous feedback, and professional isolation (Adedoyin & Soykan, 2020). Students reported fatigue, disconnection, and perceived irrelevance of assignments. Inconsistent attendance, reduced interaction, and asynchronous pacing contributed to a "crisis of belonging" in digital learning environments (Borup et al., 2020b). Although instruction continued, it did not always foster community, engagement, or cognitive rigor.

These conditions led to a more serious and lasting consequence: widespread student learning loss. While the term "learning loss" has been debated for its deficit framing, it remains a useful descriptor for the academic regression experienced during this period. According to the NWEA, students began the 2021–2022 school year several months behind in reading and mathematics, with the most significant setbacks occurring in high-poverty schools and among historically marginalized groups (Kuhfeld et al., 2022).

It is important to contextualize these findings. Standardized assessments were normed for in-person learning under stable conditions. Students learning during the pandemic faced elevated stress, masked interactions, and social distancing, all of which likely diminished focus and academic engagement, calling into question the reliability of these benchmarks.

The implications extended beyond academic content. Motivation, self-efficacy, and student–teacher relationships were deeply affected. A Brookings Institution report found that chronic absenteeism rose sharply after the pandemic, indicating a fundamental shift in how some students relate to school (Balfanz & Byrnes, 2023). Teachers, in turn, were left to support disengaged and anxious learners without sufficient tools or training.

Exacerbating these challenges was the continued reliance on conventional accountability systems. Metrics such as attendance, participation, and high-stakes assessments remained misaligned with the realities of digital instruction. Teachers often prioritized compliance over connection because that was the expectation and that was a tangible result. This, though, revealed a disconnect between what was measurable and what truly mattered.

These compounding issues affirm a critical insight that effective digital learning requires more than tools and content; it requires a pedagogical transformation grounded in relevance, engagement, and human connection. As Hodges et al. (2020) explained, what most students experienced during the pandemic was not true online learning, but emergency remote teaching as a temporary response to crisis, not a sustainable model. These compounding issues affirm a critical insight: effective digital learning requires more than just tools and content. It demands a pedagogical transformation rooted in relevance, engagement, and human connection. As Hodges et al. (2020) clarified, what most students experienced during the pandemic was not genuine online learning, but emergency remote teaching, a temporary crisis response, not a sustainable model.

Looking ahead, educational systems must go beyond remediation to reimagine what meaningful, equitable learning can be. This includes building digital and hybrid environments that prioritize social presence, autonomy, and authentic engagement; equipping educators with ongoing professional learning; and implementing systemic, data-informed interventions. If the lessons of the pandemic are to drive lasting progress, schools must resist slipping back into outdated models and instead commit to bold, learner-centered transformation.

When Infrastructure Meets Inequity: The Hidden Costs of Unprepared Systems

Although instructional gaps and engagement struggles drew much of the public's attention during the early stages of pandemic learning, they pointed to a deeper and more pervasive issue. These challenges were symptoms of long-standing inequities that had been embedded within the education system for decades. The pandemic did not create these disparities. It made them impossible to ignore. These challenges revealed how systemic readiness, or lack thereof, shaped student access, educator preparedness, and instutional capicity during the most significan educational distruption of our life time.

The COVID-19 pandemic did not create inequities within American public education; rather, it rendered them unmistakably visible. While students in affluent districts rapidly transitioned to synchronous online instruction, supported by well-established learning management systems and existing 1:1 device initiatives, their peers in under-resourced urban and rural communities were often left in educational limbo, awaiting basic tools such as laptops, tablets, or reliable internet access (Dorn et al., 2020). These disparities were not merely technological; they were deeply systemic, reflecting decades of uneven investment in educational infrastructure and digital readiness.

In my previous role as a middle school principal, I proactively championed a 1:1 Chromebook initiative, ensuring that every student had access to a device well before the onset of the pandemic. This strategic foresight paid dividends, enabling our school to transition to distance learning within a week of statewide closures. However, this level of preparedness was atypical. For example, Hartford Public Schools in Connecticut faced significant digital infrastructure deficits at the start of the pandemic. Although the district received $24 million in combined state and federal COVID-19 relief funding to purchase devices, expand Wi-Fi access, and support remote learning, substantial delays in distributing devices and hotspots revealed the limitations of reactive, rather than proactive, investment (Connecticut State Department of Education [CSDE], 2021).

Similar challenges unfolded across the country. In the Los Angeles Unified School District (LAUSD), more than 100,000 students were initially without access to either a device or the internet, prompting the district to allocate over $100 million in emergency funds to address the digital divide (Los Angeles Unified School District [LAUSD], 2020). Detroit Public Schools Community District (DPSCD) launched the Connected Futures initiative, a $23 million public–private partnership aimed at providing every student with a device and home internet access (Connected Futures, 2020). While these interventions were commendable, they also highlighted the precarious dependency on emergency relief funds to compensate for long-standing systemic deficiencies.

These disparities extended beyond access to technology and connectivity and were equally evident in the availability and quality of professional development and instructional support. While some districts mobilized quickly to provide structured, job-embedded professional learning, collaborative planning time, and tiered support for staff, others failed to offer even basic training. Educators in underprepared districts were left to navigate unfamiliar digital tools and instructional models independently, often without formal onboarding, peer collaboration, or centralized guidance (Dorn et al., 2020). This lack of systemic readiness amplified instructional inconsistencies, eroding both implementation fidelity and student engagement, particularly among vulnerable populations.

As a school leader during the pandemic's onset, I witnessed firsthand the widening gulf between teachers who had previously embraced educational technology and those who had resisted it. Prior to COVID-19, some educators within my building viewed digital tools as optional enhancements rather than essential components of instructional practice. Their reliance on traditional methods, often sufficient for producing satisfactory state assessment results, fostered a belief that innovation was unnecessary so long as measurable outcomes were achieved.

When the pandemic demanded an abrupt shift to distance learning, that comfort with outdated structures quickly became a liability. Teachers who had previously dismissed platforms such as Google Classroom or Canvas were now expected to master them within days. The learning curve was steep and unforgiving. Many experienced a sharp drop in instructional efficacy as they struggled to adapt their pedagogy to virtual environments. In contrast, educators who had already integrated technology into their practice transitioned more smoothly, leveraging existing workflows to preserve continuity in student learning. This disparity in preparedness translated directly into disparities in student experience, further entrenching the inequities the pandemic had laid bare and underscoring the urgent need to redesign education around resilience, equity, and learner-centered models.

The lack of uniform professional development, compounded by years of underinvestment in instructional innovation, meant that teachers' capacity to deliver effective digital instruction varied widely, even within the same school building. For some, the crisis catalyzed growth and transformation; for others, it led to frustration, demoralization, and burnout. Ultimately, the uneven distribution of digital fluency among educators became yet another axis of inequity, underscoring the urgent need for sustained and equitable investment in both human and technological capital. To ensure future resilience, school systems must prioritize not only access to devices and connectivity but also the cultivation of professional learning ecosystems that equip all educators, not just early adopters, with the skills and support necessary to thrive in digitally mediated environments.

Data collected during my doctoral research affirmed that three interdependent factors most strongly predicted successful transitions to remote learning: (a) implementation fidelity, (b) community engagement, and (c) prior investment in educational technology infrastructure. Where these components were embedded into district strategy, continuity and innovation were possible. Where they were absent, the digital divide widened, exacerbating disparities in access, opportunity, and outcomes.

A foundational prerequisite to equitable digital learning is reliable home broadband access. According to the Pew Research Center (2024), 80% of US adults report having broadband at home. However, access remains uneven: 86% of suburban residents have home broadband, compared to 77% in urban and 73% in rural areas. Furthermore, mobile dependency is disproportionately high among lower-income households. Vogels (2021) found that only 71% of rural residents own smartphones, compared to 83% of their urban counterparts. In many such households, mobile phones serve as the sole internet-connected device, a poor substitute for a computer when completing complex educational tasks.

This disparity is particularly evident in households with children. While 80% of such households report owning a tablet, digital access still varies significantly by income and geography (US Census Bureau, 2023). Moreover, research from Common Sense Media (2024) shows that more than half of children aged eight and younger now own a mobile device, often in place of more suitable educational tools. This substitution reflects both economic constraints and cultural norms, but its implications for digital literacy and long-term academic achievement are concerning.

Technology, therefore, must be redefined as a critical element of instructional equity, not as a supplementary resource. Access to devices and high-speed internet is no longer a luxury; it is a prerequisite for participation in contemporary learning environments. To achieve true resilience, school systems must transition from crisis-driven solutions to proactive digital ecosystem design. This includes sustained investments not only in hardware and connectivity, but also in professional development, inclusive instructional design, and community partnerships. Digital equity must be recognized as a civil rights imperative, one that ensures every student has the opportunity to thrive in a digitally connected world.

Beyond the Bell Schedule: Early Signs of Personalized and Competency-Based Learning

While the pandemic exposed widespread inequities in infrastructure and preparedness, it also created the conditions for experimentation with alternative instructional models. In the absence of conventional constraints, some educators began to explore practices that prioritized mastery, personalization, and learner autonomy. These early signals of pedagogical innovation suggested a shift not only in tools but also in the very assumptions underpinning instructional design.

Amid the upheaval of emergency remote learning, an unexpected development began to surface: the nascent contours of personalized, competency-based education (CBE). Freed from rigid schedules and traditional seat time requirements, educators increasingly questioned the efficacy of conventional pacing guides, homework policies, and summative assessments. In their place, emergent strategies emphasized formative feedback loops, individualized goal setting, and task-based progression, which are the hallmarks of

CBE and allowed students to advance upon demonstrated mastery rather than arbitrary deadlines (Aurora Institute, 2018; Pane, 2021).

For students who had previously struggled within time-bound instructional models, this shift created an opportunity to demonstrate understanding at their own pace. Educators began to tailor expectations based on individual learning profiles, home environments, and mental health considerations. Digital tools enabled differentiated instruction through video lectures, simulations, and asynchronous discussion boards, thereby supporting diverse learner needs. These adaptations signaled a transition toward learner-centered pedagogies in which instruction conforms to students' individual contexts, rather than requiring conformity to standardized models (Reich et al., 2020; Sharratt, 2019).

With personal experiences throughout my career in public education, it has been observed that there is a strong correlation between student engagement and autonomy: increased flexibility in accessing materials and demonstrating understanding was associated with greater persistence through academic challenges. This finding aligns with broader literature on CBE, which identifies student agency, personalized learning pathways, and equitable support structures as essential to modern educational systems (Patrick & Sturgis, 2015).

While these practices were often implemented unevenly and improvised in response to the crisis, they represented a pivotal inflection point in educational practice. Educators came to recognize the inadequacy of rigid, time-based instructional models and began exploring alternatives centered on student growth and demonstrated mastery. As Sharratt and Fullan (2022) argue, "putting faces on the data requires knowing the whole learner, including their identity, community, and lived experience," a sentiment that underscores the philosophical shift catalyzed by pandemic-era teaching.

Formative feedback loops consist of continuous, low-stakes assessments that provide timely, actionable information to both students and educators. These iterative cycles enable real-time instructional adjustments and foster a responsive, adaptive learning environment. As Sharratt (2019) explains, "real time assessment enables the teacher to determine how it's going and to decide to abandon the original lesson plan if it is not working in favor of a more relevant approach." Feedback that is descriptive, specific, and learner-focused, what Sharratt refers to as "descriptive feedback," has been shown to enhance student metacognition and motivation, especially when aligned with success criteria (Sharratt, 2019).

The consistent use of feedback within digital platforms during the pandemic allowed students to receive just-in-time interventions through auto-scored quizzes, peer discussions, and comments on digital workspaces, thereby reinforcing CBE principles that emphasize formative learning over compliance-based assessment (Budhai & Skipwith, 2022).

Individualized goal setting fosters student autonomy and self-regulated learning by helping learners articulate and pursue personal academic objectives. Sharratt (2019) identifies this as the "ultimate destination of assessment for and as learning," where students take an active role in evaluating their progress and charting future directions. Research suggests that students who set measurable, personalized goals exhibit increased motivation, resilience, and engagement (Schippers et al., 2015). This aligns with competency-based structures where progress is measured by growth rather than norm-based comparisons.

During pandemic distance learning, students who were supported in setting and monitoring goals demonstrated a higher degree of persistence and agency, particularly in environments that allowed for flexible timelines and individualized support (Rowe & Leach, 2021). These findings echo Fullan's (2007) assertion that "students, parents, and teachers must share the same vision of success and be involved in shaping it together" (p. 38).

Task-based progression, central to CBE, enables students to advance through curricular content by demonstrating mastery rather than by accumulating seat time. This model acknowledges that learning is nonlinear and must be adaptable to varying paces of student comprehension. As Budhai and Skipwith (2022) explain, "competency-based learning is measured by demonstrating a competency or mastery of knowledge and skills … while not worrying about the set time prerequisites in traditional classrooms" (p. 94).

The pandemic highlighted the limitations of seat time models and showcased the viability of mastery-based progression. Digital learning environments made it easier to embed interactive tasks, portfolios, and scenario-based assessments into instruction, which allowed for multiple pathways toward demonstrating understanding (Keengwe, 2021). These practices not only fostered deeper learning but also aligned with the ethical imperative to tailor education to the learner rather than the system (Fullan, 2007).

While formative feedback, goal setting, and task-based progression are not new educational innovations, the pandemic thrust these strategies into the spotlight. As Fullan (2007) argues, systemic reform often requires disruption to established routines: "the status quo is remarkably resilient, but change accelerates when core beliefs and systems are challenged simultaneously." What was once the purview of progressive or pilot programs became a necessity for daily instruction, particularly in schools serving diverse and historically marginalized populations.

The shift toward personalized and competency-based learning represents not merely a temporary adaptation but a fundamental rethinking of instructional purpose. As Sharratt and Fullan (2022) articulate, this transformation occurs when educators make student learning visible and take collective responsibility for every learner's progress. In this way, the crisis served as a catalyst for pedagogical innovation, positioning the principles of CBE at the forefront of the contemporary educational change our public institutions so desperately need.

The Subtle Emergence of Machine Learning and AI in K–12 Classrooms

As educators explored flexible, learner-centered practices during the pandemic, they increasingly turned to digital tools that supported personalization and mastery-based progression. This shift, initially rooted in pedagogy, soon intersected with emerging technologies. Among these, artificial intelligence (AI) began to play a subtle yet significant role in shaping instructional delivery, often without being explicitly recognized as such.

Although AI was not widely recognized or adopted in K–12 classrooms during the initial stages of the COVID-19 pandemic, the crisis catalyzed conditions conducive to its subtle and incremental introduction. As schools rapidly transitioned to digital environments, educators sought scalable tools to maintain instructional continuity and differentiate learning across a range of student abilities. In this context, AI-powered platforms such as DreamBox, Lexia, and Khan Academy emerged as essential supports that were often framed as stopgap solutions rather than intentional pedagogical innovations. These technologies offered real-time feedback, adaptive instruction, and automated scaffolding, features that began to redefine how educators conceived of individualized learning paths.

Although educators may not have immediately recognized these tools as AI, they were engaging with machine learning algorithms designed to analyze student responses, identify learning gaps, and recommend next steps. This reflected a quiet yet profound pedagogical shift: a move away from static, one-size-fits-all instructional models toward dynamic systems that adjusted content delivery based on real-time learner data. As Fullan (2007) observed, educational transformation does not always result from large-scale mandates but often emerges through a series of incremental changes in daily practice that gradually reshape systemic norms.

This moment marked a critical turning point. For the first time, many educators encountered digital tools that not only supported instruction but also automated traditionally time-consuming tasks such as grading, progress monitoring, and report generation. This reduction in managerial burden enabled teachers to reinvest their time and energy into relationship building, instructional design, and the cultivation of higher-order thinking skills. However, the rapid adoption of AI technologies also revealed a significant gap: the absence of robust professional development. Most educators began their AI journey at a foundational level, often without the training or time necessary to explore its full instructional potential and thereby negating the time available for relationship building.

Simon Sinek's (2009) insights into leadership and innovation offer a valuable lens. In his concept of the "Diffusion of Innovation," Sinek distinguishes between innovators, early adopters, and the more reluctant majority. The pandemic spotlighted this divergence in real time: while some educators emerged as trailblazers, experimenting with AI-powered tools and leading grassroots innovation, others remained cautious and rightly concerned about data privacy, equity, and pedagogical purpose. As Fitzpatrick et al. (2023) assert, when implemented with intentionality, AI allows educators to outsource the doing and focus on the thinking. In the best cases, educators experienced a professional redefinition, not as content transmitters or "sages on the stage," but as designers of student-centered, inquiry-driven learning experiences.

Simultaneously, the education technology market responded with a surge of products branded as "AI-powered," regardless of whether those tools employed machine learning in meaningful or transparent ways. This trend underscores the need for critical discernment and clear definitions. As Mamlok (2021) warns, the uncritical embrace of digital innovation risks reducing education to a commodity, where personalization becomes synonymous with consumption rather than empowerment.

Nevertheless, these developments align with broader shifts toward personalization, equity, and learner agency. As Sharratt and Fullan (2022) emphasize, truly data-informed instruction begins with the learner in mind, recognizing each student's identity, lived experience, and community context. When deployed ethically and equitably, AI tools can augment this vision by providing educators with immediate insights that inform targeted interventions and responsive pedagogy (Budhai & Skipwith, 2022). The early integration of AI set the stage for deeper reflection on the ethical and pedagogical consequences of algorithm-driven decision-making. Questions of bias, transparency, and accountability remain urgent. As the field continues to explore AI's potential, it must also grapple with its limitations, ensuring that innovation strengthens rather than supplants the human relationships that anchor meaningful learning.

While the introduction of AI into K–12 classrooms may have been quiet, its implications are anything but marginal. The pandemic served as both disruptor and accelerant, prompting educators and systems alike to reconsider the role of technology in teaching and learning. Moving forward, the challenge lies not only in sustaining momentum but also in ensuring that AI serves as a complement to, rather than a replacement for, the thoughtful, relational, and human-centered work that defines high-quality education.

A Glimpse of What Could Be: Lessons from Crisis, Blueprints for Transformation

As AI and digital platforms quietly reshaped aspects of instruction, a broader vision of what education could become began to take shape. Educators and systems were no longer just responding to crisis; they were glimpsing new models of learning that prioritized adaptability, equity, and student agency. These glimpses offered not just temporary solutions, but a roadmap for long-term transformation.

The COVID-19 pandemic forced public education to confront its fragilities, revealing not just systemic inadequacies but also previously unimagined possibilities. Amid the tumult of remote learning, educators glimpsed a vision of education that embraced genuine flexibility, personalized instruction, and learner-centered pedagogies. However transient, these experiences illuminated pathways toward a fundamentally reimagined educational ecosystem grounded in equity, adaptability, and human-centered innovation.

Central to this future is the concept of "learning ecosystems," an approach advocating interconnected, adaptable, and learner-driven educational environments (Brown-Martin, 2014). Learning ecosystems transcend the rigid structures of traditional schooling by integrating formal education with informal, community-based, and digital learning opportunities, emphasizing learner agency, lifelong learning, and continuous feedback loops. By cultivating ecosystems rather than isolated institutions, education can respond dynamically to individual and community needs, fostering resilience and adaptability at systemic levels.

Expanding on this vision, a recent scholarship on "hybrid pedagogies" offers promising frameworks for combining the strengths of face-to-face and digital learning environments. According to Castañón et al. (2023), effective hybrid pedagogy is not merely an operational blend of physical and virtual classrooms, but rather a transformative practice that leverages each environment's unique affordances. Hybrid learning, when implemented intentionally, provides a balance of direct human engagement and technology-enhanced flexibility, fostering environments that support diverse learning preferences and needs while reinforcing student agency.

Furthermore, the emerging notion of "Universal Design for Learning (UDL) 2.0" proposes a more expansive interpretation of inclusive education. UDL 2.0 extends the principles of representation, engagement, and expression to proactively address educational inequities exposed by the pandemic (Gravel et al., 2023). By embedding universal design deeply within digital and hybrid instructional models, schools can ensure learning environments are inherently accessible, reducing barriers that disproportionately affect historically marginalized students. This proactive approach aligns with equity-focused reform, emphasizing systemic rather than reactive accommodations (Novak Educational Consulting, 2024).

Integral to this vision is the role of educators as "facilitators of agency," a concept that redefines the teacher's role from content expert to guide and collaborator. Sahlberg (2023) argue that when educators shift their focus toward facilitating learner autonomy and critical inquiry, they cultivate intrinsic motivation, deeper learning, and greater student resilience. Technology, particularly AI-driven platforms, can augment this facilitative role by automating routine tasks, allowing educators more time to build relationships, mentor individual students, and nurture higher-order cognitive skills (Budhai & Skipwith, 2022).

"Futures literacy" emerges as a critical competency for students navigating an unpredictable global landscape. According to Miller (2018), developing futures literacy, the capacity to imagine and prepare for diverse future scenarios, is essential for equipping students to adapt and thrive amidst uncertainty. Incorporating futures literacy into the curriculum encourages critical thinking, adaptability, and proactive problem-solving, qualities increasingly vital in an era defined by rapid technological and societal change.

Finally, the integration of "digital ethical citizenship" into K–12 curricula represents a crucial step forward in addressing the ethical implications of an increasingly digital educational landscape. Pangrazio and Selwyn (2023) highlight that cultivating digital ethical citizenship helps students navigate complex issues related to privacy, digital identity, AI biases, and responsible online behaviors. As educational institutions embrace greater digital integration, explicitly embedding ethical and responsible technology use into learning processes ensures that innovation is both empowering and equitable.

Together, these concepts create a transformative vision of an educational future marked by adaptability, personalization, equity, and ethical digital citizenship. The pandemic, despite its disruptions, presented an invaluable opportunity to dismantle entrenched barriers and rethink education as a responsive, inclusive ecosystem. For a brief moment, educators and students stepped beyond traditional schooling boundaries into a space where innovation was not only necessary but also achievable. These lessons, born of crisis, should be harnessed to build an agile and equitable educational system that prepares every learner for future complexities.

References

Adedoyin, O. B., & Soykan, E. (2020). Covid-19 pandemic and online learning: The challenges and opportunities. *Interactive Learning Environments*, *28*(7), 1–13. https://doi.org/10.1080/10494820.2020.1813180

Aurora Institute. (2018). *Moving toward mastery: Growing, developing, and sustaining competency-based education*. https://aurora-institute.org/resource/moving-toward-mastery-growing-developing-and-sustaining-competency-based-education/

Balfanz, R., & Byrnes, V. (2023). *Chronic absenteeism in the wake of COVID-19*. Brookings Institution. https://www.brookings.edu

Borup, J., Graham, C. R., Short, C. R., & Archambault, L. (2020a). Supporting students during COVID-19 through flexible online learning. *Educational Technology Research and Development, 68*, 309–312. https://doi.org/10.1007/s11423-020-09831-2

Borup, J., Graham, C. R., West, R. E., Archambault, L., & Spring, K. (2020b). The adolescent community of engagement framework: A model for research on adolescent online learning. *Journal of Technology and Teacher Education, 28*(2), 299–318.

Brown-Martin, G. (2014). *Learning reimagined: How the connected society is transforming learning (N. Tavakolian, Photographs)*. Bloomsbury Qatar Foundation Publishing.

Budhai, S. S., & Skipwith, K. (2022). *Best practices in engaging online learners through active and experiential learning strategies*. Routledge.

Castañón, M., Rice, M., & Filiss, T. (2023). Emergent themes from a study of a highly flexible hybrid learning program. *Online Learning, 27*(4), 220–243. https://doi.org/10.24059/olj.v27i4.4020

Common Sense Media. (2024). *The state of kids and media*. https://www.commonsensemedia.org

Connected Futures. (2020). *Connected Futures initiative: Closing the digital divide in Detroit*. https://www.connectedfutures.net

Connecticut State Department of Education. (2021). *COVID-19 digital access report*. https://portal.ct.gov/SDE

Deci, E. L., & Ryan, R. M. (2000). The "what" and "why" of goal pursuits: Human needs and the self-determination of behavior. *Psychological Inquiry, 11*(4), 227–268. https://doi.org/10.1207/S15327965PLI1104_01

Dorn, E., Hancock, B., Sarakatsannis, J., & Viruleg, E. (2020). *COVID-19 and learning loss: Disparities grow and students need help*. McKinsey & Company. https://www.mckinsey.com

Fitzpatrick, D., Fox, A., & Weinstein, B. (2023). *The AI classroom: The ultimate guide to artificial intelligence in education*. TeacherGoals Publishing.

Fullan, M. (2007). *The new meaning of educational change (4th ed.)*. Teachers College Press.

Gravel, J. W., Rose, D. H., & Tucker-Smith, T. N. (2023). Universal Design for Learning in its third decade: A focus on equity, inclusion, and design. In R. J. Tierney, F. Rizvi, & K. Erkican (Eds.) *International Encyclopedia of Education* (4th ed., Vol. 6, pp. 712–720). Elsevier. https://doi.org/10.1016/B978-0-12-818630-5.14079-5

Hodges, C., Moore, S., Lockee, B., Trust, T., & Bond, A. (2020, March 27). The difference between emergency remote teaching and online learning. *EDUCAUSE Review*. https://er.educause.edu/articles/2020/3/the-difference-between-emergency-remote-teaching-and-online-learning

Katz, V. S., Jordan, A. B., & Ognyanova, K. (2025). Digital inequalities and U.S. undergraduate outcomes over the first two years of the COVID-19 pandemic. *PLOS One, 20*(3), e0319000. https://doi.org/10.1371/journal.pone.0319000

Keengwe, J. (Ed.). (2021). *Handbook of research on equity in computer science in P-16 education*. IGI Global.

Kuhfeld, M., Tarasawa, B., Johnson, A., Ruzek, E., & Lewis, K. (2022). *Learning during COVID-19: Initial findings on students' reading and math achievement and growth*. NWEA. https://www.nwea.org

Li, G., Luo, H., Lei, J., Xu, S., & Chen, T. (2022). Effects of first-time experiences and self-regulation on college students' online learning motivation: Based on a national survey during COVID-19. *Education Sciences, 12*(4), 245. https://doi.org/10.3390/educsci12040245

Los Angeles Unified School District. (2020). *Schoology and digital learning resources*. https://achieve.lausd.net/Page/10174

Mamlok, D. (2021). Rethinking educational technology: Ethical implications of AI in education. *AI & Society, 36*(2), 679–689. https://doi.org/10.1007/s00146-020-01056-6

Maryland Department of Legislative Services. (2021). *Blueprint for Maryland's future implementation report*. https://mgaleg.maryland.gov

Miller, R. (2018). *Transforming the future: Anticipation in the 21st century*. Routledge/UNESCO.

Novak Educational Consulting. (2024). *UDL 2.0 framework overview*. https://www.novakeducationalconsulting.com

Pane, J. F. (2021). *Strategies for implementing personalized learning while acknowledging potential pitfalls*. RAND Corporation. https://www.rand.org

Pangrazio, L., & Selwyn, N. (2023). Digital ethical citizenship: Rethinking youth digital literacies. *Learning, Media and Technology, 48*(1), 1–16. https://doi.org/10.1080/17439884.2022.2116517

Patrick, S., & Sturgis, C. (2015). *Maximizing competency education and blended learning: Insights from experts*. Aurora Institute. https://aurora-institute.org

Pew Research Center. (2024). *Internet/broadband fact sheet*. https://www.pewresearch.org

Reich, J., Buttimer, C. J., Fang, A., Hillaire, G., Hirsch, K., Larke, L. R., & Slama, R. (2020). *Remote learning guidance from state education agencies during the COVID-19 pandemic: A first look* (EdWorkingPaper No. 20–226). Annenberg Institute at Brown University. https://doi.org/10.26300/cdrv-yw05

Rowe, D., & Leach, T. (2021). Goal setting and student agency in online learning. *International Journal of Educational Technology, 18*(1), 101–117.

Sahlberg, P. (2023). Trends in global education reform since the 1990s: Looking for the right way. *International Journal of Educational Development, 98*, 102748. https://doi.org/10.1016/j.ijedudev.2023.102748

Schippers, M. C., Scheepers, A. W. A., & Peterson, J. B. (2015). A scalable goal-setting intervention closes both the gender and ethnic minority achievement gap. *Proceedings of the National Academy of Sciences, 112*(42), 12399–12404. https://doi.org/10.1073/pnas.1506047112

Sharratt, L. (2019). *Clarity: What matters most in learning, teaching, and leading.* Corwin Press.

Sharratt, L., & Fullan, M. (2022). *Putting FACES on the data* (Updated ed.). Corwin Press.

Sinek, S. (2009). *Start with why: How great leaders inspire everyone to take action.* Portfolio.

Trust, T., & Whalen, J. (2021). K–12 teachers' experiences and challenges with remote learning during the COVID-19 pandemic: Insights from a national survey. *TechTrends, 65*(4), 1–12. https://doi.org/10.1007/s11528-021-00625-2

US Census Bureau. (2023). *Computer and internet use in the United States: 2023.* https://www.census.gov

Vogels, E. A. (2021). *Digital divide persists even as Americans with lower incomes make gains in tech adoption.* Pew Research Center. https://www.pewresearch.org

Vygotsky, L. S. (1978). *Mind in society: The development of higher psychological processes.* Harvard University Press.

Wrye, T. P. (2022). *The great equalizer: Distance learning and its impact on education equity* (Doctoral dissertation), Drexel University. https://doi.org/10.17918/00001294

Yue, M., Jong, M. S. Y., & Ng, D. T. K. (2024). Understanding K–12 teachers' technological pedagogical content knowledge readiness and attitudes toward artificial intelligence education. *Education and Information Technologies, 29*(15), 19505–19536. https://doi.org/10.1007/s10639-024-12621-2

Zhang, B., Taub, M., & Chen, G. (2021). Examining the impact of students' motivation on performance and engagement in distance learning. *Educational Technology Research and Development, 69*(3), 1545–1565. https://doi.org/10.1007/s11423-021-09995-2

Section 2
Equity by Design
Building Personalized Pathways for All Learners

Personalized systems must honor learner variability across pace, pathway, and support, rather than treat students as uniform. As Darling-Hammond argues, effective schooling recognizes individual learning trajectories and designs environments that respect them (Darling-Hammond et al., 2020). Moving from industrial-era education models to adaptive, inclusive, and student-centered systems requires a fundamental redesign of the principles guiding schooling. Public education continues to face persistent challenges, including achievement gaps, disengagement, and systemic inequities. Personalized learning has gained attention as a promising response, yet its application remains inconsistent. When thoughtfully constructed, personalized learning disrupts standardization, honors learner variability, and expands access to relevant, rigorous opportunities. Without an intentional focus on equity, however, such models risk becoming exclusive to well-resourced environments, deepening rather than narrowing opportunity gaps.

Ensuring that personalized learning supports equity involves more than the use of digital tools. It demands a comprehensive framework grounded in inclusive pedagogy, learner agency, and authentic engagement. Foundational concepts must be clarified to distinguish personalization from differentiation or individualization. A clear emphasis on mastery-based progression, cultural

DOI: 10.4324/9781003739050-5

relevance, and structural support is essential to avoid superficial or inequitable implementations.

The role of AI further complicates and enhances the conversation. AI offers unprecedented possibilities for responsive, real-time learning pathways, yet it also introduces significant concerns related to bias, transparency, and access. Addressing these tensions requires ethical oversight, professional development, and inclusive design principles. Educators are central to this transformation. As roles shift from content delivery to facilitation and design, professional identity and instructional practice must evolve accordingly.

Embedding equity into the core of personalized learning creates the conditions for educational justice. When aligned with culturally responsive teaching, universal design, and systemic investment, these approaches can offer every learner a pathway defined by individual strengths, affirmed identity, and preparation for a complex and rapidly changing world.

Reference

Darling-Hammond, L., Schachner, A., Edgerton, A. K., Badrinarayan, A., Cardichon, J., Cookson, P. W., Jr., Griffith, M., Gulati, S., Institute, J., & Ramos, M. (2020). Restarting and reinventing school: Learning in the time of COVID and beyond. Learning Policy Institute. https://learningpolicyinstitute.org/product/restarting-reinventing-school-learning-time-covid

4

Defining Personalized Learning

Foundations for the Future

Personalized learning has emerged as a central component of contemporary educational reform, driven by the need to tailor instruction to individual learner profiles, diverse academic needs, and unique personal interests (Fullan et al., 2018; Hatch et al., 2021). Consistent with Lubbock's argument that schools should cultivate a desire to learn rather than only deliver instruction (Lubbock, 2010), personalized learning extends beyond a pedagogical rebrand. Unlike previous instructional trends that often faded without systemic transformation, personalized learning presents a scalable and sustainable framework grounded in learner agency, real-time data, and flexible pacing. It responds not only to instructional needs but also to structural and systemic challenges, aligning with the evolving demands of mid-21st-century education.

Traditional models of education, which continue to rely on uniform content delivery and standardized assessments, increasingly fall short amid technological advancements, global instability, and shifting political landscapes (Lehmann & Chase, 2015; Mitchell et al., 2018). In contrast, forward-leaning initiatives such as Vermont's Act 77 Flexible Pathways Initiative, New Hampshire's transition to competency-based education, and Maine's proficiency-based diploma policy have begun to redefine public schooling. These models prioritize student voice, adaptability, and mastery-based progression.

DOI: 10.4324/9781003739050-6

By integrating core tenets of personalized learning, formative feedback, flexible scheduling, and individualized goal setting into the learning process, these initiatives challenge traditional time-bound instructional structures. In doing so, they offer a foundation for dismantling historic structural inequities and preparing learners with the critical thinking, adaptability, and collaborative skills required for success in a complex and evolving world (DePaoli et al., 2021; Pane et al., 2015, 2017; Patrick et al., 2018).

Beyond the Buzzwords: The Pillars of Personalized Learning

Personalized learning is increasingly recognized as a transformational framework in contemporary education, one that challenges the traditional architecture of standardized, time-bound instructional systems. Rather than merely adjusting content delivery, personalized learning reorients the entire learning ecosystem around the student, leveraging data, learner input, and flexible pathways to support holistic development. Grounded in research and responsive to the demands of the mid 21st century, this pedagogical model seeks to ensure that all students, regardless of background or ability, can access meaningful, relevant, and future-ready learning opportunities (Pane et al., 2015, 2017; Patrick et al., 2018).

Across the educational landscape, multiple frameworks have attempted to define and structure personalized learning. The components presented here synthesize key insights from the work of Patrick et al. (2018), Fullan et al. (2018), and LeGeros (2022), among others, into six interdependent pillars: learner agency, differentiated instruction through Universal Design for Learning (UDL), competency-based progression, formative assessment and feedback supported by real-time data, flexible learning environments, and personalized pathways. Taken together, these components reflect a systems-level model of personalization designed for equity, engagement, and scalability.

Learner agency constitutes the epistemological core of personalized learning. It refers to the degree to which students are empowered to set goals, make instructional choices, monitor progress, and reflect critically on their learning trajectories (Fullan,

2007; Lehmann & Chase, 2015). Unlike traditional models in which students assume passive roles, agency-based instruction cultivates metacognition and fosters a sense of ownership over the learning process. Empirical research indicates that increased agency correlates positively with academic motivation, self-efficacy, and engagement, particularly among students historically marginalized by conventional schooling (Fitzpatrick et al., 2023; Reber et al., 2021).

Differentiated instruction, operationalized through Universal Design for Learning (UDL), addresses learner variability with intentionality and precision. Tomlinson (2017) defines differentiation as the adaptation of content, process, product, and learning environment to meet individual needs. UDL provides a proactive framework that embeds flexibility and equity into curriculum design by offering multiple means of engagement, representation, and expression (CAST, 2020; Fullan et al., 2018; Keengwe, 2021). Together, differentiated instruction and UDL enable personalized learning to move beyond reactive accommodations, becoming a coherent and inclusive design principle.

Competency-based progression restructures how time and advancement are organized in the learning process by allowing students to move forward based on demonstrated mastery rather than age or the amount of instructional time completed. This model challenges the one-size-fits-all structure of traditional education by shifting the focus from compliance to proficiency (Pane et al., 2017; Sturgis & Casey, 2018). It requires clearly defined learning targets, rigorous assessment of skills, and flexible pacing, all of which contribute to deeper learning and authentic performance (Patrick et al., 2018).

Formative assessment and real-time feedback systems serve as the instructional engine of personalized learning. Ongoing assessment practices enable educators to gather timely data on student understanding, adapt instruction responsively, and provide targeted feedback that supports remediation, enrichment, and self-regulation (Sharratt, 2019; Heritage, 2022). When coupled with learning analytics and adaptive technologies, formative feedback not only enhances instructional precision but also empowers students to make informed decisions about their learning, reinforcing agency and metacognitive development.

Flexible learning environments and modalities expand the where, when, and how of instruction. These may include virtual or hybrid classrooms, flexible pacing models, flipped instruction, and experiential or project-based learning. By removing spatial and temporal constraints, flexible environments accommodate diverse learning needs and support personalized access (Patrick et al., 2018). Tools such as Summit Learning, Altitude Learning, and adaptive platforms have demonstrated effectiveness in increasing engagement and academic performance, particularly in rural and underserved districts (Pane et al., 2015, 2017).

Personalized pathways and interest-based learning opportunities serve as the capstone of this model. These approaches allow students to pursue learning experiences aligned with their passions, goals, and identities through interdisciplinary studies, service learning, capstone projects, and community-based internships. These experiences promote relevance, deepen engagement, and foster purpose-driven learning (DePaoli et al., 2021). Incorporating futures literacy, the capacity to anticipate, imagine, and prepare for multiple possible futures further enhances adaptability and prepares students for a volatile, uncertain, complex, and ambiguous world (Miller, 2018).

Together, these six interwoven pillars form the philosophical, pedagogical, and structural foundation of personalized learning. The breadth and depth of these components may appear ambitious, yet such complexity reflects the magnitude of the shift being proposed. This is not a marginal adjustment to existing systems, but a fundamental reimagining of what schooling can and should be in the middle 21st century. Personalized learning redefines educators as facilitators, mentors, and designers of learning experiences, while positioning students as active agents in their educational development. Far from being a fragmented approach, it offers a coherent, equity-driven framework for systemic transformation, one capable of addressing long-standing limitations while equipping learners for the complexity of the future. To operationalize these six pillars in practice, leaders and educators can draw on established pedagogical frameworks that guide the integration and evaluation of technology within personalized learning environments.

Project-Based Learning: Agency, Equity, and Deeper Learning

Project-based learning (PBL) has become a central vehicle for operationalizing personalized learning because it positions students as active investigators rather than passive recipients of knowledge. In contrast to traditional instructional approaches that emphasize compliance and repetition, PBL emphasizes inquiry, sustained engagement, and authentic problem-solving. Students learn by pursuing complex questions, applying interdisciplinary skills, and producing artifacts that demonstrate mastery in real-world contexts (Larmer et al., 2015; Thomas, 2000).

Driving Agency and Deeper Learning

PBL is uniquely aligned with the six pillars of personalized learning. It fosters learner agency by requiring students to set goals, make design choices, and reflect on their progress. It strengthens competency-based progression through performance assessments where mastery is demonstrated by application rather than test scores. Finally, PBL supports flexible pathways by allowing students to integrate their personal interests, cultural backgrounds, and community contexts into learning tasks. Research shows that students engaged in PBL report higher levels of motivation, critical thinking, and collaborative problem-solving compared to peers in traditional classrooms (Condliffe et al., 2017).

Integration of Technology and Personalization

Technology enhances PBL by expanding access to information, collaboration, and authentic audiences. Platforms such as Google Workspace, multimedia creation tools, and adaptive feedback systems enable students to design, iterate, and share projects with peers and external stakeholders. When grounded in pedagogical frameworks such as TPACK or Triple E, technology integration in PBL moves beyond novelty to authentically enhance engagement and extend learning beyond the classroom (Kolb, 2017; Koehler & Mishra, 2009). Extended reality (XR) environments also enrich PBL by allowing learners to simulate scientific phenomena or engage in immersive historical re-creations, bridging access gaps for schools with limited physical resources.

Equity and Culturally Responsive Pedagogy

PBL is not only an instructional strategy but also a lever for equity. By valuing diverse cultural perspectives and lived experiences, PBL aligns with culturally responsive pedagogy and Universal Design for Learning (Gay, 2018; CAST, 2020). Students are encouraged to draw upon their identities and communities as resources in problem-solving. This emphasis on relevance ensures that historically marginalized learners, such as multilingual students, students of color, and those from under-resourced contexts, see their experiences reflected in academic inquiry. When combined with competency-based education, PBL disrupts tracking systems by providing multiple pathways to demonstrate mastery through authentic performance tasks rather than standardized assessments (Sturgis & Casey, 2018).

Case Examples of District Implementation

Several schools and districts illustrate how PBL operationalizes equity and personalization:

- **Science Leadership Academy (Philadelphia, PA)**: Students engage in interdisciplinary projects tied to civic and scientific challenges, culminating in public exhibitions. This model advances student voice, collaboration, and agency while connecting learning to real-world issues (Lehmann & Chase, 2015).
- **High Tech High (San Diego, CA)**: PBL forms the core of the curriculum. Students present their work through exhibitions, portfolios, and public performances. This model redefines assessment as an authentic demonstration, promoting equity by recognizing multiple forms of knowledge and expression (Fullan et al., 2018).
- **Vermont Act 77 Flexible Pathways**: The statewide initiative embeds PBL within personalized learning plans,

work-based learning, and proficiency-based graduation requirements. This policy-level integration ensures that PBL is not an isolated practice but a structural driver of personalization and equity (DePaoli et al., 2021).

Together, these models show that PBL is both a pedagogical method and a systems-level reform strategy. It exemplifies how personalized learning can advance deeper engagement, equitable participation, and mastery-based outcomes when aligned with technology and culturally responsive design.

Pedagogical Frameworks to Guide Technology-Enhanced Personalized Learning

Personalized learning requires more than access to digital tools; it demands pedagogical frameworks that ensure technology supports, rather than supplants, instructional goals. Several established models provide leaders and educators with practical approaches to align technology integration with learning outcomes. These frameworks help ensure that digital tools are not adopted for novelty or compliance, but instead advance meaningful, equitable, and student-centered learning.

The first framework, Technological Pedagogical Content Knowledge (TPACK), emphasizes the intersection of technology, pedagogy, and content as the core of effective instructional design. Koehler and Mishra (2009) argue that technology integration is most successful when teachers understand not only the subject matter and pedagogical strategies but also how technology reshapes and mediates both. For school and district leaders, TPACK provides a decision-making guide to align technology purchases, professional learning, and instructional design with academic standards and curricular goals. In this sense, it supports coherence across policy, pedagogy, and practice.

Complementing TPACK is the Triple E Framework, developed by Kolb (2017) to evaluate the effectiveness of technology integration. Triple E focuses on whether digital tools engage students in learning, enhance instructional goals, and extend learning beyond the classroom. Its emphasis on measurable impact makes it particularly relevant for leaders navigating competing vendor claims and budgetary pressures. By applying Triple E, districts can prioritize technologies that demonstrate clear instructional value and avoid investments that reinforce passive or superficial use.

A third perspective is provided by the Student Engagement, Technology, and Instruction (SETI) model, which highlights the relational and instructional dimensions of technology use (Hernandez-Ramos & De La Paz, 2009). SETI underscores that technology integration must account for the interplay of student engagement, teacher practice, and contextual factors, rather than being treated as an isolated intervention. For leaders, this model reinforces the idea that successful technology adoption requires systemic alignment that includes professional development, curriculum design, and classroom culture.

Together, these frameworks offer complementary approaches for guiding personalized learning. TPACK ensures a balanced alignment between content, pedagogy, and technology. Triple E provides criteria to evaluate whether technology supports engagement and learning goals. SETI situates these decisions within the broader instructional context, emphasizing the centrality of relationships and student experience. When applied collectively, they create a roadmap for leaders to ensure that technology integration advances equity, agency, and mastery rather than reinforcing outdated models of compliance or consumption. These frameworks establish a foundation for evaluating technology choices and instructional strategies, and their value becomes most evident when applied to real-world models where schools and districts have translated the principles of personalization into action.

Empowering Learners through Personalization

Building on these guiding frameworks, personalized learning enhances educational experiences by aligning them with each learner's strengths, challenges, interests, and sociocultural contexts. It also responds to diverse cognitive and learning preferences, including visual, auditory, reading–writing, and kinesthetic modalities, as well as hands-on and experiential learning styles. A key advantage of this approach is its potential to advance educational equity by addressing systemic disparities and ensuring that historically marginalized populations, including students with disabilities, multilingual learners, and those from underserved communities, receive targeted support tailored to their specific needs (Fullan et al., 2018; Pane et al., 2017). When implemented with fidelity, personalized learning creates inclusive environments where students are active participants in shaping their educational trajectories.

Numerous public school models across the United States illustrate how personalized learning can be embedded in both district and state-level strategies. Lindsay Unified School District in California offers one of the most comprehensive examples. Its system-wide use of competency-based progression, personalized learning plans, and digital dashboards reflects deep integration of all six foundational pillars (Patrick et al., 2018). Similarly, Vermont's Act 77 Flexible Pathways Initiative exemplifies statewide personalization through dual enrollment, work-based learning, and proficiency-based graduation requirements. These mechanisms elevate student agency and align learning with real-world relevance (DePaoli et al., 2021).

Another group of models demonstrates the power of personalized learning to align with career pathways and industry partnerships. Westbrook Public Schools in Connecticut, in collaboration with General Dynamics Electric Boat, prepares students for careers through welding certifications and industry-specific training during high school. This model reinforces personalized pathways, learner agency, and competency-based advancement (Westbrook Public Schools, 2024). Granby Memorial High School, also in Connecticut, emphasizes mentorship and postsecondary planning through community partnerships and structured advising. These programs support flexible environments and student-driven exploration of life after graduation (Connecticut Association of Schools, 2022).

Several schools integrate personalization through inquiry-based, project-centered learning. At the Science Leadership Academy in Philadelphia, students co-design interdisciplinary projects to investigate civic and scientific problems. This model strongly reinforces learner agency, flexible environments, and personalized pathways (Lehmann & Chase, 2015). Similarly, in Massachusetts, Andover High School's Global Pathways Program encourages students to explore global challenges through community collaboration. Although it is not formally grounded in competency-based progression, its emphasis on relevance, collaboration, and interdisciplinary inquiry aligns closely with the principles of personalized learning (Jacobs & Alcock, 2017). High Tech High extends these principles through student-led conferences and public exhibitions, embedding authenticity, feedback, and agency into learning demonstrations (Fullan et al., 2018).

Technology-supported models also contribute significantly to the personalization landscape. Montour School District in Pennsylvania uses adaptive learning platforms such as DreamBox and Carnegie Learning to customize pacing and content delivery. These tools support formative assessment, responsive intervention, and differentiated instruction, especially in math and literacy (Fitzpatrick et al., 2023). In the Winton Woods City School District in Ohio, the integration of Universal Design for Learning with artificial intelligence (AI)-enabled platforms creates multisensory, accessible instructional environments tailored to individual learning profiles (CAST, 2020; Fitzpatrick et al., 2023).

Some districts also embed culturally responsive pedagogy into personalized learning structures. Wayne Township in Indiana affirms student identity by incorporating language, lived experiences, and cultural narratives into instruction. This model emphasizes learner agency, differentiation, and relevance, particularly for students underserved by standardized systems (Keengwe, 2021).

Taken together, these cases demonstrate that effective personalized learning is not dependent on any single platform, pedagogical technique, or policy initiative. Its success lies in the intentional and integrated application of the six foundational pillars: learner agency, differentiated instruction, competency-based progression, formative assessment, flexible environments, and personalized pathways. These elements work in concert to form a coherent, inclusive, and future-oriented educational design.

While the philosophical and structural foundations of personalized learning provide a critical blueprint, its true value emerges through implementation. Across the country, forward-thinking districts and schools have translated these core principles into practice, adapting the six pillars to meet the needs of their local communities. These models offer concrete evidence that personalized learning, when thoughtfully designed and executed, leads to meaningful shifts in student engagement, academic growth, and real-world readiness.

Empowering Resilient Learners: Futures Literacy, Adaptive Competencies, and Universal Design

As schools deepen their commitment to personalized learning, the imperative extends beyond academic customization to include the cultivation of adaptable, future-ready individuals. This section explores how futures literacy, adaptive competencies, and UDL function not as separate innovations but as critical extensions of the six foundational pillars. Each contributes to the creation of learning environments that are inclusive, anticipatory, and designed to prepare students not only for the world they will inherit but also for the systems they will shape.

As personalized learning continues to evolve from a classroom-based strategy to a systemic educational model, its aims must extend beyond individualized content mastery. The model must now address the broader imperative of preparing learners for an unpredictable, interconnected, and rapidly changing world. Achieving this requires the deliberate integration of futures literacy, adaptive competencies, and UDL. These three domains do not constitute a new framework but rather deepen and extend the six foundational pillars of personalized learning by reinforcing agency, mastery, and access within equitable and future-focused learning systems.

Futures literacy, as defined by UNESCO, refers to the capacity to imagine, critique, and navigate multiple potential futures (Miller, 2018). In educational contexts, it involves equipping learners not only to succeed within existing systems but also to engage in shaping the systems that will succeed them. This book itself embraces a futures-oriented perspective by challenging the structural inertia of traditional education and proposing frameworks designed for adaptability, inclusion, and long-term relevance. When embedded in personalized learning environments, futures literacy encourages students to consider long-term social, technological, and environmental trajectories. This anticipatory mindset directly supports learner agency, personalized pathways, and flexible environments by empowering students to co-create learning experiences that are meaningful, context-aware, and aligned with their evolving identities and aspiration.

Global and local applications illustrate how futures literacy is being operationalized in schools. In Singapore, secondary-school students participate in structured scenario planning exercises that explore the implications of climate change, technological advancements, and economic transformation (Miller, 2018). Similarly, the Global Pathways Program at Andover High School in Massachusetts engages students in interdisciplinary inquiries into civic and global challenges through partnerships with community organizations. The program is a three-year sequence that includes language study, immersive experiences, service learning, and a capstone project that culminates in an endorsement for global engagement. These experiences foster essential skills such as collaboration, ethical reasoning, and systems thinking. In doing so, they position students not merely as recipients of knowledge but as emerging architects of the future (Andover High School, n.d.).

Closely aligned with futures literacy is the development of adaptive competencies, which are skills necessary for success in complex, uncertain environments. These competencies include creativity, critical thinking, emotional intelligence, resilience, and digital fluency (Fullan et al., 2018). They are not supplementary to academic success; they are foundational. Personalized learning environments naturally support the emergence of these competencies through interdisciplinary projects, authentic performance assessments, and opportunities for student-driven inquiry. These experiences cultivate intellectual flexibility, metacognitive awareness, and the ability to respond constructively to new challenges.

Several schools featured earlier in this chapter exemplify the integration of adaptive competencies. At High Tech High, student-led conferences and public exhibitions develop communication, project management, and reflective practice. In Westbrook Public Schools, students pursuing industry certifications engage in real-world applications of learning through partnerships with Electric Boat, gaining practical skills, confidence, and workplace readiness. In both cases, students are engaged in learning that is purposeful, situated, and responsive to their future trajectories.

UDL plays a critical enabling role in ensuring that futures literacy and adaptive competencies are accessible to all learners. Developed by CAST (2020), UDL is a research-informed framework that promotes multiple means of engagement, representation, and expression. It operationalizes core pillars of personalized learning, particularly differentiated instruction, formative assessment, and flexible environments, by proactively designing curriculum and instruction to accommodate diverse learning needs from the outset. In districts such as Winton Woods City Schools in Ohio, UDL is paired with adaptive technologies to create inclusive and rigorous learning experiences that support all students, regardless of ability, background, or profile.

Beyond ensuring access, UDL enhances the development of adaptive competencies by removing barriers to engagement and expression. When students can demonstrate understanding through modalities such as video, prototypes, podcasts, or collaborative presentations, they are more likely to engage deeply, reflect critically, and persist through academic challenges. Similarly, by offering authentic choices in how students interact with content and express mastery, UDL fosters the learner autonomy and agency that futures literacy demands.

Integrating futures literacy, adaptive competencies, and UDL does not replace the original pillars of personalized learning. Rather, it strengthens and operationalizes them. This convergence transforms personalized learning from a model of individual customization to a framework for educational transformation. Students are not simply navigating current systems more efficiently. They are acquiring the tools and dispositions required to analyze, adapt, and redesign those systems with vision, resilience, and ethical responsibility. When grounded in inclusive design and oriented toward long-term readiness, personalized learning becomes both a moral and pedagogical imperative for public education in the 21st century.

Extending the Vision: From Personalized Learning to Intelligent Design

The personalized learning movement represents more than a pedagogical shift. It is a reimagining of the purposes, processes, and outcomes of public education. As this chapter has illustrated, personalization, when grounded in the six foundational pillars of learner agency, differentiated instruction, competency-based progression, formative assessment, flexible learning environments, and personalized pathways, serves as a powerful framework for advancing equity, engagement, and academic success. Through illustrative models from Lindsay Unified, Westbrook Public Schools, Summit Public Schools, and others, it is evident that personalization can be implemented at both the classroom and system levels, producing measurable and meaningful outcomes for diverse learners.

The integration of UDL ensures that personalized environments are not only responsive but also inclusive by design. The deliberate incorporation of adaptive competencies, including resilience, creativity, and critical thinking, expands the reach of personalization into long-term learner development. Futures literacy further reinforces this progression by equipping students with the capacity to anticipate, navigate, and influence the complex challenges that lie ahead. Taken together, these elements position personalization as both a moral imperative and a strategic necessity in an era defined by uncertainty and accelerating change.

Yet even as schools and districts advance toward more personalized, equitable, and future-ready learning models, new questions emerge. How can these approaches be scaled without compromising depth? What role should emerging technologies play in supporting or accelerating personalization? And most critically, how can educators ensure that innovations such as AI are used ethically, inclusively, and in service of student-centered learning?

As education systems begin to integrate futures literacy, adaptive competencies, and UDL into the fabric of personalized learning, the landscape of possibility continues to expand. At the same time, the pace of technological and social transformation demands new forms of leadership, pedagogy, and foresight. Among the most consequential developments is the rise of AI. Positioned at the intersection of personalization, automation, and data-informed instruction, AI holds the potential to strengthen and scale many of the principles explored in this chapter. It also introduces a new set of ethical, infrastructural, and professional challenges. As we turn to examine the evolving role of AI in public education, the question is not whether intelligent tools will shape learning but how they can be designed and deployed to extend, not replace, the human-centered foundations on which meaningful education depends.

References

Andover High School. (n.d.). *Global pathways program.* https://www.andoverhighschool.k12.ma.us/globalpathways

CAST. (2020). *Universal design for learning guidelines version 2.2.* http://udlguidelines.cast.org

Condliffe, B., Quint, J., Visher, M. G., Bangser, M. R., Drohojowska, S., Saco, L., & Nelson, E. (2017). *Project-based learning: A literature review.* MDRC. https://www.mdrc.org/publication/project-based-learning

Connecticut Association of Schools. (2022). *Granby Memorial High School profile.* https://www.casciac.org/granby

DePaoli, J. L., Bridgeland, J., Balfanz, R., Atwell, M., & Ingram, E. S. (2021). *Building a grad nation: Progress and challenge in raising high school graduation rates.* Civic Enterprises and Everyone Graduates Center.

Fitzpatrick, D., Fox, A., & Weinstein, B. (2023). *The AI classroom: The ultimate guide to artificial intelligence in education.* Routledge.

Fullan, M. (2007). *The new meaning of educational change* (4th ed.). Teachers College Press.

Fullan, M., Quinn, J., & McEachen, J. (2018). *Deep learning: Engage the world, change the world.* Corwin.

Gay, G. (2018). *Culturally responsive teaching: Theory, research, and practice* (3rd ed.). Teachers College Press.

Hatch, T., Corson, D., & Gerth van den Berg, J. (2021). *The education we need for a future we can't predict.* Corwin.

Heritage, M. (2022). *Formative assessment: Making it happen in the classroom.* Corwin.

Hernández-Ramos, P., & De La Paz, S. (2009). Learning history in middle school by designing multimedia in a project-based learning experience. *Journal of Research on Technology in Education, 42*(2), 151–173. https://doi.org/10.1080/15391523.2009.10782545

Jacobs, H. H., & Alcock, M. (2017). *Bold moves for schools: How we create remarkable learning environments*. ASCD.

Keengwe, J. (Ed.). (2021). *Handbook of research on equity in computer science in P–16 education*. IGI Global.

Koehler, M. J., & Mishra, P. (2009). What is technological pedagogical content knowledge? *Contemporary Issues in Technology and Teacher Education, 9*(1), 60–70.

Kolb, L. (2017). *Learning first, technology second: The educator's guide to designing authentic lessons*. ISTE.

Larmer, J., Mergendoller, J. R., & Boss, S. (2015). *Setting the standard for project based learning: A proven approach to rigorous classroom instruction*. ASCD.

LeGeros, L. (2022). Informing the implementation of technology-supported personalized learning. *Journal of Educational Technology Development and Exchange, 15*(1). https://doi.org/10.1080/19404476.2022.2009707

Lehmann, C., & Chase, Z. (2015). *Building school 2.0: How to create the schools we need*. Jossey-Bass.

Lubbock, J. (2010). *The pleasures of life*. Scholar Select. (Original work published 1890)

Miller, R. (2018). *Transforming the future: Anticipation in the 21st century*. UNESCO Publishing.

Mitchell, D. E., Shipps, D., & Crowson, R. L. (2018). *Shaping education policy: Power and process*. Routledge.

Pane, J. F., Steiner, E. D., Baird, M. D., & Hamilton, L. S. (2015). *Continued progress: Promising evidence on personalized learning*. RAND Corporation. https://www.rand.org/pubs/research_reports/RR1365.html

Pane, J. F., Steiner, E. D., Baird, M. D., & Hamilton, L. S. (2017). *Informing progress: Insights on personalized learning implementation and effects*. RAND Corporation. https://doi.org/10.7249/RR2042

Patrick, S., Worthen, M., Frost, D., & Truong, N. (2018). *Current to future state: Issues and action steps for personalized learning implementation*. Aurora Institute. https://aurora-institute.org/resource/current-to-future-state-issues-and-action-steps-for-personalized-learning-implementation/

Reber, R., Pedro, L., & Schwartz, B. (2021). Metacognitive awareness and academic motivation: How reflection enhances learning. *Journal of Educational Psychology, 113*(5), 912–927. https://doi.org/10.1037/edu0000657

Sharratt, L. (2019). *Clarity: What matters most in learning, teaching, and leading.* Corwin.

Sturgis, C., & Casey, K. (2018). *Designing for equity: Leveraging competency-based education to ensure all students succeed.* CompetencyWorks at iNACOL. https://aurora-institute.org/resource/designing-for-equity/

Thomas, J. W. (2000). *A review of research on project-based learning.* Autodesk Foundation. https://www.asec.purdue.edu/lct/HBCU/documents/AReviewofResearchofProject-BasedLearning.pdf

Tomlinson, C. A. (2017). *How to differentiate instruction in academically diverse classrooms* (3rd ed.). ASCD.

UNESCO. (n.d.). *Futures literacy.* https://en.unesco.org/themes/futures-literacy

Westbrook Public Schools. (2024). *Work-based learning program overview.* https://www.westbrookctschools.org/workbasedlearning

5

Beyond Smart

How AI and XR Are Reshaping the Architecture of Learning

As Ignacio Estrada is often credited with saying, "If a child cannot learn the way we teach, maybe we should teach the way they learn." This principle captures the essence of education's next transformation and aligning instructional design with learner diversity through adaptive technologies and responsive pedagogy. The current pace of technological change means that education systems can no longer afford to lag behind industry expectations. Lifelong learning and adaptability are no longer optional; they are essential survival skills (Brynjolfsson & McAfee, 2014).

Artificial intelligence (AI) has emerged as one of the most consequential forces in education's ongoing transition into the digital age. In the aftermath of the COVID-19 pandemic, as schools expanded their digital ecosystems, AI became more than a technical enhancement. It now represents a potential engine for personalization, equity, and deeper student engagement. For educators navigating heterogeneous student needs, constrained resources, and expanding expectations, AI offers scalable tools capable of reconfiguring instructional design and delivery.

AI, however, tells only part of the story. The future of learning will also be immersive. Extended reality (XR), which includes augmented, virtual, and mixed reality, introduces the spatial dimension of educational transformation. Where AI adapts instruction to the learner, XR reshapes the environment itself, enabling embodied, place-agnostic experiences that transcend static content and the physical classroom. Together, AI and XR constitute a new architecture of learning that is responsive, fluid, and unconstrained by industrial-era models.

These technologies must not be understood as discrete interventions. Their significance lies in how they align with a broader structural shift toward student-centered learning. Personalized education is already anchored in six core pillars: learner agency, flexible pacing, authentic assessment, competency-based progression, meaningful relationships, and data-informed practice. When embedded in frameworks such as Universal Design for Learning (UDL), futures literacy, and adaptive competencies, AI and XR extend these pillars into practice, enabling inclusive design at scale and preparing students for a rapidly changing world.

The pace of development is unprecedented. Tools such as ChatGPT, Gemini, and Claude, alongside education-specific platforms like MagicSchool AI, Khanmigo, and DreamBox, are evolving faster than institutional structures can adapt. This volatility underscores the need for leadership grounded in pedagogy, ethics, and equity rather than novelty or expedience (Trust, 2024).

Despite their promise, integration across public education remains inconsistent. Policy gaps, infrastructure disparities, and unresolved ethical concerns continue to stall meaningful adoption. At the same time, enthusiasm for innovation often eclipses urgent questions about bias, privacy, accessibility, environmental sustainability, and educator readiness. Without deliberate attention to these concerns, technologies that hold the potential to close gaps risk instead entrenching them.

This chapter interrogates the dual role of AI and XR in advancing personalized learning. It situates these technologies within the widening divide between education and workforce demands, identifies systemic barriers to adoption, applies the framework of vulnerable versus durable learning, and evaluates how immersive and adaptive tools can be harnessed to promote accessibility and equity. The chapter concludes by arguing that successful integration depends not on the tools themselves, but on how schools position them within a broader vision of human dignity, learner agency, and sustainable transformation.

From Workforce Readiness to Future Fluency

The integration of AI and XR across nearly every sector of the global economy reinforces the urgent need for educational systems to evolve. Once considered speculative, these technologies now permeate professional domains such as healthcare, logistics, marketing, journalism, education, and software development. Trust (2024) observes that generative AI platforms including ChatGPT, Gemini, and Microsoft Copilot are no longer peripheral but embedded in daily workflows across industries (Trust, 2024). Recent survey data confirms this shift, with more than 70 percent of employees who use AI in their jobs identifying ChatGPT as their primary tool (Martin, 2025). This finding demonstrates that generative AI has moved beyond experimentation and into routine professional practice. Students therefore need more than basic exposure. They must develop fluency in collaborating with intelligent systems in ways that reflect authentic workplace demands.

XR represents an equally significant dimension of this transformation. XR tools, including virtual, augmented, and mixed reality, are increasingly deployed in advanced manufacturing, aerospace, construction, product design, and health sciences. These technologies provide experiential learning in simulated environments that replicate real-world complexity while reducing physical risk. Surgical trainees can rehearse procedures, architects can conduct virtual walk-throughs of buildings in design, and engineers can refine precision tasks through interactive models. The rise of spatial computing, illustrated by platforms such as Apple Vision Pro and Meta Quest, signals that learners will be expected not only to interact with AI systems but also to co-navigate and co-create within immersive digital environments (World Economic Forum, 2023). Emerging visual translation tools, capable of rendering written or spoken language in real time through wearables, further extend this potential by allowing students to engage with peers and experts around the world without linguistic barriers. Preparing students for this future requires schools to position XR as a central element of instructional design and workforce readiness, rather than as an optional enhancement.

These developments reflect broader macroeconomic and societal transformations. The World Economic Forum (2023) projects that by 2027, nearly 44 percent of the skills required in the global workforce will have changed, with routine cognitive tasks increasingly displaced by dynamic problem-solving, AI interaction, and digital collaboration. In response, education faces a dual imperative. First, it must equip students with durable and transferable competencies that extend beyond disciplinary boundaries. Second, it must ensure that learners are ethically and practically prepared to navigate an automated, immersive, and data-driven society.

The Skills We Must Cultivate

Children entering kindergarten in the 2025–2026 school year will graduate in 2038. Over the next 13 years, K–12 systems must prepare these learners for an economy shaped not only by AI but also by spatial computing, immersive collaboration, and continuous technological convergence. This future will be defined by human–machine interaction across intelligent systems and extended reality environments, requiring fluency in both data interpretation and embodied digital experience. The following ten workforce competencies, synthesized from labor market forecasts, AI education frameworks, and futures thinking research, are foundational to navigating this rapidly evolving landscape (OECD, 2021; World Economic Forum, 2023; Trust, 2024).

- **Human–AI and XR Collaboration**: Co-designing, co-creating, and critically evaluating outcomes alongside intelligent systems and immersive platforms.
- **Ethical and Responsible Technology Use**: Addressing dilemmas involving algorithmic bias, surveillance, data monetization, and automation's social impact.
- **Systems Thinking and Interdisciplinary Problem-Solving**: Connecting global systems and leveraging tools such as simulations and immersive XR models to design adaptive solutions.

- **Cognitive Flexibility and Futures Thinking**: Adapting to change, engaging in scenario planning, and anticipating emerging challenges.
- **Data and Computational Literacy**: Interpreting, visualizing, and questioning the data that powers AI systems, with a focus on accuracy, bias, and purpose.
- **Creative Expression and Generative Innovation**: Using multimodal AI, XR, and spatial computing to produce novel content, simulate experiences, and generate original solutions across disciplines.
- **Civic and Cultural Intelligence**: Promoting inclusion, accessibility, and cultural fluency in civic technology systems, extended reality spaces, and hybrid learning or work environments.
- **Self-Direction and Agency in Learning**: Setting goals, leveraging adaptive tools, and engaging in lifelong reskilling.
- **Eco-Ethical and Sustainability Mindsets**: Understanding the environmental consequences of digital infrastructure and advocating for regenerative technologies.
- **Interpersonal Communication and Empathic Leadership**: Leading diverse, distributed teams and building trust in digitally mediated workspaces.

The Changing Nature of Work: Then, Now, and Next

To convey the scope of this transformation, Table 5.1 compares how core workforce competencies have evolved across three generational benchmarks: the year 2000, the present, and the projected demands of 2038. In 2000, technology functioned primarily as a peripheral tool for routine tasks. Workers were expected to operate word processors, manage email, and follow standardized procedures. By contrast, the emerging workforce will be required to collaborate with intelligent systems, exercise ethical judgment in technology use, and continuously adapt to shifting environments and tools.

From Legacy Systems to Future Readiness

The most profound difference between 2000 and 2038 is not merely the proliferation of digital tools, but the changing nature of how humans and machines interact. In 2000, technology was a tool for

TABLE 5.1 Evolution of workforce competencies, 2000–2038

Skill area	2000	2025	2038
Communication	Verbal, written, phone-based	Digital, asynchronous, multimodal	Multilingual, AI-mediated, immersive, and XR-enabled
Collaboration	In-person teamwork	Hybrid and remote teamwork	Human and AI collaboration in physical and virtual environments
Problem-solving	Independent and task based	Complex and technology augmented	Systems-level, ethical, and interdisciplinary
Adaptability	Willingness to learn	Continuous reskilling	Cognitive flexibility and scenario planning
Ethics and responsibility	Dependability and loyalty	Digital ethics and compliance	AI ethics, environmental justice, civics
Technology use	Basic digital tools	AI copilots and data analytics	Immersive, spatial, ambient, and intelligent systems

Note: XR = extended reality. Values for 2038 are projected.

execution. By 2038, it will be a cognitive partner in ideation, creation, and decision-making. The modern workforce demands individuals who can learn continuously, reason ethically, collaborate with AI, and adapt to futures that are still emerging.

This disconnect between the demands of an AI-enabled economy and the structure of most K–12 education systems is increasingly untenable. Traditional schooling models that are organized around seat time, standardized curricula, and fixed pacing are misaligned with the competencies needed in an AI-infused world. As Trust (2024) argues, preparing students to engage critically with AI-generated content and understand how their personal data is used, stored, and monetized is a form of civic literacy (Trust, 2024).

One district that exemplifies this future-ready and responsive framework is the Montour School District in Pennsylvania. In partnership with Carnegie Mellon University and the Readiness

Institute at Penn State, Montour has implemented a district-wide AI strategy grounded in data literacy, ethical reasoning, and project-based learning. Their approach aligns closely with the six pillars of personalized learning: learner agency, differentiated instruction, competency-based progression, formative assessment, flexible learning environments, and personalized pathways. Students engage with tools such as Khanmigo and MagicSchool AI to support inquiry-driven learning, while educators integrate UDL principles to ensure that these innovations are inclusive and accessible from the outset. Additionally, Montour cultivates futures literacy and adaptive competencies such as resilience, creativity, and critical thinking, preparing students not only for emerging technologies but also for the complex challenges of the future (Getting Smart, 2019; Carnegie Mellon University Machine Learning Department, 2018; CMU LearnLab, 2024).

Carnegie Mellon University has formally recognized Montour's leadership in AI education through multiple initiatives. CMU's School of Computer Science partnered with Montour to create and implement one of the first K–12 AI curricula in the United States (Getting Smart, 2019). The district has also been actively involved in CMU-hosted initiatives such as the World Artificial Intelligence Competition for Youth (WAICY), providing students with authentic experiences in applied AI (CMU Machine Learning Department, 2018). Moreover, Montour collaborates with CMU's LearnLab to pilot and scale research-based educational strategies that support AI and cognitive science integration in classrooms (LearnLab, 2024). These efforts reflect a systemic alignment between K–12 innovation and university-led research, offering a compelling model for bridging traditional educational practices with the demands of an AI-powered world (Getting Smart, 2019; Carnegie Mellon University Machine Learning Department, 2018; CMU LearnLab, 2024).

In parallel with AI, XR is also becoming a core component of future-ready education. XR platforms are not limited to entertainment or postsecondary settings; they are increasingly integrated into K–12 classrooms to enhance experiential learning, especially in STEM, career and technical education, and global studies. For example, VictoryXR has partnered with school districts across multiple states to implement virtual reality classrooms where students explore scientific concepts, conduct virtual dissections, and participate in historical simulations (Dede et al., 2023). These immersive experiences support deeper engagement, spatial reasoning, and equity in access to environments that may otherwise be inaccessible due to geographic, financial, or safety constraints. As with AI, the thoughtful use of XR must be guided by principles of inclusivity, pedagogical alignment, and ethical awareness to ensure it enhances rather than fragments student learning (Dede et al., 2023; VictoryXR, 2023).

Making Readiness Real: Policy, Pedagogy, and Practice

The path toward future-ready learning is not simply a matter of introducing new technologies, but of redesigning educational systems through aligned action. Policy must provide clear guardrails for ethical and effective AI use, ensuring privacy, transparency, and equitable access. Pedagogy must evolve to prioritize student agency, interdisciplinary competencies, and authentic engagement with intelligent tools. Practice must reflect a culture of continuous learning, where educators are supported in experimenting, iterating, and collaborating. The readiness gap will not close on its own. It must be addressed through deliberate structures and leadership committed to transformation. Without this alignment, districts risk reinforcing outdated models under the guise of innovation.

Anchoring Emerging Technologies in Pedagogical Frameworks

The rapid development of AI and XR has generated considerable enthusiasm across K–12 education. Yet these technologies risk being adopted for their novelty rather than their instructional value. Without clear frameworks, leaders and educators may pursue innovation in ways that amplify inequities or fail to improve outcomes. To avoid this trap, AI and XR must be evaluated and integrated through established pedagogical models that clarify how technology interacts with content, pedagogy, and context.

The Technological Pedagogical Content Knowledge (TPACK) framework provides one such model (Koehler & Mishra, 2009). It emphasizes that effective instructional design emerges from the intersection of content expertise, pedagogical knowledge, and technological fluency (Koehler & Mishra, 2009). Recent studies confirm its relevance in the era of AI. Yue et al. (2024) found that teachers' readiness for AI education is strongly tied to their technological and pedagogical knowledge, while Ning et al. (2024) expanded this into an "AI–TPACK" framework that highlights the integration of AI-specific knowledge, ethics, and instructional practices. These findings reinforce that emerging technologies cannot be added in isolation; they must be integrated in ways that sustain curricular coherence and equity.

Kolb's (2017) Triple E Framework provides another evaluative lens. Triple E asks whether technologies engage learners in active and meaningful work, enhance the achievement of instructional goals, and extend learning beyond classroom walls. For AI and XR, this framework is critical, as both are often accompanied by inflated claims about personalization or immersion. By applying Triple E, district and school leaders can distinguish between tools that authentically enrich learning experiences and those that serve primarily as expensive substitutes for traditional practices.

The Student Engagement, Technology, and Instruction (SETI) model adds a relational dimension by situating technology use within the cultural and instructional fabric of classrooms (Hernandez-Ramos & De La Paz, 2009). Hernandez-Ramos and De La Paz (2009) argue that effective technology adoption must account for engagement, collaboration, and instructional design. Recent research on teacher preparation supports this perspective: Goldman et al. (2024) show that using TPACK to frame AI integration in special education leads to more inclusive and relationally grounded applications. SETI reinforces that AI and XR adoption should strengthen, rather than disrupt, the social fabric of learning.

Taken together, these frameworks establish continuity between established instructional principles and emerging innovations. They help ensure that AI and XR are not treated as isolated experiments but as components of coherent, equity-driven learning systems. By applying TPACK, Triple E, and SETI, leaders and educators can evaluate whether new tools genuinely expand student agency and mastery or simply reinforce outdated models under the guise of innovation.

No Policy, No Progress: Navigating AI without a Map

The promise of AI in K–12 education is clear, yet the absence of coherent policy and coordinated leadership continues to undermine its potential. While many districts acknowledge AI's transformative possibilities, few have successfully developed large-scale transformative governance structures to guide ethical and effective use. As a result, schools often stall. Leaders are uncertain about how to proceed, reluctant to take risks, and unprepared to provide guidance. In some cases, districts have even used AI itself to generate policy language, creating a paradox in which critical decision-making is outsourced to tools that remain poorly understood and insufficiently regulated. Without a clear roadmap, even well-intentioned efforts can erode student trust, damage institutional credibility, and compromise instructional integrity (US Department of Education, 2023; Trust, 2023).

One critical concern is the lack of district-level clarity regarding responsible AI use and compliance with federal privacy law. As Trust (2023) and others note, few districts have frameworks to evaluate or govern tools that rely on generative models or machine learning algorithms to process student data. Without defined guardrails, educators risk violating the Family Educational Rights and Privacy Act (FERPA) or state regulations by uploading personally identifiable information into unsecured platforms (US Department of Education, 2023). The absence of policy introduces significant risk, as illustrated by cases in which AI experimentation has led to data exposure incidents, compliance reviews, or public backlash (US Department of Education, 2023; Trust, 2023).

The 2023 lawsuit in Hingham, Massachusetts, made these risks visible. Parents sued the district after their son was accused of academic dishonesty for using AI on a history project. Although the court upheld the disciplinary decision, the controversy revealed the consequences of policy ambiguity: conflict between families and schools, reputational harm, and legal distraction from the educational mission (JDSupra, 2024; Patriot Ledger, 2024).

This uncertainty produces a climate of hesitation. Administrators, especially in compliance-focused districts, often default to blanket restrictions or passive avoidance. Instead of building frameworks for ethical implementation, they sideline tools that could advance equity and engagement. This vacuum reflects a deeper challenge. Lacking expertise and clear guidance, decision-makers fear that rapid action could produce legal or reputational consequences. Yet inaction also carries costs. When policies are absent or vague, educators are left to interpret boundaries independently, leading to inconsistent practices, inequitable access, and missed opportunities for innovation.

A more constructive path requires intentionality and structure. AI readiness rubrics, such as those developed by Trust and colleagues (2023), provide districts with practical tools for self-assessment and capacity building. These frameworks help schools evaluate preparedness across infrastructure, data governance, instructional alignment, and professional learning. When paired with locally developed policies that reflect legal requirements and community values, they can transform uncertainty into strategic direction. Districts must take ownership of their role as ethical stewards of AI integration rather than waiting for top-down mandates. This includes policies that are adaptive, transparent, and anchored in educational purpose (Trust, 2023).

Leadership in this context means more than approving tools. It requires cultivating a culture of inquiry, transparency, and professional learning. Superintendents, chief technology officers, and school boards must create collaborative spaces where educators, families, students, and technologists co-design policies that are both responsible and practical. The central question is no longer whether AI will be used, but how. Avoiding that question is itself a decision, and one that public education cannot afford.

Even the most thoughtful AI policies will fail if they are not grounded in digital equity. Access to devices, reliable internet, and high-quality digital learning experiences remains uneven across districts and communities. If these foundational disparities are not addressed, AI will not close opportunity gaps. It will deepen them.

Equity is not a secondary concern or enhancement to responsible AI integration. It is the prerequisite.

Digital Equity as a Prerequisite for AI Integration

A core maxim in the Spider-Man canon holds that greater power demands greater responsibility. In education, the growing power of AI requires a corresponding responsibility to design for equity from the start. As AI becomes increasingly embedded in K–12 education, its potential to personalize learning, automate feedback, and expand instructional reach will only be realized if digital equity is treated as a foundational condition. AI cannot be equitably integrated into systems that are already inequitable. Emerging technologies do not dismantle injustice on their own. They inherit and often intensify the disparities embedded within existing educational structures.

Beyond Access: The Four Dimensions of the Digital Divide

Dr Torrey Trust (2023) identifies three critical divides that shape digital equity: access, usage, and quality of use. To these, a fourth must be added: digital fluency. Collectively, these four divides must be addressed before AI can serve as a tool for equitable transformation.

The access divide concerns the availability of modern devices, broadband, and infrastructure capable of supporting AI. While many districts have achieved one-to-one device deployment, too many students still rely on outdated hardware, experience inconsistent connectivity, or lack high-speed internet at home. Economic barriers compound this divide, as subscription-based services such as ChatGPT Plus create a tiered environment where wealthier students gain enhanced access while others are left with limited functionality.

The usage divide involves how technology is applied in classrooms. In well-resourced schools, students often use AI to create, design, and solve authentic problems. They experiment with simulations, generate research questions, or code applications. In contrast, lower-income schools frequently limit AI to remediation, surveillance, or rote content delivery. These patterns reinforce inequity by narrowing student agency and framing AI as a tool for control rather than exploration.

The quality-of-use divide reflects the instructional conditions that shape how students engage with AI. Tools do not enhance learning independently; their value depends on how educators integrate them. In schools with trained teachers and technology specialists, students are guided to use AI critically, ethically, and creatively. In under-resourced environments, where professional support is limited, students often engage with AI without context or guidance, reducing its effectiveness and raising risks of misuse.

The digital fluency divide extends beyond access and instruction. Fluency refers to the ability to apply digital tools critically, adaptively, and ethically across contexts. Students with fluency can evaluate AI outputs for bias, use XR to collaborate across cultures and languages, and engage in multimodal exchanges through emerging translation and accessibility tools. Without fluency, even well-resourced students risk remaining passive consumers of content rather than active contributors to knowledge, civic life, and innovation.

The Uneven Ground beneath AI Integration

These divides are not incidental. They are rooted in long-standing inequities in school funding, policy, and infrastructure. Public schools financed primarily through local property taxes create vast disparities between communities. Wealthier districts often sustain robust technology ecosystems, while rural and underfunded schools struggle to meet basic operational needs. Approximately 15 million K–12 students in the United States still lack reliable internet access at home (Anderson & Perrin, 2020), disproportionately affecting students of color, rural learners, and first-generation students.

Language, culture, and disability further complicate the landscape. Generative AI platforms frequently default to dominant cultural perspectives and academic English, limiting accessibility for multilingual learners. Students with disabilities face barriers when platforms lack closed captioning, screen reader compatibility, or tools that support executive functioning. When universal design principles are not embedded from the outset, AI risks reproducing ableist assumptions and excluding learners with diverse needs.

The COVID-19 pandemic exposed these inequities starkly. Students without stable internet, accessible devices, or adult support experienced severe disruptions, particularly those with individualized education plans or from historically marginalized communities. As Wrye (2022) documents, digital platforms often amplified inequity during this period rather than mitigating it. Unless addressed, AI risks replicating this same pattern.

A Fragile Foundation for AI Integration

Digital inequity shapes instruction, assessment, and opportunity in compounding ways. Well-resourced districts are more likely to use AI for personalized learning, real-time feedback, and authentic inquiry (Trust, 2023). Under-resourced schools often use AI superficially or lack access altogether, creating fundamentally different learning environments.

Student agency is also shaped by these disparities. Where AI is integrated thoughtfully, students act as researchers, designers, and problem-solvers (ISTE, 2022). Where it is absent or poorly implemented, students remain passive recipients of algorithmic output, leaving them underprepared for an AI-mediated workforce and civic landscape (OECD, 2021).

Assessment practices illustrate the divide further. AI tools can provide timely, personalized feedback that supports iteration and metacognition (Means et al., 2021). Without access, schools continue to rely on static, one-size-fits-all assessments that obscure growth and variability in learning. These divides extend beyond graduation. Digital and AI fluency are now prerequisites for higher education pathways, competitive internships, and emerging careers (World Economic Forum, 2023). Students without these opportunities face compounding disadvantages in both professional and civic life, including reduced capacity to evaluate algorithmic bias or participate meaningfully in democratic processes (Benjamin, 2019).

Historical missteps highlight the stakes. In *Robbins v. Lower Merion School District* (2010), a Pennsylvania district activated webcams on student-issued laptops without consent, capturing thousands of images from students' homes. The resulting $610,000 settlement, often referred to as "WebcamGate," underscored the dangers of deploying technology without adequate governance

(Electronic Frontier Foundation, 2010). While not an AI case, it illustrates how poorly designed oversight can erode trust and deepen inequity.

Reframing Equity as the Starting Point

Equity must not be treated as an afterthought. It is the foundation for AI integration. Districts must conduct comprehensive digital equity audits that assess disparities in access, usage, quality, and fluency. True equity requires not only modern devices and broadband but also conditions that ensure students engage meaningfully, critically, and ethically with digital tools.

Professional learning is essential. Teachers must be prepared not just to operate AI tools but to guide students in developing AI literacy, ethical reasoning, and critical thinking. Inclusive design must also be embedded from the outset, ensuring that platforms reflect multilingual, multicultural, and disability-responsive principles. Finally, authentic community engagement is necessary. Students, families, and local stakeholders must co-shape technology priorities, increasing transparency and building trust.

Without systemic commitment, AI risks becoming another mechanism of exclusion. With equity as the blueprint, schools can ensure that digital transformation expands opportunity, strengthens agency, and advances justice.

Designing for All Learners: Technologies Promise in Personalized, Accessible, and Hybrid Education

Realizing the pedagogical promise of AI requires more than technical adoption. Schools must intentionally align AI integration with the principles of personalized learning and UDL. Personalized learning is grounded in six foundational pillars: learner agency, flexible pacing, authentic assessment, competency-based progression, meaningful relationships, and data-informed instruction. UDL complements this framework by ensuring inclusivity from the outset, offering multiple means of engagement, representation, and expression. When combined with future-focused competencies such as adaptability, critical thinking, and digital fluency, AI-supported personalization can advance both accessibility and durable learner development across traditional and hybrid models.

AI's adaptive capabilities enable real-time customization of content, pacing, and modality to meet learner needs. Tools such as Google Gemini and Microsoft Copilot, as described by Trust (2024), demonstrate how generative AI can support multimodal learning by generating and interpreting text, speech, images, and video. These features expand access for students with diverse linguistic, cognitive, and sensory profiles, enhancing personalization and inclusivity.

Real-time translation technologies provide a compelling example of UDL in action. Audio translation via wearable hearables allows students and educators to participate in multilingual discussions without language becoming a barrier. Visual translation through augmented reality or egocentric-vision systems enables instant recognition and rendering of written text, such as signage, books, or community text, into preferred languages or accessible formats. These tools support learners who are multilingual, neurodivergent, or otherwise underserved by conventional print-based materials. They exemplify how AI can expand representation and engagement by embedding inclusive access into learning environments rather than layering it on afterward.

Classroom practice illustrates these possibilities. A student who struggles with writing may use voice input to brainstorm, receive AI-generated scaffolding through sentence starters, and later transform a draft into a multimedia presentation. A peer who prefers visual learning might collaborate with AI to produce concept maps, annotated diagrams, or video explanations. Creative platforms such as Canva Magic Write, Adobe Firefly, and MagicSchool AI extend these opportunities by enabling flexible outputs that align with learner strengths and goals.

At the same time, meaningful integration of UDL with AI requires critical awareness of limitations. Trust (2024) cautions that AI systems are prone to hallucinations, embedded bias, and overconfidence in fabricated outputs. Educators must therefore teach students how to validate AI content, interrogate sources, and identify ethical concerns, particularly when marginalized groups are misrepresented or excluded. Concerns also arise around authorship and intellectual property. Tools such as Google's Help Me Write may compromise student ownership when they rewrite or replace original work without transparency or instructional framing. Without careful guidance, these risks can undermine critical thinking and creativity.

To fulfill AI's potential in advancing UDL and personalization, educators need sustained professional learning, access to student-centered design tools, and policy frameworks that support ethical and equitable implementation. These supports ensure that AI enhances differentiation and accessibility rather than reinforcing standardization. Personalized learning must remain a human-led endeavor, with AI functioning as a responsive companion that amplifies teacher expertise, broadens student agency, and enriches engagement across all learning environments.

Depth over Automation: Redefining Learning in the Age of AI

As AI becomes more embedded in classrooms, educators face a critical decision. Will these tools be used to cultivate deep, transferable learning, or will they be deployed to automate thinking and encourage shortcuts? The distinction between surface-level automation and purposeful engagement lies at the heart of how AI will shape the next era of public education. This section frames that divide through the lens of vulnerable and durable learning, offering a pathway toward instructional design that prioritizes reflection, inquiry, and agency.

Vulnerable learning emphasizes replication and task completion. It relies on automation to meet immediate goals but lacks cognitive depth. *Durable learning*, in contrast, develops metacognition, critical thinking, and transferable skills. It prepares students to question, adapt, and construct meaning in complex contexts while cultivating digital fluency as a civic and workforce competency.

Without intentional design, AI can reinforce vulnerable patterns. A student who generates an essay outline through AI may bypass the processes of organizing ideas, evaluating evidence, and refining claims. Trust (2024) warns that such automation risks outsourcing thought, eroding executive function, and weakening independent learning strategies. Learners may appear proficient yet lack conceptual understanding and the ability to transfer knowledge to new settings (Trust, 2024; Zhai et al., 2024).

Durable learning emerges when AI augments cognition rather than replaces it. Generative tools can foster inquiry by presenting multiple perspectives, suggesting counterarguments, or supporting revision. In these cases, AI functions as a cognitive partner that deepens engagement and reflection. Trust (2024) identifies platforms such as Gemini and Copilot as capable of supporting iterative thinking when guided by purposeful prompts and instructional scaffolding.

Durable learners interrogate outputs, evaluate sources, and revise iteratively. These dispositions must be explicitly taught and reinforced. Porayska-Pomsta et al. (2024) argue that AI must be designed and implemented in ways that support autonomy and reflective judgment. Instruction must prioritize cultivating these durable habits of mind.

Equity concerns amplify the stakes. Students in under-resourced schools are more likely to encounter AI without ethical framing or instructional scaffolds, leading to task automation and passive consumption. Students in better-resourced schools are more likely to receive guidance on critical evaluation and strategic application. This divergence risks creating two distinct AI literacies: one grounded in efficiency, the other in discernment and empowerment.

Tools such as Google's Help Me Write highlight the risks of misuse. When AI-generated text overwrites student work without transparency, authorship and intellectual property are compromised. Trust (2024) and Li et al. (2023) caution that such practices may erode student voice and diminish authentic expression.

Moving toward a durable model requires recalibrating instructional design. Educators must ask: Are students using AI to build intellectual stamina, or to bypass challenge? Are practices prompting them to interrogate outputs, or to accept them uncritically? Are ethical habits scaffolded, or are opaque systems shaping cognition without reflection?

Formative assessment should emphasize process over product, with greater attention to reflection, peer feedback, and critique of AI-generated content. Rubrics must evolve to assess originality, revision, and ethical engagement, not only correctness. Frameworks such as Understanding by Design and UDL provide strong foundations. Backward design ensures alignment with enduring understandings, while UDL supports multiple pathways for students to demonstrate meaning and growth (US Department of Education, 2023).

The goal is not to reject AI but to reframe its role. When AI supports inquiry, strengthens metacognition, and reinforces learner agency, it contributes to durable learning. When it functions as a shortcut, it fosters vulnerability. As education systems confront rapid technological change, durability must become a guiding principle for instruction, assessment, and policy. Cultivating digital fluency within this framework ensures that students can not only use AI responsibly but also navigate, critique, and shape the digital systems that increasingly define civic life and the global workforce.

Operationalizing AI: Practical Tools for Ethical and Personalized Instruction

The integration of AI into K–12 classrooms presents both opportunities and responsibilities. The question is not whether AI supports instruction but how it is implemented to strengthen, rather than diminish, learning. Educators must consider whether generative tools foster intellectual engagement or enable surface-level task completion. The distinction between vulnerable and durable learning provides a useful framework for this challenge.

Vulnerable learning prioritizes efficiency and replication. It often relies on automation to achieve short-term goals but lacks depth and transferability. Trust (2024) describes this as the outsourcing of cognitive labor, where learners bypass the processes of analyzing, synthesizing, and refining ideas. Zhai et al. (2024) caution that repeated use of generative tools without scaffolding can weaken the development of executive function and independent problem-solving.

Durable learning, by contrast, positions AI as a partner in inquiry. Generative tools can encourage revision, provide alternative perspectives, and support feedback loops when embedded in thoughtful instructional design. Trust (2024) points to platforms such as Gemini and Copilot as examples of systems that, when paired with guided prompts, sustain iterative thinking and deeper engagement. In this model, AI extends rather than replaces cognition.

Durable learning also depends on explicit instruction. Students must be taught to interrogate AI outputs, validate evidence, and revise based on feedback. Porayska-Pomsta et al. (2024) argue that this requires both intentional system design and teacher-led scaffolding to promote autonomy, reflection, and critical judgment.

Implementation practices matter. In some classrooms, AI is used mainly to generate outlines or summaries, which risks diminishing authentic student authorship and creativity. Tools such as Google's Help Me Write illustrate this tension, as they can overwrite student work without transparency if used without instructional framing (Li et al., 2023). In contrast, when educators design assignments that require critique of AI outputs, peer feedback, and iterative revision, students develop stronger habits of analysis and originality.

Shifting toward durable learning requires recalibrated pedagogy and assessment. Formative assessments should emphasize process, reflection, and critique rather than product alone. Rubrics must evolve to reward originality, ethical engagement, and revision practices, not just surface-level fluency. Frameworks such as Understanding by Design and UDL provide strong foundations. Backward design ensures that AI supports enduring understandings, while UDL promotes multiple pathways for demonstrating mastery (US Department of Education, 2023).

The goal is not to limit AI use but to align it with principles of deep learning. When used as a shortcut, AI fosters dependence and superficial outcomes. When embedded with purpose, it cultivates reflection, adaptability, and intellectual stamina. The durability of learning must guide curriculum, pedagogy, and policy if AI is to strengthen rather than weaken the architecture of public education.

When Learning Becomes Place-Agnostic: The Role of Extended Reality (XR)

While AI has received significant attention for its capacity to personalize instruction and support cognitive scaffolding, extended reality (XR) is equally important for reimagining how learning is experienced in the mid-21st century. XR, which encompasses virtual reality (VR), augmented reality (AR), and mixed reality (MR), provides immersive, multisensory experiences that allow learners to engage with content spatially and interactively. These environments replicate complex systems, simulate historical or scientific phenomena, and create contexts that may be inaccessible due to geography, cost, or safety.

XR shifts learning from fixed locations to a flexible, place-agnostic model. In this framework, students can conduct virtual dissections in biology, test engineering designs in augmented space, or explore sustainable city models through immersive simulations. These activities promote durable learning by activating spatial memory and situating knowledge in embodied experiences. During the COVID-19 pandemic, for example, my son, then an elementary school student, used a Meta Quest 1 headset to participate in physical education through Rec Room. The platform allowed him to engage in movement-based challenges with peers in virtual space, fostering agency, physical engagement, and connectedness at a time when traditional schooling was disrupted. What began as a stopgap solution revealed XR's potential to sustain motivation and continuity of learning in nontraditional contexts.

This potential is increasingly visible in schools. VictoryXR has partnered with districts across the United States to deliver VR-based science and social studies content aligned with academic standards (VictoryXR, 2023). Students in these programs conduct virtual labs, tour reconstructed historical landmarks, and collaborate with teachers and peers in three-dimensional classrooms (Dede et al., 2023). Similarly, platforms such as ClassVR and PrismsVR bring immersive applications into mathematics, physics, and career and technical education, making abstract concepts more tangible through visualization and interaction.

XR's adoption reflects broader shifts in the workforce. Industries including healthcare, manufacturing, aerospace, and construction now use XR for professional training and certification. As spatial computing platforms such as Apple Vision Pro and Meta Quest continue to evolve, students will be expected not only to interact with AI systems but also to co-navigate and co-create within immersive digital environments. Preparing learners for this reality requires schools to treat XR as a core element of instructional design and workforce readiness rather than an optional enhancement.

As with AI, XR's integration must be deliberate and pedagogically aligned. Without planning and attention to access, representation, and instructional goals, XR risks reinforcing existing inequities. When implemented with clarity and care, however, XR expands what is possible in teaching and learning. It removes the constraints of the physical classroom and creates opportunities for deeper understanding, collaboration, and creativity. In this way, XR redefines not only where learning occurs but also what learning can become.

Ethics across Time: AI and the Replication of Inequity

The integration of AI into K–12 education cannot be approached as if technology operates in a neutral space. AI systems are trained on data that reflect existing cultural and social hierarchies, which means they carry forward the biases embedded within them. Without intentional safeguards, AI risks becoming another mechanism that reproduces historical patterns of exclusion. Scholars warn that algorithmic systems often disproportionately disadvantage marginalized groups, including students of color, English learners, and students with disabilities (Shelton & Lanier, 2024).

This challenge is consistent with broader patterns in public education. For more than two centuries, schools have been shaped by tensions between civic ideals and structural inequities. From the assimilationist aims of the Civilization Fund Act of 1819 to the persistence of segregation long after *Brown v. Board of Education*, innovations in education have historically advantaged some populations while marginalizing others (Anderson, 1988; Lomawaima & McCarty, 2006; Nasir & Darling-Hammond, 2025). If left unchecked, AI may encode this legacy into decision-making processes such as student placement, resource allocation, or disciplinary action.

Ethical integration therefore requires a confrontation with history. Schools must evaluate not only whether AI tools improve outcomes but also whether their use dismantles or reinforces inequities. This work involves interrogating datasets for bias, creating accountability systems that include diverse perspectives, and preparing educators to act as stewards of responsible technology use. Equity in the age of AI cannot be achieved by expanding access alone; it requires an explicit commitment to preventing the digital continuation of historical harms.

Equity by Design: Centering Ethics in Educational AI

As AI becomes part of everyday schooling, the question is no longer whether students will use these tools, but under what conditions. Ethics cannot be an afterthought. They must be embedded from the beginning, in adoption, in design, and in classroom use.

The risks are not abstract. Large language models are trained on massive datasets that carry forward historical and social inequities. Students with disabilities are often missing from these data, which means tools may reinforce ableist assumptions or fail to meet accessibility needs (Trust, 2024; Whittaker et al., 2019). Multilingual learners face similar exclusion when models default to dominant cultural norms and academic English, narrowing what counts as legitimate knowledge (Bender et al., 2021). Without deliberate intervention, inequities that schools have struggled with for generations will be reproduced under a digital veneer.

Ethics also extend beyond equity. Sustainability is rarely discussed in education, yet the environmental costs of training and maintaining large models are significant. Strubell et al. (2019) estimate that training one model can generate as much carbon output as five cars over their lifetimes. These trade-offs cannot be ignored. Educators and policymakers must weigh educational benefit against environmental cost and consider alternatives when they exist.

Privacy adds another layer. Li et al. (2023) and others have warned of the dangers of entering student information into public-facing platforms with no binding protections. Without district policies and secure agreements in place, teachers are left to make decisions on their own, often without knowing the risks. This places both students and educators in vulnerable positions.

A sustainable approach requires policy, professional learning, and student engagement. Teachers need preparation not only to use AI tools but also to guide students in questioning where outputs come from, whose voices are missing, and how algorithms shape knowledge. Students must learn that AI does not produce neutral truths but reflections of cultural and historical contexts (Zhai et al., 2024; Trust, 2024).

Equally important is involving students in setting the rules. When learners help draft classroom policies for responsible AI use, they share ownership and develop the capacity to decide when these tools support creativity and when they undermine it (Porayska-Pomsta et al., 2024). Co-construction fosters democratic practice in addition to ethical reasoning, provided it is paired with clear schoolwide accountability.

Ethical integration is not a one-time checklist. It is a commitment that evolves with technology, requiring ongoing reflection and adjustment. The goal is not simply to prevent misuse but to ensure that AI strengthens inclusion, transparency, and student agency. The same applies to XR. As XR becomes more common, questions of access, representation, safety, and sensory inclusion must be addressed at the design stage, not after harm occurs.

Technology will not decide these questions for us. Educators and leaders must. The challenge is not whether AI and XR will shape the future of schools but whether they will do so in ways that honor justice and human dignity.

References

Anderson, J. D. (1988). *The education of Blacks in the South, 1860–1935.* University of North Carolina Press.

Anderson, M., & Perrin, A. (2020, October 29). Nearly one-in-five teens cannot always finish their homework because of the digital divide. *Pew Research Center.* https://www.pewresearch.org/internet/2020/10/29/nearly-one-in-five-teens-cannot-always-finish-their-homework-because-of-the-digital-divide/

Bender, E. M., Gebru, T., McMillan-Major, A., & Shmitchell, S. (2021). *On the dangers of stochastic parrots: Can language models be too big?* Proceedings of the 2021 ACM Conference on Fairness, Accountability, and Transparency, pp. 610–623. https://doi.org/10.1145/3442188.3445922

Benjamin, R. (2019). *Race after technology: Abolitionist tools for the new Jim Code.* Polity Press.

Brynjolfsson, E., & McAfee, A. (2014). *The second machine age: Work, progress, and prosperity in a time of brilliant technologies.* W. W. Norton & Company.

Carnegie Mellon University Machine Learning Department. (2018). *World Artificial Intelligence Competition for Youth (WAICY)*. https://www.ml.cmu.edu/news/news-archive/2018/november/waicy-2018.html

CMU LearnLab. (2024). *Research-based educational strategies for AI integration*. https://learnlab.org/

Dede, C., Richards, J., & Saxberg, B. (2023). *The octopus effect: How technology is transforming education*. Harvard Education Press.

Electronic Frontier Foundation. (2010). *WebcamGate: Lower merion school district spying scandal*. https://www.eff.org/cases/webcamgate

Getting Smart. (2019, August 4). *Montour school district: A K–12 leader in AI education*. https://www.gettingsmart.com/2019/08/04/montour-school-district-a-k-12-leader-in-ai-education/

Goldman, S. R., Carreon, A., & Smith, S. J. (2024). Exploring the integration of artificial intelligence into special education teacher preparation through the TPACK framework. *Journal of Special Education Preparation*, 4(2), 52–64. https://doi.org/10.33043/6zx26bb2

Hernandez-Ramos, P., & De La Paz, S. (2009). Learning history in middle school by designing multimedia in a project-based learning experience. *Journal of Research on Technology in Education*, 42(2), 151–173. https://doi.org/10.1080/15391523.2009.10782545

International Society for Technology in Education. (2022). *Artificial intelligence in education: Considerations for teaching and learning*. https://www.iste.org/areas-of-focus/ai

JDSupra. (2024, December 10). *Court backs school in AI cheating case: 5 things your school should do now*. https://www.jdsupra.com/legalnews/court-backs-school-in-ai-cheating-case-5936746/

Koehler, M. J., & Mishra, P. (2009). What is technological pedagogical content knowledge (TPACK)? *Contemporary Issues in Technology and Teacher Education*, 9(1), 60–70. https://citejournal.org/volume-9/issue-1-09/general/what-is-technological-pedagogicalcontent-knowledge/

Kolb, L. (2017). *Learning first, technology second: The educator's guide to designing authentic lessons*. International Society for Technology in Education.

Li, X., Li, Y., & Wei, L. (2023). Ethical concerns in generative AI use for education. *Journal of Educational Technology Development and Exchange*, 16(1), 1–20. https://doi.org/10.18785/jetde.1601.01

Lomawaima, K. T., & McCarty, T. L. (2006). *To remain an Indian: Lessons in democracy from a century of Native American education.* Teachers College Press.

Martin, J. (2025, August 26). The hidden AI workforce: 29 percent of employees pay for their own AI tools while bosses provide no training. *Exploding Topics.* https://explodingtopics.com/blog/ai-workforce-research

Means, B., Neisler, J., & Langer Research Associates. (2021). *Learning in the time of COVID-19: The student experience.* Digital Promise. https://digitalpromise.org/wp-content/uploads/2021/05/DP_Learning-in-the-Time-of-COVID-19_Paper_FINAL.pdf

Miller, R. (2018). *Transforming the future: Anticipation in the 21st century.* UNESCO Publishing. https://unesdoc.unesco.org/ark:/48223/pf0000260424

Nasir, N. S., & Darling-Hammond, L. (Eds.). (2025). *Equity and education since Brown v. Board: Where do we go from here?* Teachers College Press.

Ning, Y., Li, S., Wang, J., & Zhang, H. (2024). Teachers' AI-TPACK: Exploring the relationship between AI integration and teaching performance. *Sustainability, 16*(3), 978. https://doi.org/10.3390/su16030978

Organisation for Economic Co-operation and Development. (2021). *AI and the future of skills: Challenges for OECD countries.* https://doi.org/10.1787/5f06c3f4-en

The Patriot Ledger. (2024, December 31). *Judge upholds Hingham High's discipline in AI plagiarism case.* https://www.patriotledger.com/story/news/local/2024/12/31/ai-plagiarism-student-paper-hingham-high-school-ma-lawsuit-research-paper-grammarly-court/77179645007/

Porayska-Pomsta, K., Holmes, W., Nematzadeh, A., & Yigit, K. (2024). Responsible artificial intelligence in education. *British Journal of Educational Technology, 55*(2), 300–316. https://doi.org/10.1111/bjet.13306

Shelton, K., & Lanier, D. (2024). *The promises and perils of AI in education: Ethics and equity have entered the chat.* Lanier Learning.

Strubell, E., Ganesh, A., & McCallum, A. (2019). *Energy and policy considerations for deep learning in NLP.* Proceedings of the 57th Annual Meeting of the Association for Computational Linguistics, pp. 3645–3650. https://doi.org/10.18653/v1/P19-1355

Trust, T. (2023). *Artificial intelligence in K–12 classrooms: Ethical integration and equity considerations.* Educational Technology Publications.

Trust, T. (2024). *AI for educators: Learning with artificial intelligence.* Routledge.

US Department of Education. (2023). *Artificial intelligence and the future of teaching and learning: Insights and recommendations.* https://tech.ed.gov/ai

VictoryXR. (2023). *Virtual reality classrooms for K–12.* https://www.victoryxr.com/

Whittaker, M., Alper, M., Bennett, C. L., Hendren, S., Kaziunas, E., & Mills, M. (2019). *Disability, bias, and AI.* AI Now Institute. https://ainowinstitute.org/disabilitybiasai-2019.pdf

World Economic Forum. (2023). *The future of jobs report 2023.* https://www.weforum.org/reports/the-future-of-jobs-report-2023/

Wrye, T. P. (2022). *The great equalizer: Distance learning and its impact on education equity* (Doctoral dissertation), Drexel University. https://doi.org/10.17918/00001294

Yue, M., Jong, M. S. Y., & Ng, D. T. K. (2024). Understanding K–12 teachers' TPACK readiness and attitudes toward AI education. *Education and Information Technologies, 29,* 12621. https://doi.org/10.1007/s10639-024-12621-2

Zhai, X., Zhao, W., Zhang, Z., & Xie, Y. (2024). ChatGPT and education: Opportunities, challenges, and future research directions. *Computers and Education: Artificial Intelligence, 5,* 100146. https://doi.org/10.1016/j.caeai.2024.100146

6

From Instructor to Architect

Transforming the Role of Educators

The integration of artificial intelligence (AI) into K–12 education is reshaping the professional role of educators. Teachers are no longer defined solely as content deliverers. They are increasingly expected to act as facilitators of inquiry, designers of learning experiences, interpreters of data, and ethical decision-makers within digital learning environments (US Department of Education, 2023). Consistent with Couros's argument that technology becomes transformational in the hands of great teachers, this shift demands intentional design and professional capacity-building (Couros, 2015; Fullan & Quinn, 2020).

AI now manages routine tasks such as grading, scheduling, and adaptive content delivery. These efficiencies create opportunities for educators to focus on strengthening human connection, cultivating critical thinking, and ensuring instructional purpose (Bransford et al., 2000). To realize this potential, professional learning must shift from isolated training sessions to sustained capacity building that develops digital fluency, collaborative problem-solving, and cultural readiness (Darling-Hammond et al., 2017).

This transformation is not merely technical. It redefines the purposes and structures of teaching, requiring shared leadership and alignment between school culture and instructional vision (Fullan, 2020). Educators remain central to this work. Their expertise and

DOI: 10.4324/9781003739050-8

ethical judgment are essential to integrating AI in ways that protect equity, expand student agency, and anchor innovation in meaningful learning outcomes (Trust, 2023).

Purpose and Positioning of the Educator in an AI Era

Educators design learning with a clear commitment to human dignity, justice, and student agency. The profession's purpose extends beyond content delivery. Teachers create environments where every learner is known, challenged, and supported through equitable access, culturally responsive practices, and transparent assessment. AI can assist this work only when educators lead its use with professional judgment, ethical awareness, and a focus on meaningful outcomes (US Department of Education, 2023).

Teacher expertise sits at the center of responsible AI integration. Educators translate standards into coherent learning progressions, select or adapt digital tools to match goals, and interpret evidence of student understanding to guide next steps. Trust within school communities strengthens this process. When educators, families, and leaders share high expectations and communicate openly, implementation quality improves, and student outcomes rise (Bryk & Schneider, 2002). Coherence across classrooms and initiatives matters as well. System actors must align vision, assessment, professional learning, and resource allocation so that technology serves learning rather than the reverse (Fullan & Quinn, 2016).

Equity provides the test for every design decision. AI must expand access, not stratify it. Educators safeguard privacy, watch for bias, and ensure that multilingual learners, students with disabilities, and historically marginalized groups benefit from supports that honor identity and raise expectations. Ethical use requires transparency about data, clarity about instructional purpose, and a human-in-the-loop stance that keeps teachers responsible for interpretation and action (US Department of Education, 2023). This stance respects students as developing citizens whose voices and choices matter in classroom decision-making.

The educator's role is therefore architectural. Teachers integrate pedagogy, content, and technology into experiences that build durable knowledge and transferable skills. They organize time for inquiry, select texts and tasks that reflect diverse perspectives, and use AI to free attention for feedback, conferencing, and small-group instruction. The goal is not efficiency alone. The goal is deeper learning with dignity at the center. When schools position educators as designers and ethical stewards, AI becomes a tool for inclusion, mastery, and belonging rather than a force that narrows purpose or substitutes judgment.

Vignette: Student-Centered Design in Practice

Ms. Grant, a middle-school humanities teacher, once relied on direct instruction and textbook comprehension tasks. While efficient for covering content, these methods left many students disengaged and struggling, particularly multilingual learners and those reading below grade level. The introduction of an AI-supported platform created an opportunity to redesign her practice around inquiry, scaffolding, and student voice.

In a unit on civil rights, students used the tool to explore historical figures and legislation through adaptive prompts and leveled texts. One student, who previously avoided primary sources, accessed a scaffolded version of *Letter from Birmingham Jail* and was able to unpack key arguments with teacher guidance. This access affirmed dignity by removing barriers to participation while preserving rigor.

Assessment shifted as well. Instead of relying on quizzes of factual recall, Ms. Grant designed collaborative projects in which students synthesized sources into multimedia presentations. The AI tool organized timelines and generated discussion prompts, allowing students to focus on interpretation and perspective-taking. In classroom discussions, students articulated their own positions and connected historical struggles to contemporary issues, demonstrating both analytical depth and personal agency.

This redesign repositioned Ms. Grant as a facilitator. Rather than serving as the sole source of information, she circulated to ask questions, deepen dialogue, and support critical thinking. Students assumed responsibility for inquiry, drawing on AI as a scaffold while engaging with one another and their teacher in more meaningful ways.

The classroom became a space where technology amplified human connection rather than replacing it. By centering student identity and cultural context in task design, Ms. Grant created opportunities for equitable access and authentic voice. Her classroom reflects research on how students learn best through active engagement, culturally responsive teaching, and scaffolded support that affirms belonging (Bransford et al., 2000; Gay, 2018).

Design Frameworks for the Architect Role

Recasting educators as architects of learning requires practical frameworks that guide intentional design. Models such as Technological Pedagogical Content Knowledge (TPACK), the Triple E Framework, and the Student Engagement, Technology, and Instruction (SETI) model provide structured approaches that align pedagogy, content, and technology with equity and student growth. When applied thoughtfully, these frameworks help teachers move beyond novelty and create environments where technology supports deeper learning and human dignity.

The TPACK framework emphasizes the interplay among pedagogy, content, and technology as the foundation of effective instructional design (Koehler & Mishra, 2009). Research shows that teachers' knowledge of these domains strongly influences their readiness to integrate AI in K–12 settings (Yue et al., 2024). More recent studies extend this model into AI-TPACK, highlighting the importance of understanding AI tools, ethics, and applications as part of professional preparation (Ning et al., 2024). This approach positions educators to evaluate whether emerging technologies serve learning goals and advance equity.

Kolb's (2017) Triple E Framework adds a clear evaluative stance. It prompts educators to ask whether technology engages learners, enhances existing goals, and extends learning beyond the classroom. Applied to AI, this framework directs attention away from digitizing low-level tasks and toward designing experiences that deepen conceptual understanding and promote agency.

The SETI model contributes a social and cultural lens by centering engagement, identity, and collaboration. Hernandez-Ramos and De La Paz (2009) show that the success of technology integration depends on how well it supports student participation and belonging. Studies in special education have found that TPACK-based approaches aligned with SETI lead to more inclusive and culturally responsive uses of AI tools (Goldman et al., 2024).

Together, these frameworks provide a coherent toolkit. TPACK clarifies the relationships among domains of teacher knowledge, Triple E compels evaluation of technology's instructional value, and SETI grounds design in relationships and equity. Used collectively, they help educators function as architects who align innovation with purpose, ensuring that AI amplifies inquiry, agency, and justice rather than reinforcing inequities.

Applying the Frameworks through Project-Based Learning

Educators who embrace the role of architect design classrooms where students construct knowledge through sustained inquiry. Project-based learning (PBL) provides a strong context for this shift, positioning teachers as facilitators, mentors, and co-designers. In PBL, students investigate complex questions and create authentic products, while teachers guide them in connecting content, skills, and technology in meaningful ways (Larmer et al., 2015).

Frameworks such as TPACK, Triple E, and SETI support this design process by aligning pedagogy, technology, and student identity. TPACK ensures that technology use is embedded in content and pedagogy rather than functioning as an add-on (Koehler & Mishra, 2009). Triple E challenges teachers to evaluate whether tools engage students actively, enhance instructional goals, and extend learning beyond the classroom (Kolb, 2017). SETI adds a social dimension by emphasizing that technology integration must sustain collaboration, belonging, and cultural identity (Hernandez-Ramos & De La Paz, 2009).

A middle-school science team provides a clear illustration. During a sustainability project, students modeled climate impacts with adaptive simulations, structured collaborative roles to ensure equitable participation, and aligned products to state standards with transparent performance criteria. Teachers used TPACK to connect simulations to content goals, applied Triple E to confirm that the tools enhanced understanding rather than replacing existing practices, and relied on SETI to validate student contributions across cultural and linguistic differences.

This example highlights that effective PBL depends not only on tools but also on teacher dispositions. Educators must be comfortable with ambiguity, accept multiple pathways to mastery, and design opportunities that affirm student identities. Gay (2018) and Sturgis and Casey (2018) underscore that culturally responsive pedagogy and competency-based approaches ensure that projects both reflect students lived experiences and honor diverse demonstrations of mastery.

By applying frameworks within PBL, teachers create environments where inquiry, equity, and voice intersect. AI and other technologies serve as scaffolds that expand access and deepen engagement, while educators design conditions that preserve human judgment, foster collaboration, and sustain dignity.

Scaling Differentiation with AI Supports

AI is changing how educators differentiate instruction, making it possible to extend equitable practices across diverse classrooms. Differentiation has long been considered essential but difficult to implement consistently. AI systems reduce some of these barriers by automating routine tasks and generating adaptive resources, which frees educators to focus on instructional design and relational teaching.

One powerful application involves content adaptation. AI tools can generate leveled texts, scaffolded prompts, and multimodal supports that allow all students to engage with core materials. For example, a teacher preparing a unit on climate change can quickly create three versions of the same text: one simplified for emerging readers, one aligned with grade-level expectations, and one enriched with advanced vocabulary. These scaffolds honor student dignity by making rigorous material accessible without reducing expectations (Diliberti et al., 2024).

Another high-impact use case is formative feedback. AI platforms can analyze student writing or problem-solving processes to provide immediate, targeted suggestions. Teachers then interpret this feedback, connect it to learning goals, and guide students in applying it. This process strengthens equity because students receive timely support while teachers preserve their central role as mentors and evaluators (US Department of Education, 2023).

While these systems expand capacity, they cannot replace teacher judgment. Educators must critically evaluate outputs, identify algorithmic bias, and ensure that supports align with instructional intent. Research underscores that the most effective use of AI occurs when teachers direct its application to enhance differentiation while maintaining relationships and cultural responsiveness (World Economic Forum, 2025).

By treating AI as a scaffold rather than a substitute, educators can create classrooms where diverse learners engage with challenging content, receive just-in-time feedback, and develop confidence as independent thinkers. Differentiation at scale becomes not only more feasible but also more aligned with principles of justice, equity, and student dignity.

Professional Learning Architecture That Builds Capacity

Preparing educators for an AI-driven future requires professional development that is continuous, job-embedded, and grounded in equity. One-time workshops or disconnected training sessions rarely shift instructional practice. Decades of research confirm that professional learning has the greatest impact when it is iterative, collaborative, and directly tied to classroom contexts (Darling-Hammond et al., 2017).

Structured capacity-building begins with models that treat professional learning as an ecosystem. Effective systems include coaching, professional learning communities, curated digital resources, and micro-credentials that validate specific competencies (Fullan & Quinn, 2020; Digital Promise, n.d.). These ecosystems respect teacher expertise by providing multiple entry points for growth while maintaining coherence across district goals.

National initiatives offer examples of scalable, high-quality programs. The AI4K12 Initiative provides guidelines for teaching AI concepts responsibly in K–12 settings (AI4K12, n.d.). The international Society for Technology in Education (ISTE)'s micro-credential system allows teachers to demonstrate mastery in areas such as AI integration and ethical technology use (ISTE, n.d.). RAND research shows that districts offering structured, ongoing AI-focused professional development report higher levels of educator confidence and instructional alignment than those offering short introductory sessions (Diliberti et al., 2024).

Equity must remain at the center of capacity-building efforts. Training should not only address technical fluency but also prepare teachers to evaluate bias, safeguard privacy, and ensure that AI tools expand opportunities for multilingual learners, students with disabilities, and historically marginalized groups (US Department of Education, 2023). Programs that provide collaborative inquiry and case-based learning help teachers practice this critical evaluation in real instructional contexts.

Sustained professional learning is an ethical responsibility. Educators are stewards of student trust and must be prepared to use AI in ways that protect dignity and affirm identity. When schools invest in coherent ecosystems that blend coaching, collaboration, and credentialing, they build professional cultures that are adaptive, reflective, and aligned with justice.

Collective Capacity: PLCs and Networked Improvement

Building the capacity for AI integration cannot rest on individual teachers alone. It requires collective structures where educators engage in shared inquiry, critique practice, and co-develop strategies that protect equity and uphold human dignity. Professional learning communities (PLCs) provide a well-established model for this type of collaborative growth.

PLCs function as spaces where teachers analyze student work, review instructional practices, and align their approaches across classrooms and grade levels. DuFour et al. (2016) emphasize that effective PLCs are defined by a focus on results, a culture of collaboration, and a commitment to continuous improvement. In the context of AI, these principles ensure that experimentation is not fragmented or isolated but coordinated and transparent.

Research in improvement science highlights the value of networked approaches to change. Bryk et al. (2015) show that educators working within structured networks of inquiry are better able to identify promising practices, refine them through iterative cycles, and share findings across contexts. When PLCs adopt this model, AI use can be tested and adapted in ways that safeguard student agency while strengthening coherence.

Practical applications of AI-focused PLCs include joint evaluation of tools, sharing effective prompt strategies, analyzing data for bias or equity gaps, and developing common protocols for responsible classroom use. These collaborative structures also surface concerns that may not emerge in isolated practice, such as how AI-generated texts represent cultural narratives or how adaptive systems support multilingual learners. CoSN (2024) stresses that these discussions are vital for building both technical capacity and ethical oversight.

Collective inquiry creates a safeguard against uncritical adoption. Teachers remain central interpreters of how AI influences learning, identity, and equity. When PLCs and networks foster reflective dialogue, they create the professional culture necessary for responsible innovation. AI integration then becomes not an individual burden but a shared endeavor rooted in collaboration, trust, and justice.

Responsible AI: Ethics, Equity, and Human Dignity

Integrating AI into K–12 education requires more than technical fluency. It requires ethical awareness and a commitment to equity. Teachers must be equipped to evaluate how AI tools influence representation, access, and student outcomes. Responsible use begins with clarity about principles such as transparency, accountability, fairness, privacy, and the protection of students from harm (European Commission, 2022).

The risks of neglecting these principles are significant. Studies have shown that AI systems often replicate and amplify social bias. Benjamin (2019) warns that algorithmic design can reproduce inequities by privileging dominant cultural narratives and marginalizing voices that are already underrepresented. Trust (2023) highlights how educators need to identify such limitations in AI outputs and scaffold content to ensure inclusion. Without deliberate oversight, AI can deepen structural barriers rather than dismantle them.

Educators must also safeguard student privacy. Many AI tools collect and analyze behavioral and performance data without clear disclosure. The US Department of Education (2023) calls for a human-in-the-loop approach that positions teachers as the interpreters and decision-makers in all AI applications. Teachers evaluate outputs, connect them to instructional intent, and apply them in ways that maintain student agency and protect data rights.

Responsible AI use must include a focus on equity. Students with disabilities, multilingual learners, and those in under-resourced schools often experience barriers when technology is not adapted to their needs. Culturally responsive practices can help ensure that AI functions as an amplifier of access rather than an additional filter. When educators apply an equity lens, they not only integrate technology but also honor justice, representation, and human dignity.

Professional learning plays a key role. Teachers need structured opportunities to practice evaluating AI-generated content, examine real cases of bias, and engage in collaborative reflection. These activities strengthen ethical literacy and prepare educators to guide students in navigating AI responsibly. Preparing learners to think critically about algorithms, authorship, and fairness is not optional. It is foundational to civic education in a digital society.

Feedback Loops for Continuous Improvement

When new technologies enter schools, teachers are the first to see both the benefits and the problems. They notice when an AI tool saves time by creating leveled texts, and they also notice when the same tool misses the mark for multilingual learners or students with disabilities. These observations are critical. Without a process for collecting and acting on them, decisions about technology risk being made without the perspective of those closest to students.

Feedback structures provide that process. Districts can create simple but consistent systems such as post-unit reflections, surveys built into professional learning communities, or scheduled check-ins during pilot programs. These mechanisms allow teachers to share not only whether a tool "worked" but also how it affected equity, student agency, and classroom relationships.

Feedback also shifts power. When educators are invited to critique tools and shape how they are used, they become co-designers rather than end-users. This strengthens trust and reduces the sense that AI is being imposed from above. Teacher advisory groups, pilot teams, or curriculum committees that review AI implementation can turn teacher voice into system-level influence (ISTE, 2023).

Well-structured feedback loops connect teachers with both district leaders and technology developers. Developers can adjust functionality based on classroom evidence, while leaders can refine policies and professional learning in response to patterns that teachers identify. CoSN (2024) stresses that these cycles are essential for responsible adoption because they keep classroom realities visible in system-level decision making.

Feedback is also an equity tool. Teachers are often the first to see when technology benefits some students while leaving others behind. Making feedback intentional ensures that these disparities inform future design rather than remaining hidden. Continuous improvement in AI use depends on this cycle of teacher observation, system response, and shared accountability.

The integration of AI into schools is not just a matter of tools and infrastructure. It is a question of leadership. District and school leaders set the tone for how innovations are framed, how resources are aligned, and how concerns about ethics and equity are addressed. Without a clear vision and shared purpose, AI risks being treated as a passing trend rather than part of a coherent instructional strategy.

Strategic leadership begins with communication. Leaders must explain why AI is being used, how it connects to learning goals, and what protections are in place for student data and teacher judgment.

When this is done openly, it builds trust. When it is absent, teachers and families often interpret new tools as mandates that erode professional autonomy. The US Department of Education (2023) emphasizes that maintaining a human-in-the-loop approach is critical to ensure that educators remain central decision-makers.

Governance also requires structures that move beyond compliance. The Consortium for School Networking (CoSN)'s (2024) AI Maturity Framework provides districts with a way to assess readiness across areas such as instruction, ethics, and infrastructure. Tools like this are useful when paired with teacher input and community engagement. Policies on data privacy, academic integrity, and ethical use should be reviewed with educators and families so that decisions reflect shared values rather than technical convenience.

A practical example comes from a mid-sized district that introduced AI supports for literacy instruction. Instead of a blanket rollout, the superintendent created a teacher-led pilot group, established clear privacy guidelines, and invited parent representatives to join an advisory council. This slowed the implementation but built trust and transparency. Teachers who participated in the pilot later shared results through learning walks, which helped scale adoption in ways that were grounded in evidence and aligned to local priorities.

Strategic leadership in AI is about balance. It requires urgency to prepare students for a changing world, but also patience to ensure that equity and trust guide each step. Leaders who listen first, set clear expectations, and model ethical responsibility create the conditions for technology to strengthen rather than weaken the public purposes of education.

Strategic Leadership and Governance

As districts move from exploration to implementation, leadership becomes the determining factor in whether artificial intelligence contributes to instructional coherence or creates fragmentation. The integration of AI in schools is not primarily a technical undertaking. It is a leadership responsibility that shapes how innovation is framed, how resources are aligned, and how ethical and equity-related concerns are addressed. In the absence of a clearly articulated vision and shared purpose, AI initiatives risk being perceived as transient innovations rather than components of a coherent instructional strategy.

At this stage, strategic leadership is grounded in deliberate communication. Leaders must explain the instructional rationale for AI use, articulate its connection to learning goals, and clarify the protections in place for student data and professional judgment. When these expectations are communicated transparently, they support trust and shared ownership. When they are unclear, educators and families may interpret new tools as externally imposed mandates that diminish professional autonomy. The US Department of Education (2023) emphasizes that maintaining a human-in-the-loop approach is essential to ensuring educators remain central to instructional and ethical decision-making.

Governance structures must extend beyond compliance-oriented policies to support alignment and shared accountability. Frameworks such as CoSN's (2024) AI Maturity Framework provide districts with mechanisms to assess readiness across instructional, ethical, and infrastructural dimensions. These tools are most effective when paired with teacher input and community engagement rather than applied as technical checklists. Policies addressing data privacy, academic integrity, and ethical use should be developed collaboratively so that governance decisions reflect shared values rather than operational convenience.

A mid-sized district provides a practical illustration of this approach. As the district introduced AI-supported literacy tools, the superintendent convened a teacher-led pilot group, established explicit privacy guidelines, and invited parent representatives to participate in an advisory council. Although this process extended the implementation timeline, it strengthened transparency and trust. Teachers involved in the pilot later shared outcomes through learning walks, supporting broader adoption that was grounded in evidence and aligned with local priorities.

Strategic leadership in AI integration requires balance. Leaders must respond with urgency to prepare students for a changing educational landscape while exercising restraint to ensure equity, trust, and professional judgment guide each step. When leaders listen intentionally, set clear expectations, and model ethical responsibility, technology can reinforce rather than undermine the public purposes of education.

Community Partnership and Ethical Digital Citizenship

The integration of artificial intelligence in education depends not only on strong leadership and instructional design but also on trust with families and communities. Schools are public institutions, and their legitimacy rests on transparency, shared responsibility, and responsiveness to community concerns.

Partnership begins with communication. When schools adopt AI tools, families need clear explanations of what the tools do, why they are being used, and how student data is protected. This information should be accessible in multiple languages and shared through forums, newsletters, and classroom conversations. Without such openness, communities may view AI as something imposed rather than a resource that serves students.

Engagement also requires listening. Parents and caregivers bring valid questions about surveillance, bias, and the impact of technology on student well-being. In communities where technology has historically been used in harmful ways, these concerns are especially acute. Benjamin (2019) reminds us that algorithmic systems often reinforce inequities, which makes community voice essential in shaping how schools approach AI adoption.

Digital citizenship must also evolve. Traditional lessons on internet safety are no longer sufficient. Students must understand how algorithms shape information, how authorship is defined in the age of generative tools, and what ethical participation in digital spaces looks like. Organizations such as ISTE (2023) and Common Sense Media (2023) provide frameworks that help educators teach students to navigate these issues critically and responsibly.

Building trust with families and preparing students for civic life in a digital world are not add-ons to AI integration. They are the conditions that determine whether AI strengthens or undermines the public purpose of education. When schools honor community voice and prepare students as ethical digital citizens, they create learning environments rooted in justice, transparency, and shared responsibility.

Honor, Justice, and Human Connection

The role of the educator is evolving in ways that affirm both the promise of technology and the enduring importance of human presence. Artificial intelligence can help teachers reduce administrative burdens, differentiate instruction, and provide new pathways for inquiry. Yet these contributions matter only when guided by educators who design with purpose and place justice, dignity, and equity at the center of their practice.

Teachers are not passive adopters of tools. They are architects of learning who determine how content, pedagogy, and technology intersect in ways that foster agency, belonging, and authentic engagement. They are also ethical stewards who safeguard student privacy, challenge bias, and model responsible digital citizenship. When professional learning, leadership structures, and community partnerships position teachers as co-creators of innovation, schools can integrate AI in ways that strengthen rather than weaken the public purposes of education.

The future of teaching is not defined by algorithms. It is defined by the capacity of educators to design systems where students learn deeply, act responsibly, and see themselves as valued members of a learning community. AI may support this work, but it is teachers who embody the values of justice and human connection that make education transformative.

References

AI4K12 Initiative. (n.d.). *AI4K12: National guidelines for K–12 AI education*. https://ai4k12.org

Benjamin, R. (2019). *Race after technology: Abolitionist tools for the new Jim Code*. Polity Press.

Bransford, J. D., Brown, A. L., & Cocking, R. R. (Eds.). (2000). *How people learn: Brain, mind, experience, and school* (Expanded ed.). National Academies Press.

Bryk, A. S., Gomez, L. M., Grunow, A., & LeMahieu, P. G. (2015). *Learning to improve: How America's schools can get better at getting better*. Harvard Education Press.

Bryk, A. S., & Schneider, B. (2002). *Trust in schools: A core resource for improvement*. Russell Sage Foundation.

Common Sense Media. (2023). *Digital citizenship and AI: Teaching students responsible technology use*. https://www.commonsensemedia.org

Consortium for School Networking. (2024). *K–12 generative AI maturity tool*. https://www.cosn.org

Couros, G. (2015). *The innovator's mindset: Empower learning, unleash talent, and lead a culture of creativity*. Dave Burgess Consulting.

Darling-Hammond, L., Hyler, M. E., & Gardner, M. (2017). *Effective teacher professional development*. Learning Policy Institute.

Digital Promise. (n.d.). *Micro-credentials for educators*. https://digitalpromise.org

Diliberti, M., Schwartz, H. L., & Grant, D. (2024). *Teacher and principal perspectives on generative AI in schools*. RAND Corporation.

DuFour, R., DuFour, R., Eaker, R., & Many, T. (2016). *Learning by doing: A handbook for professional learning communities at work* (3rd ed.). Solution Tree.

European Commission. (2022). *Ethics guidelines for trustworthy AI*. https://digital-strategy.ec.europa.eu

Fullan, M. (2020). *The devil is in the details: System solutions for equity, excellence, and well-being*. Corwin.

Fullan, M., & Quinn, J. (2016). *Coherence: The right drivers in action for schools, districts, and systems*. Corwin.

Fullan, M., & Quinn, J. (2020). *The right drivers for whole system success*. Centre for Strategic Education.

Gay, G. (2018). *Culturally responsive teaching: Theory, research, and practice* (3rd ed.). Teachers College Press.

Goldman, S., Carreon, A., & Smith, S. (2024). Exploring the integration of artificial intelligence into special education teacher preparation through the TPACK framework. *Journal of Special Education Preparation*, 4(2), 52–64. https://doi.org/10.33043/6zx26bb2

Hernandez-Ramos, P., & De La Paz, S. (2009). Learning history in middle school with laptops: A comparison of groupwork with and without technology. *Journal of Research on Technology in Education, 42*(2), 151–173. https://doi.org/10.1080/15391523.2009.10782545

International Society for Technology in Education. (2023). *AI in education: A guide for policy makers and educators.* https://www.iste.org

International Society for Technology in Education. (n.d.). *Artificial intelligence explorations and their practical use in schools.* https://www.iste.org

Koehler, M. J., & Mishra, P. (2009). What is technological pedagogical content knowledge? *Contemporary Issues in Technology and Teacher Education, 9*(1), 60–70.

Kolb, L. (2017). *Learning first, technology second: The educator's guide to designing authentic lessons.* International Society for Technology in Education.

Larmer, J., Mergendoller, J. R., & Boss, S. (2015). *Setting the standard for project-based learning: A proven approach to rigorous classroom instruction.* ASCD.

Ning, W., & Inan, F. A. (2024). Impact of social media addiction on college students' academic performance: An interdisciplinary perspective. *Journal of Research on Technology in Education, 56*(5), 616–631.

Sturgis, C., & Casey, K. (2018). *Designing for equity: Leveraging competency-based education to ensure all students succeed.* CompetencyWorks. ERIC Document ED589907.

Trust, T. (2023). Artificial intelligence in K–12 classrooms: Ethical integration and equity considerations. *Educational Technology, 63*(5), 3–12.

US Department of Education, Office of Educational Technology. (2023). *Artificial intelligence and the future of teaching and learning: Insights and recommendations.* https://tech.ed.gov/ai

World Economic Forum. (2025). *The future of jobs report 2025.* https://www.weforum.org

Yue, K. Y., Jong, M. S. Y., & Ng, O. L. (2024). Understanding K–12 teachers' technological pedagogical content knowledge readiness and attitudes toward artificial intelligence education. *Education and Information Technologies, 29,* 19505–19536. https://doi.org/10.1007/s10639-024-12621-2

Section 3

The Architecture of Resistance

Systems, Structures, and the Challenge of Reform

Educational change is impossible without systemic change, and systemic change is impossible without confronting policy (Fullan et al., 2018). The most persistent barriers to educational transformation are structural. Despite the proliferation of innovative models, tools, and pedagogies, public education remains constrained by a legacy framework rooted in compliance, standardization, and institutional preservation. This architecture consists of policy mandates, funding mechanisms, hierarchical governance, and deeply ingrained cultural norms that prioritize stability over adaptability.

Policy and practice must move together. Educational change depends on what teachers do and think, which makes professional culture and capacity central to any reform effort (Hargreaves & Fullan, 2012). To move forward, we must redesign structures to elevate flexibility, equity, and student-centered learning. This means shifting from compliance-driven accountability to outcomes that measure authentic growth, from rigid funding models to sustainable investment strategies, and from hierarchical governance to collaborative leadership that empowers educators, families, and students. Only by restructuring these foundations will innovation move from the margins to the core of public education.

Resistance to innovation is not merely the result of individual reluctance or ideological opposition. It is engineered and sustained by systemic interdependencies that reinforce existing power dynamics and operational models. These mechanisms of resistance often remain hidden beneath layers of bureaucratic logic, resource limitations, and accountability frameworks that suppress deviation from normative practices.

This part critically examines how these forces manifest, the forms they take, and the implications they hold for those attempting to lead meaningful change. The first analysis focuses on the psychological and organizational roots of resistance, exploring how leadership decisions, trust-building, and communication strategies shape the conditions for stakeholder engagement. The second inquiry turns to infrastructure and governance, interrogating outdated financial systems, procedural inefficiencies, and fractured oversight that hinder systemic progress. The final discussion highlights the unintended consequences of reform, particularly when equity is not embedded into the design of technological and artificial intelligence (AI)-related innovation efforts (US Department of Education, 2023; International Society for Technology in Education [ISTE], 2023).

Taken together, these examinations argue that transformation requires more than programmatic change. It demands a reengineering of the structures and systems that shape the daily realities of schools. Educational stakeholders, especially leaders, must move beyond the easy temporary fixes and confront the underlying architecture of resistance with strategic, equity-centered intent.

References

Fullan, M., Quinn, J., & McEachen, J. (2018). *Deep learning: Engage the world change the world.* Corwin Press

Hargreaves, A., & Fullan, M. (2012). *Professional capital: Transforming teaching in every school.* Teachers College Press.

International Society for Technology in Education. (2023). *Bringing AI to school: Tips for school* leaders. https://cms-live-media.iste.org/Bringing_AI_to_School-2023_07.pdf

U.S. Department of Education, Office of Educational Technology. (2023). *Artificial intelligence and the future of teaching and learning: Insights and recommendations* (ED631097). https://www2.ed.gov/documents/ai-report/ai-report.pdf

# From Instructor to Architect

Transforming the Role of Educators

Resistance to change is not a problem to be fixed; it is a sign that people care (Fullan, 2001). Although there is growing consensus that personalized learning and artificial intelligence enhanced instruction represent a critical direction for the future of education, widespread adoption remains limited. Even strong reforms face skepticism rooted in fears of automation, loss of human connection, and disruption of familiar practices. Resistance often stems from genuine investment in what currently works and concern for what could be lost. Recognizing this emotional and cultural dimension of change is essential for building trust, sustaining innovation, and creating shared ownership of transformation.

The introduction of technologies such as artificial intelligence, adaptive platforms, and extended reality often triggers apprehension among educators, families, and stakeholders. The immersive nature of extended reality (XR) can raise concerns about screen time, physical disconnection, and the perceived erosion of traditional instructional methods. These concerns are not irrational. They reflect a desire to preserve the relational, ethical, and human dimensions of education.

This chapter examines the psychology of resistance, challenges myths that hinder innovation, and presents strategies to build trust and guide change. Drawing on research from organizational behavior and educational leadership, it reframes resistance not as defiance but as evidence that people care. When addressed through transparency, empathy, and collaboration, resistance can strengthen reform efforts and reveal the conditions necessary for success.

Transforming public education will require more than new tools or revised policy. It demands a cultural shift grounded in trust, shared purpose, and inclusive leadership.

Rethinking Replacement: The Educator's Role in an AI-Augmented Future

On August 29, 2025, *The Atlantic* published "AI Has Broken High School and College," which documents how generative AI has normalized AI-assisted work across secondary and postsecondary classrooms. The reporting underscores a core fear in education that AI will cheapen thinking and displace authentic learning, yet it also points to a different path. Rather than framing AI as a substitute for educators, districts should define educator roles that orchestrate human–AI collaboration, safeguard academic integrity, and design tasks that require judgment, discourse, and original creation (Beres, 2025).

Although culturally resonant, this narrative is conceptually flawed. Educators have consistently adapted to technological shifts, from blackboards to search engines. Yet the myth of professional obsolescence persists, often amplified by dystopian media, limited educator voice in policymaking, and opaque implementation. When these conditions exist, technology is no longer seen as an instructional tool, but as a threat to professional identity.

Historical comparisons are instructive. When Google became widely used in the early 2000s, critics warned that students would lose critical thinking skills. In practice, Google elevated the educator's role, requiring teachers to guide students in evaluating sources, synthesizing information, and thinking across disciplines. The warning that "Google will make students lazy" has evolved into "AI will make teachers irrelevant." Both reflect a misunderstanding of how roles evolve alongside broader technological change.

The language of replacement itself is misleading. To replace implies elimination. Educational roles, however, are continually redefined. Calculators did not remove the need for math instruction;

they allowed educators to focus on conceptual reasoning. Similarly, AI is unlikely to eliminate teachers. It will redistribute tasks, reducing time spent on grading, content curation, and routine data entry, and expanding opportunities for mentorship, instructional design, ethical reasoning, and social-emotional development.

This redefinition extends to the structure of schooling. As AI integrates with immersive tools such as XR, the traditional schoolhouse model will continue to shift. XR can dissolve the boundaries between school and the wider world, offering students access to virtual laboratories, simulations, and collaborative global learning spaces. These environments are flexible, asynchronous, and responsive to individual needs. For students in rural, urban, and historically underserved communities, XR expands access to high-quality learning once limited by geography or funding, offering students virtual labs and global collaboration spaces. These tools do not make schools obsolete, but they call for more adaptive, connected, and experience-driven models. Educators remain essential not to control these environments, but to ensure ethical use, support engagement, and preserve community and belonging.

It is also critical to recognize that today's AI limitations are not fixed. While current models cannot replicate empathy, cultural responsiveness, or ethical discernment yet, these must remain central to teaching. The educator's role has always adapted to changing contexts. AI does not mark the end of that trajectory. It signals the next chapter.

Empirical research reinforces this view. The World Economic Forum (2023) identifies teaching as one of the most human-dependent professions due to its reliance on interpersonal judgment and moral reasoning. Fitzpatrick et al. (2023) argue that AI is most effective when it augments educators, enabling more time for feedback, mentorship, and planning. Mamlok (2021) emphasizes that the risk of dehumanization comes not from the tools themselves, but from implementation that lacks ethical oversight and educator involvement. When AI and XR tools are used within student-centered frameworks, they can strengthen equity, agency, and teacher autonomy.

To move beyond fear-based narratives, education leaders must prioritize inclusive design, transparent policy, and sustained professional learning. Educators should not be passive recipients of technological change. They must serve as co-designers of the systems that shape their work. Implementation must uphold core values of privacy, autonomy, and pedagogy. The true risk is not that AI or XR will replace humanity. The greater threat is that, without foresight and ethical leadership, education will lose its human purpose.

Redefining the educator's role is one part of the challenge. Reducing fear is necessary, but not sufficient. The success of any innovation depends as much on the conditions of implementation as on the quality of the tool. Even the most promising technologies will falter if educators do not feel valued, supported, and engaged. Meaningful transformation begins not with devices or policies, but with psychological safety, shared purpose, and leadership that builds lasting trust.

Trust before Tools: Foundations for Sustainable Innovation in Schools

Meaningful change in education rarely results from policy mandates alone. It depends on people. Transformation requires a willingness to shift mindsets, embrace uncertainty, and engage in sustained professional effort. Yet initiatives are often introduced rapidly, with little attention to the emotional, psychological, and cultural dimensions of educators' work. Teachers are frequently expected to implement new tools or instructional models with limited clarity, inadequate support, and minimal input, while remaining accountable for successful outcomes. The result is often not engagement but resistance. In these cases, the primary obstacle is not the innovation itself but the absence of trust and the conditions necessary for meaningful change.

Research consistently demonstrates that trust is foundational to sustainable educational improvement. Bryk and Schneider (2002) showed that relational trust among teachers, leaders, and families is essential for school effectiveness. Without trust, even well-intentioned reforms are met with skepticism or passive compliance. Educators are unlikely to take instructional risks if they expect judgment or lack support. Families question new approaches when communication is inconsistent. Students quickly perceive when change is superficial or disconnected from care.

Effective leadership does not compel compliance. It fosters professional growth. Fullan (2001) argues that successful change agents build shared meaning, support ongoing learning, and lead through relationships rather than authority. This stands in contrast to mandates that treat resistance as defiance rather than a signal of exclusion. When educators are treated as collaborators, innovation becomes relational, purposeful, and more likely to succeed.

Psychological safety is a critical, yet often underexamined, element of effective leadership. Edmondson (2018) defines it as the belief that individuals can speak up, take risks, and make mistakes without fear of humiliation or retaliation. In psychologically safe school cultures, educators feel empowered to experiment, reflect, and offer feedback. These conditions support iterative improvement and long-term innovation.

Simon Sinek reinforces this view in *Leaders Eat Last*, asserting that trust begins with a "Circle of Safety" where individuals feel valued and supported (Sinek, 2014). When teachers feel secure in their roles and identities, they are more likely to engage in inquiry and change. In *The Infinite Game*, Sinek (2019) adds that improvement in education must be guided by enduring values such as equity, trust, and growth, rather than short-term wins or test-based metrics. Leaders who adopt this mindset are better equipped to foster resilience and coherence, especially when introducing technologies like artificial intelligence.

Coherence is another essential element of trust. Educators often encounter fragmented initiatives that lack alignment with district goals or classroom realities. This leads to initiative fatigue and a perception that change is disjointed or performative. Leithwood et al. (2020) stress the importance of a clear vision that connects new tools or models to an overarching strategy. When educators see how a reform aligns with their purpose, they are more likely to engage with intention and ownership.

In practice, cultivating trust requires consistent leadership behaviors and structural commitments. These include offering relevant professional learning, establishing feedback loops, and involving educators in planning and implementation. Leaders must model humility by acknowledging limitations, soliciting input, and learning alongside staff. In districts where AI implementation has been successful, common practices include pilot teams, opt-in participation, and phased rollouts that allow for adjustment based on feedback. These approaches signal that educators are not passive recipients of change but are integral to shaping it.

Sustainable innovation is not driven by technology alone. It is sustained by people who believe that change is meaningful, respectful, and aligned with their professional identity. Trust cannot be legislated or outsourced. It must be built intentionally, through leadership that listens, adapts, and shares responsibility for the future of teaching and learning.

Building What Comes Next: Models of Trust-Based, Student-Centered Reform

The following case studies highlight how schools and districts across varied contexts are advancing personalized learning, competency-based education, culturally responsive pedagogy, experiential learning, school autonomy, STEAM education, equitable grading, and technology integration. Each example reflects systemic reform grounded in trust, educator voice, and measurable outcomes.

Personalized Learning
Champlain Valley Union High School in Vermont integrates student agency and social consciousness through reflective, project-based learning, including student-produced documentaries on social justice (Gewertz, 2017). Captain Isaac Paine Elementary School in Rhode Island combines adaptive software with differentiated instruction to improve formative outcomes (Kamenetz, 2018). Montour School District in Pennsylvania pioneered AI-powered math platforms that boosted test scores and instructional differentiation (Hughes & Pane, 2020).

Competency-Based Education (CBE)
Melrose Public Schools in Massachusetts overhauled grading practices with professional development and policy reform to support mastery-based learning (Hechinger Report, 2018). The Virtual

Learning Academy Charter School (VLACS) in New Hampshire delivers asynchronous, modular CBE with strong completion rates (Singer, 2016). Lindsay Unified School District in California eliminated grade levels, allowing progression based on proficiency, which led to gains in graduation rates and equity outcomes (Pane et al., 2017; Patrick et al., 2019).

Culturally Responsive Pedagogy

Milwaukee Urban Waldorf School serves a predominantly African American population using arts integration and storytelling, improving engagement and outcomes (Dover, 2013). Thomasville Heights Elementary in Georgia redesigned its curriculum to respond to demographic shifts, investing in culturally relevant pedagogy (Wright, 2019). In Australia, Northern Metropolitan Adelaide Schools implemented a region-wide initiative informed by student cultural contexts, increasing teacher–student connection and engagement (Queensland University of Technology, 2020).

Experiential Learning

South Burlington High School in Vermont uses the Big Picture Learning model and internship-based curricula for personalized planning and postsecondary success (Gewertz, 2017). Statesboro STEAM Academy in Georgia blends arts and technology through project-based learning, improving engagement (Statesboro STEAM Academy, 2023). Baxter Academy for Technology and Science in Maine structures inquiry-driven, interdisciplinary learning through weekly "Flex Friday" projects, with strong capstone results and increased STEM interest (Rennie Center, 2018).

School Autonomy

Boston Public Schools implemented decentralized decision-making to increase responsiveness, improving parent satisfaction and leadership assessments (Boston Foundation, 2014). A.D. Henderson University School in Florida uses autonomous curriculum design and project-based instruction, resulting in strong academic performance and teacher retention (AP News, 2023). Winter Hill and Paul Revere Innovation Schools in Massachusetts leverage autonomy in staffing and budgeting to improve achievement and retention (Rennie Center, 2018).

STEAM Education

Ignite Institute in Kentucky offers interdisciplinary STEAM academies in biomedical science, engineering, and design, yielding strong capstone performance (Kentucky Department of Education, 2023). Salamanca City Central School District in New York built a rural K–12 STEAM ecosystem through partnerships and innovation centers (Salamanca CSD, 2023). Baxter Academy demonstrates integrated STEAM through student-led science and arts projects that elevate student agency and performance (Rennie Center, 2018).

Equitable Grading Practices
Modesto City Schools in California adopted standards-based grading and skill-specific report cards to improve accuracy and equity (Modesto Bee, 2024). Saint Francis High School diversified assessment to reduce bias using portfolios and performance tasks, improving student choice and reducing grade inflation (Saint Francis High School [Internal Report], 2023). Highline Public Schools in Washington used equity audits to drive grading reform, leading to fewer failing grades and better outcomes for underserved populations (Feldman, 2019).

Technology Integration
A coordinated AI pilot in Connecticut from the State Department of Education embedded tutoring tools into instruction, improving engagement and achievement (Vaznis, 2025). Nauset Public Schools in Massachusetts expanded broadband, device access, and digital literacy training, earning high usage and feedback scores (Cape Cod Commission, 2024). Montour School District continues to lead in AI integration with sustained academic gains and teacher adoption (Hughes & Pane, 2020).

These cases show that innovation succeeds when grounded in coherence, trust, and educator agency, not mandates. Infrastructure and policy must create the conditions for such reform at scale.

References

AP News. (2023). *A.D. Henderson University School continues to excel.* https://apnews.com/article/a-d-henderson-university-school-excel

Beres, D. (2025, August 29). AI has broken high school and college. *The Atlantic.* https://www.theatlantic.com/newsletters/archive/2025/08/ai-high-school-college/684057/

Boston Foundation. (2014). *The Boston Public Schools' school autonomy initiative: Lessons from implementation.* https://www.tbf.org

Bryk, A. S., & Schneider, B. (2002). *Trust in schools: A core resource for improvement.* Russell Sage Foundation.

Cape Cod Commission. (2024). *Broadband needs assessment: CTC report (August 2024).* https://capecodcommission.org/resource-library/file/?url=/dept/commission/team/Website_Resources/broadband/Broadband%20Needs%20Assessment%20-%20CTC%20Report%20%28August%202024%29.pdf

Dover, A. G. (2013). Teaching for social justice: From conceptual frameworks to classroom practices. *Multicultural Perspectives, 15*(1), 3–11. https://doi.org/10.1080/15210960.2013.754285

Edmondson, A. C. (2018). *The fearless organization: Creating psychological safety in the workplace for learning, innovation, and growth.* John Wiley & Sons

Feldman, J. (2019). *Grading for equity: What it is, why it matters, and how it can transform schools and classrooms.* Corwin.

Fitzpatrick, D., Fox, A., & Weinstein, B. (2023). *The AI classroom: The ultimate guide to artificial intelligence in education.* TeacherGoals Publishing.

Fullan, M. (2001). *Leading in a culture of change.* Jossey-Bass.

Gewertz, C. (2017). *Personalized learning models catch on in rural and urban schools.* Education Week. https://www.edweek.org

Hechinger Report. (2018). *Competency-based education gains traction in Massachusetts schools.* https://hechingerreport.org

Hughes, J., & Pane, J. F. (2020). *AI in K–12 education: Early lessons and promising applications.* RAND Corporation. https://www.rand.org

Kamenetz, A. (2018). *Personalized learning and its pitfalls.* NPR. https://www.npr.org

Kentucky Department of Education. (2023). *Ignite Institute profile.* https://education.ky.gov

Leithwood, K., Harris, A., & Hopkins, D. (2020). Seven strong claims about successful school leadership revisited. *School Leadership & Management, 40*(1), 5–22. https://doi.org/10.1080/13632434.2019.1596077

Mamlok, D. (2021). Rethinking the digital divide: Perspectives from education. *Technology in Society, 66,* 101640. https://doi.org/10.1016/j.techsoc.2021.101640

Modesto Bee. (2024). *Modesto City Schools adopts standards-based grading.* https://www.modbee.com

Pane, J. F., Steiner, E. D., & Baird, M. D. (2017). *Informing progress: Insights on personalized learning implementation and effects.* RAND Corporation. https://www.rand.org

Patrick, S., Worthen, M., Frost, D., & Truong, N. (2019). *Maximizing competency education and personalized learning: Insights from practitioners.* Aurora Institute.

Queensland University of Technology. (2020). *Culturally responsive teaching in Australian schools.* https://www.qut.edu.au

Rennie Center. (2018). *From the ground up: Building comprehensive school redesign.* https://www.renniecenter.org

Saint Francis High School. (2023). *Equitable grading practices: Report on progress and outcomes* [Internal report].

Salamanca City Central School District. (2023). *Salamanca STEAM innovation center.* https://www.salamancany.org

Sinek, S. (2014). *Leaders eat last: Why some teams pull together and others do not.* Portfolio.

Sinek, S. (2019). *The infinite game.* Portfolio.

Singer, N. (2016, May 21). The virtual charter school experiment. *The New York Times.* https://www.nytimes.com

Statesboro STEAM Academy. (2023). *Integrating arts and technology: Program overview.* https://www.statesborosteam.org

Vaznis, J. (2025). Connecticut pilots AI tutoring program across districts. *The Boston Globe.* https://www.bostonglobe.com

World Economic Forum. (2023). *The future of jobs report 2023.* https://www.weforum.org

Wright, C. (2019). Culturally relevant teaching transforms Atlanta school. *Education Week.* https://www.edweek.org

8

Modernizing Infrastructure and Governance

Modernizing public education depends on systems that make innovation routine, not rare. Technology upgrades and new buildings matter, yet they succeed only when governance, funding, data, and procurement align to a long-term instructional vision. This chapter presents a practical architecture: treat governance as the operating system, invest sustainably after ESSER, mandate interoperability and privacy, plan physical and digital improvements together, make cybersecurity core school safety, procure for trust and accessibility, and coordinate local, state, and federal roles.

Governance as the Operating System of Modernization

Governance determines authority, decision speed, and whether choices serve a multiyear vision rather than short-term convenience. The most durable gains come from redesigning time, data, and roles so that strategy drives operations.

Time as Infrastructure

The academic calendar functions as infrastructure. The University of Connecticut's Center for Education Policy Analysis, Research, and Evaluation distinguishes between single-track year-round

DOI: 10.4324/9781003739050-11

calendars, which redistribute instructional time for all students, and multi-track models that stagger enrollment to expand facility capacity. The review finds that single-track calendars can reduce summer learning loss, especially for students furthest from opportunity, while multi-track calendars primarily address overcrowding and introduce family scheduling challenges. Benefits emerge when calendar redesign are paired with targeted supports and sustained family engagement (Center for Education Policy Analysis, Research, and Evaluation, 2025).

New London Public Schools illustrates these principles. Beginning in 2023, the district offered a year-round option with six-week terms and two-week intersessions that include tutoring and enrichment. Reports indicate improvements in reading and mathematics, reductions in chronic absenteeism, and higher engagement tied to the combined effect of redistributed time, enrichment, and family partnership (New London Public Schools, 2024; Ritchie, 2024).

Calendar reform is not a quick fix. It is a governance test that touches policy, collective bargaining, transportation, childcare, and facilities. Districts that succeed pair calendar redesign with resource alignment, community engagement, and instructional supports.

Sustainable Investment after ESSER

The Elementary and Secondary School Emergency Relief funds delivered an unprecedented national infusion that allowed districts to accelerate recovery and modernize core systems. Federal guidance estimates the total allocation at approximately 190 billion dollars across three rounds, with final obligation dates in 2024 and liquidation windows that extend beyond the obligation deadline (US Department of Education, 2022a).

State allocations show both the scale and the limits. Massachusetts districts received approximately $2.9 billion across all ESSER phases. Connecticut districts received approximately $1.7 billion. These amounts stabilized operations and expanded services, yet many districts now face fiscal cliffs where recurring costs outlive one-time dollars (Connecticut State Department of Education, 2021; Massachusetts Department of Elementary and

Secondary Education, n.d.; Rennie Center for Education Research & Policy, 2023).

Federal efforts now emphasize resilience. In 2024, the FCC launched a 200 million dollar Cybersecurity Pilot to test sustainable models for protections such as endpoint detection and identity security. The pilot recognizes that digital safety is essential infrastructure for learning (Federal Communications Commission, 2024).

District leaders should convert ESSER-era progress into durable plans by shifting from one-time purchases to lifecycle funding, consolidating overlapping tools, and tying operating budgets to measurable service levels for connectivity, security, devices, and support.

Data Interoperability, Privacy, and AI Governance

Interoperability is a governance requirement. The Consortium for School Networking defines interoperability as secure, seamless, and controlled exchange of data across systems to support effective decision-making and privacy (Consortium for School Networking, 2023). Districts that do not standardize data in turn create data silos, duplicate work, and delay interventions.

Districts and vendors should adopt recognized interoperability standards and demonstrate compliance through formal certification. 1EdTech publishes widely used specifications, including Learning Tools Interoperability (LTI) and OneRoster, which enable secure connections among platforms for sharing rosters, instructional content, and assessment data. Project Unicorn's Interoperability Rubric provides districts and vendors with a practical framework to evaluate readiness and embed clear interoperability expectations into procurement and contract language. The Ed-Fi data standard further supports interoperability by enabling states and districts to unify student information, assessment, and program data for near real time use across systems (1EdTech Consortium, n.d.-a; 1EdTech Consortium, n.d.-b; Ed-Fi Alliance, n.d.; Project Unicorn, n.d.).

Privacy remains foundational. FERPA and COPPA set federal baselines for student data rights and protections. Districts should publish data inventories, include model privacy terms in vendor contracts, conduct privacy impact reviews for AI tools, and maintain public registers of approved applications. Guidance from the US Department of Education, the Federal Trade Commission, and the Future of Privacy Forum supports these practices (Federal Trade Commission, 2013; Future of Privacy Forum, 2024; US Department of Education, 2022b).

For AI, align to principles that are concrete and testable. The EDSAFE AI Alliance emphasizes efficacy, safety, accountability, and fairness, with human-in-the-loop and impact assessment as defaults for K–12 deployment. Data governance boards should adopt these criteria and require vendors to disclose model purpose, data use, and known limitations before procurement (EDSAFE AI Alliance, 2023).

Physical, Digital, and Community Connectivity

Physical and digital planning must operate as one process. The 2024 National Educational Technology Plan calls for coherent, learner-centered systems in which space, devices, networks, and content design reinforce each other. Flexible environments, reliable connectivity, and platform interoperability enable student-centered instruction across settings (US Department of Education, 2024).

Community broadband is part of the instructional infrastructure. Hundreds of municipal networks improve affordability and competition. At the same time, statutes in many states still restrict or prohibit municipal broadband, which limits local problem solving in communities where commercial providers have underinvested or where cost remains a barrier (BroadbandNow, 2025; Institute for Local Self-Reliance, 2024).

Local models demonstrate feasibility. Syracuse, New York launched Surge Link in 2023 and expanded it in 2025 with state support to reach additional households, offering symmetrical service at a subsidized monthly rate for eligible families and aligning the service with digital skills programming. These initiatives help reduce the homework gap (City of Syracuse, 2024, 2025).

State digital equity plans funded through the Infrastructure Investment and Jobs Act, the Broadband Equity, Access, and

Deployment Program, and the Digital Equity Act can align infrastructure with affordability and device access. Rhode Island's ConnectRI plan integrates infrastructure buildout with inclusion and skills and offers a useful model for states and municipalities (Rhode Island Commerce Corporation, 2024).

Cyber Resilience as Core School Safety

Cybersecurity disruptions now threaten instruction, finance, and student privacy. Two recent incidents illustrate systemic risk. In December 2024, PowerSchool experienced a major breach in which criminal actors accessed sensitive student records and demanded a ransom. Reporting indicates the company paid the ransom and that some districts later faced continued extortion attempts (Culliford, 2025; Robertson, 2025). In 2023, New Haven Public Schools experienced a business email compromise that diverted more than six million dollars before partial recovery. The incident shows how a single compromised account can trigger cascading financial and operational harm (CT Mirror, 2023; K–12 Dive, 2023).

Districts should adopt the NIST Cybersecurity Framework version 2.0, which adds a "govern" function to place risk management and accountability at the leadership level. Leaders can use the framework to establish profiles, measure maturity, and prioritize controls that match district risk. Identity and access management should be paired with endpoint detection and response, advanced firewalls, immutable backups, and tested incident response. Districts should train every employee, conduct independent audits annually, and perform tabletop exercises on a regular cadence (National Institute of Standards and Technology, 2024).

The FCC Cybersecurity Pilot can offset costs for critical controls and generate evidence for longer-term funding solutions. Districts should build regional consortia and applications that align with their risk profiles and modernization plans (Federal Communications Commission, 2024).

Trust by Design: Procurement and Accessibility

Procurement must move beyond price and features to evidence, privacy, accessibility, and interoperability. Use evaluation rubrics that require alignment to standards, accessibility conformance reports, and clear data-handling disclosures. Require 1EdTech certification where relevant and use Project Unicorn's rubric to score vendor data exchange claims. Build performance review cycles and off-ramp language into contracts to retire tools that lack impact or compliance (1EdTech Consortium, n.d.-a; Project Unicorn, n.d.).

Accessibility is nonnegotiable. Districts that treat the Web Content Accessibility Guidelines and Section 508 as core requirements reduce barriers for students with disabilities and improve usability for all learners. Universal Design for Learning provides a practical framework for inclusive materials and environments. Accessibility checks must be tied to procurement, content creation, and professional learning, not only to legal compliance (CAST, 2018; US Access Board, 2017; W3C Web Accessibility Initiative, 2023, 2024).

Coordinated Governance: Local, State, and Federal Roles

Local boards and superintendents set vision and implement change with communities. States create policy frameworks, fund standards-aligned modernization, and enforce privacy and security baselines. The federal role sets national equity markers, funds connectivity and security at scale, and leads research and guidance.

Capacity matters. Professionalizing district technology leadership improves outcomes. The Certified Education Technology Leader credential and state chapter programs such as the Massachusetts Educational Technology Administrators Association's CTO Certificate build shared competencies in leadership, data, security, finance, and interoperability (Consortium for School Networking, 2025; Massachusetts Educational Technology Administrators Association, 2025).

National coordination also requires stable institutions. The 2024 National Educational Technology Plan signaled federal commitment to coherent digital ecosystems. Sustained capacity and cross-agency collaboration are necessary to steward interoperability, digital equity, and AI guidance across administrations (US Department of Education, 2024).

Implications for Practice

Modernization succeeds when governance, funding, and infrastructure operate as one system in service of teaching and learning. Districts must turn strategy into disciplined practice with clear decision rights, durable budgets, and accountable implementation.

Formalize decision rights through a cross-functional modernization council with authority over time, data, and security. Convert ESSER-era purchases into lifecycle funding for networks, devices, security, and support tied to multiyear plans. Mandate interoperability and privacy in procurement so new tools align to open standards, protect student data, and integrate into the district ecosystem. Build accessibility and UDL into everyday practice to ensure materials, platforms, and classrooms work for every learner. Plan facilities and technology as a single program so space, power, acoustics, and connectivity reinforce instruction in every renovation and deployment. Treat cybersecurity as core school safety through leadership ownership, tested controls, and routine exercises.

These actions make improvement repeatable. With transparent metrics and steady community engagement, districts create conditions where equity, resilience, and innovation are not pilots but the norm.

References

1EdTech Consortium. (n.d.-a). *Learning tools interoperability.* https://www.1edtech.org/standards/lti

1EdTech Consortium. (n.d.-b). *OneRoster.* https://www.1edtech.org/standards/oneroster

BroadbandNow. (2025). *Municipal broadband is restricted in many states.* https://broadbandnow.com/report/municipal-broadband-roadblocks/

CAST. (2018). *Universal design for learning guidelines version 2.2.* http://udlguidelines.cast.org

Center for Education Policy Analysis, Research, and Evaluation. (2025). *Year-round school schedules: An overview of costs and benefits.* University of Connecticut Neag School of Education. https://cepare.uconn.edu/

City of Syracuse. (2024). *Surge link community broadband launches.* https://www.syr.gov/

City of Syracuse. (2025). *Surge link expansion announcement.* https://www.syr.gov/

Consortium for School Networking. (2023). *Interoperability in K–12 education.* https://www.cosn.org/

Consortium for School Networking. (2025). *Certified education technology leader.* https://www.cosn.org/careers-certification/cetl-certification/

Connecticut State Department of Education. (2021). *ESSER funding overview.* https://portal.ct.gov/SDE

CT Mirror. (2023, August 31). *City recovers most of the $6 million stolen from New Haven schools.* https://ctmirror.org/

Culliford, E. (2025, January 27). PowerSchool pays ransom after cyberattack. *Reuters.* https://www.reuters.com/

EDSAFE AI Alliance. (2023). A framework for safe, effective, and equitable AI in education. *InnovateEDU.* https://www.edsafeai.org/

Ed-Fi Alliance. (n.d.). Ed-Fi data standard overview. https://www.ed-fi.org/ed-fi-data-standard/

Federal Communications Commission. (2024, June 6). *FCC adopts 200 million dollar cybersecurity pilot program for schools and libraries.* https://www.fcc.gov/

Federal Trade Commission. (2013). *Complying with COPPA: Frequently asked questions.* https://www.ftc.gov/

Future of Privacy Forum. (2024, October). *Vetting generative AI tools for use in schools.* https://fpf.org/

Institute for Local Self-Reliance. (2024). *Community broadband networks: State preemption map.* https://communitynets.org/

K–12 Dive. (2023, August 31). *District recovers most funds after 6 million dollar cyber fraud.* https://www.k12dive.com/

Massachusetts Department of Elementary and Secondary Education. (n.d.). *ESSER dashboards and reports.* https://www.doe.mass.edu/

Massachusetts Educational Technology Administrators Association. (2025). *CTO Certificate online course.* https://www.techdirectors.org/

National Institute of Standards and Technology. (2024, February 26). *The NIST cybersecurity framework 2.0.* https://www.nist.gov/

New London Public Schools. (2024). *Year-round learning update.* https://newlondon.org/

Project Unicorn. (n.d.). *Project unicorn interoperability rubric.* https://www.projectunicorn.org/project-unicorn-rubric

Rennie Center for Education Research & Policy. (2023). *A closer look at ESSER spending in four Massachusetts districts.* https://eric.ed.gov/

Ritchie, C. (2024). *Superintendent update on year-round option.* New London Public Schools. https://newlondon.org/

Robertson, A. (2025, March 14). PowerSchool reportedly paid a ransom, but districts still face threats after breach. *The Verge.* https://www.theverge.com/

Rhode Island Commerce Corporation. (2024). *ConnectRI digital equity plan.* https://commerceri.com/

US Access Board. (2017). *Revised 508 standards and guidelines.* https://www.access-board.gov/ict/

US Department of Education. (2022a). *ESSER fund information.* https://oese.ed.gov/

US Department of Education. (2022b). *FERPA general guidance.* https://studentprivacy.ed.gov/

US Department of Education. (2024, January 22). *US Department of education releases the 2024 national educational technology plan.* https://www.ed.gov/

W3C Web Accessibility Initiative. (2023). *What is new in WCAG 2.2.* https://www.w3.org/WAI/standards-guidelines/wcag/new-in-22/

W3C Web Accessibility Initiative. (2024). *Web content accessibility guidelines 2.2.* https://www.w3.org/TR/WCAG22/

9

Advancing Equity in the Age of AI

Artificial intelligence (AI) in education is often framed through innovation, efficiency, and personalization. Yet as Benjamin (2019) reminds us, the problem is not only bad data but the unjust categories we use to collect it. Without a parallel focus on equity, AI can intensify the very disparities it aims to address (Benjamin, 2019; Eubanks, 2017; Noble, 2018). Ensuring just and inclusive outcomes requires a moral, structural, and pedagogical commitment to serving all learners, not only those who are most resourced, represented, or connected. This chapter examines how data practices, algorithmic design, and implementation choices can either reproduce harm or advance equity, and it outlines practical standards for transparency, accountability, and community participation.

The common combination of access with equity overlooks critical structural realities. While broadband and device access remain foundational, they do not guarantee opportunity. Rural communities continue to struggle with stable connectivity, while students in densely populated urban districts often navigate over surveilled or fragmented digital environments (EducationSuperHighway, 2023; Siefer & Callahan, 2021). Equitable inclusion requires a broader lens that encompasses accessibility, neurodiversity, and language justice, grounded in principles such as UDL and federal legal frameworks including the Web Content Accessibility Guidelines (WCAG) and Section 508 of the Rehabilitation Act (US Department of Education, 2022; CAST, 2018).

Algorithmic bias and opaque data practices risk replicating historical patterns of exclusion. Automated decision systems used in grading, behavior monitoring, and student grouping may encode societal inequities unless developers prioritize transparency, representation, and accountability (Benjamin, 2019; Keddell, 2022; West et al., 2021). Data privacy must be treated not merely as a technical safeguard but as a civil rights imperative, particularly for students from historically marginalized populations (Gilliard, 2021; US Department of Education, 2023).

Public concern aligns with these risks. A 2025 cross-national survey found that respondents ranked deepfakes of politicians, AI-driven disinformation, and cyberattacks among their highest fears, and a large majority favored human oversight for AI decisions (Seismic, 2025). Families also reported worry about scams, nonconsensual imagery, and cyberbullying. Equity planning must therefore pair instructional use with safeguards against manipulative and exploitative applications that disproportionately target marginalized communities.

These concerns reflect wider public sentiment. In a 2025 cross-national survey, half of adults identified AI as a major societal problem, and nearly seven in ten said AI should never make decisions without human oversight (Seismic, 2025). Women expressed more than twice the level of pessimism compared to men, underscoring how inequities already shape perceptions of risk. For schools, this signals that addressing bias is not only a technical necessity but also a social responsibility to build community trust and protect vulnerable learners.

Cultural and cognitive inclusion is essential for equitable AI integration. AI literacy should be a core component of civic and workforce readiness, particularly for students in underrepresented communities (Fitzpatrick et al., 2023; World Economic Forum, 2020). Curriculum frameworks and educational tools must reflect diverse epistemologies and cultural narratives. Without deliberate intervention, AI systems may reinforce dominant cultural norms while minimizing or erasing marginalized perspectives (Benjamin, 2019; Gray, 2022).

Family and educator engagement is foundational to equitable implementation. Digital divides in the home, including shared device access, language barriers, and limited caregiver support, must be addressed through inclusive outreach and policy design (Digital Equity Laboratory, 2021; Wrye, 2022). Professional learning opportunities must be equitably distributed so that all educators, regardless of school context or grade level, are prepared to integrate AI-supported instructional models with confidence and purpose (Darling-Hammond et al., 2020; Fullan et al., 2018).

Predictive analytics introduces the risk of a modernized form of academic gatekeeping. Unexamined use of these tools may result in the reclassification of students based on biased or incomplete datasets, reinforcing stratification under the guise of objectivity (Kizilcec & Lee, 2022; Long & Magerko, 2020). Ethical foresight, decentralized models of data stewardship, and greater community ownership of educational technology decisions are essential for advancing a more just digital future (Project Unicorn, 2023; World Privacy Forum, 2022).

Neutrality is not an option. Equity in the age of AI demands the active dismantling of exclusionary systems and assumptions. Advocacy, design justice, and principled innovation must guide the transformation of public education.

The Digital Access Continuum: Equity beyond the Device

The pandemic-era surge in federal technology funding brought overdue national attention to the digital divide in American public education. As schools rapidly expanded Wi-Fi access and distributed devices such as Chromebooks, a persistent misconception remained: access to a device or internet connection is not equivalent to access to educational opportunity (Siefer & Callahan, 2021; Wrye, 2022). Equity requires a more comprehensive understanding of geography, infrastructure, device quality, and inclusive design.

Structural disparities between rural and urban districts illustrate this complexity. Urban systems often struggle with bandwidth congestion, aging infrastructure, and multiple devices competing for limited connectivity within multi-family households. In contrast, rural districts face sparse broadband coverage, few provider options, and significant service delays. As of 2024, the average download speed in rural areas of the United States is approximately 111.87 Mbps, with a median of 45.66 Mbps, well below the averages in urbanized states such as Maryland and Virginia, which exceed 500 Mbps (Speedtest Global Index, 2024). The Federal Communications Commission (FCC) continues to define broadband as 25 Mbps download and 3 Mbps upload, a benchmark now widely regarded as inadequate for AI-enhanced learning environments, cloud-based applications, and video conferencing (FCC, 2022). In districts where infrastructure does not meet modern instructional demands, remote or blended learning initiatives often result in inconsistent engagement or educational exclusion.

Temporary funding through the Elementary and Secondary School Emergency Relief (ESSER) program, which provided nearly $190 billion across three federal relief packages, enabled many districts to address urgent infrastructure and staffing needs (US Department of Education, 2021). Investments in mobile hotspots, cloud platforms, and network upgrades improved digital access in the short term. Yet the expiration of ESSER funding has revealed the fragility of these gains. Without sustained investment, schools in economically disadvantaged or geographically isolated regions are returning to pre-pandemic inequities, lacking the resources to maintain devices, staffing, and infrastructure.

The presence of devices and connectivity does not eliminate disparities in the quality of digital experiences. Basic internet connected devices with limited processing capabilities are inadequate for running AI-supported tools or multimodal multimedia platforms used in advanced instruction. While students in well-funded districts engage with generative AI applications for writing or science simulations, their peers in under-resourced settings are often limited to restricted platforms or aging devices with lagging performance (Fitzpatrick et al., 2023; Wexler, 2022). Equitable access must be assessed through metrics of functionality, adaptability, and sustainability rather than simple distribution counts.

Global usage data reinforces the urgency of this shift. In 2025, ChatGPT reached 700 million weekly active users worldwide, with adoption spreading fastest in low and middle-income countries (Chatterji et al., 2025). While the gender gap in adoption has closed and younger users dominate non-work use such as tutoring, higher education levels still correlate with professional applications like writing and decision-making. Without deliberate intervention, these patterns risk concentrating the greatest benefits among those already advantaged. For public schools, equitable access must mean preparing all students to use AI effectively, not only those with resources or prior exposure.

Staffing inequities further undermine digital participation. Many districts operate with minimal IT personnel, with some relying on a single technician across multiple campuses (Consortium for School Networking, 2023). Limited staff capacity results in slower troubleshooting, delayed updates, and inadequate professional development. These disparities diminish instructional quality and reinforce structural inequities. Sustaining equitable access requires baseline standards for technical staffing and coordinated support models across schools.

Conditions beyond the classroom also shape access. Students experiencing energy insecurity or housing instability may lack reliable electricity, making it impossible to charge or use digital devices consistently (Snyder et al., 2021). In these contexts, equity efforts must consider partnerships with libraries, community centers, and other public spaces. Akron Public Schools, for example, transformed buildings into community learning centers, offering internet access, academic assistance, and secure environments for after-hours learning (Parsons, 2016). In a similar effort, Coachella Valley Unified School District deployed Wi-Fi–enabled school buses that park in underserved neighborhoods each evening, creating mobile internet zones for students lacking home broadband (Harwin, 2016). These community-driven interventions reflect scalable models of infrastructure designed through an equity lens.

Definitions of accessibility must also evolve in response to AI-integrated learning. Legal standards such as Section 508 and WCAG provide essential baselines for digital inclusion, but they do not address the emerging implications of intelligent systems (US

Department of Education, 2022). Tools offering voice navigation, real-time transcription, and adaptive interfaces can improve accessibility, yet they may also introduce complexity, cognitive strain, or algorithmic bias (Gray, 2022; Keddell, 2022). UDL remains a foundational framework for inclusive pedagogy, offering multiple means of engagement, representation, and expression. However, the rapid evolution of AI technologies requires continuous refinement of UDL principles to account for shifting modes of interaction and learning.

Access should be understood as a continuum, not a binary condition. The availability, quality, usability, and sustainability of digital tools and environments are shaped by infrastructure, geography, human labor, and intentional design. A district cannot claim equity based solely on device distribution. True access requires that all students meaningfully engage with technology in ways that support their learning needs, cultural identities, and lived circumstances.

This continuum continues to evolve as emerging technologies expand what students can access and how they experience learning. Extended reality (XR) technologies, including virtual, augmented, and mixed reality, are beginning to reshape how students access learning across content areas. XR can simulate laboratory environments, recreate historical moments, and provide immersive vocational experiences that are often unavailable in under-resourced schools. A student in a rural district can dissect a virtual organism or tour a museum thousands of miles away. These tools expand what is possible, but they require modern infrastructure, strong internet connectivity, and educator preparation. When XR is only accessible in well-funded schools, it reinforces opportunity gaps. Equitable implementation demands that XR be approached not as a novelty, but as part of a broader access strategy grounded in UDL. This includes ensuring compatibility with assistive technologies, offering culturally responsive content, and designing interfaces that reflect the diverse needs of learners. Without intentional planning, XR may replicate the same disparities that device distribution alone failed to resolve.

Digital Fluency as an Equity Imperative

Equity in the age of AI cannot be achieved solely through access to devices or connectivity. While closing the digital divide remains essential, ensuring equitable participation requires moving beyond digital literacy toward digital fluency. Digital literacy refers to the ability to use technologies for basic tasks such as information retrieval, communication, and content consumption. Digital fluency, by contrast, emphasizes adaptability, problem-solving, creativity, and ethical participation in digital environments (Ng, 2012; Voogt & Pareja Roblin, 2012). It reflects a learner's capacity not just to operate tools but also to navigate evolving technological landscapes with critical judgment and agency.

The distinction carries particular importance in the context of AI. Digital fluency enables students and educators to interrogate algorithmic recommendations, recognize bias in digital platforms, and adapt to emerging tools without being dependent on static skills. As Buckingham (2023) argues, fluency entails understanding how technologies shape power, identity, and participation, not only how they function. In this sense, digital fluency is both a technical and a civic competency. It equips learners to act as ethical participants in digital ecosystems rather than passive recipients of automated decisions.

For school leaders, cultivating digital fluency requires systemic strategies that extend across professional development, curriculum design, and community partnerships. Professional development must move beyond tool-specific training toward capacity building that empowers educators to critically evaluate platforms, integrate AI responsibly, and design inclusive digital learning environments. Recent research on AI-Technological Pedagogical Content Knowledge (TPACK) confirms that teacher competence in combining technological, pedagogical, and ethical knowledge is a predictor of readiness for AI integration (Ning et al., 2024; Yue et al., 2024). Building digital fluency among educators thus involves strengthening these knowledge domains while addressing emotional and cultural barriers to adoption.

Curriculum design should likewise embed opportunities for students to develop digital fluency through inquiry-based projects, problem-solving with real-world applications, and reflective practices. For example, students might analyze bias in AI-driven language models, design multimedia projects that address community challenges, or participate in scenario planning exercises that anticipate the social impacts of emerging technologies. Such activities not only build technical adaptability but also foster civic responsibility and ethical reasoning.

Examples of promising practice are already emerging. Districts participating in Project Unicorn's interoperability initiatives are designing data transparency modules that teach students to interpret and question how their information is collected and used. Professional development programs aligned with the International Society for Technology in Education (ISTE) standards are incorporating digital citizenship and AI ethics into teacher training, reinforcing the idea that fluency includes both technical and ethical dimensions. These efforts illustrate how districts can reframe digital equity as not just providing devices but also equipping learners with the skills, dispositions, and critical awareness needed to thrive in dynamic digital environments.

Positioning digital fluency as a core outcome of equity-driven schooling ensures that learners are not left vulnerable to technological change or manipulation. Instead, they are empowered to adapt, innovate, and participate as informed citizens in digitally mediated societies. For both students and educators, digital fluency transforms access into agency, bridging the gap between opportunity and meaningful participation in the age of AI.

From Digital Literacy to Digital Fluency

Equity requires more than closing access gaps. While digital literacy ensures students can log in, navigate platforms, and complete digital tasks, digital fluency emphasizes adaptability, problem-solving, and ethical participation in digital environments (Ng, 2012; Voogt & Pareja Roblin, 2012). Literacy equips learners to function; fluency equips them to thrive in complex, evolving, and often inequitable digital landscapes.

Skills. Digital literacy encompasses basic competencies such as operating devices, searching for information, and submitting assignments online. Digital fluency extends to creating, critiquing, and adapting across multiple technologies. It includes the ability to interrogate algorithmic outputs, identify bias, and apply critical judgment to data-driven recommendations (Buckingham, 2023).

Outcomes. Literacy outcomes are often measured through task completion, such as the ability to perform research online or communicate through digital platforms. Fluency outcomes are measured by transfer and agency: the ability to adapt to new tools, solve open-ended problems, and participate ethically in civic and cultural digital spaces. In the context of AI, fluency requires students to question how recommendations are generated and how decisions influence opportunity.

Leadership strategies. District leaders must move beyond tool-specific training toward systemic approaches that cultivate fluency for both educators and students. Professional development should strengthen teachers' AI-TPACK readiness by integrating technological, pedagogical, and ethical knowledge (Ning et al., 2024; Yue et al., 2024). Curriculum design should embed inquiry-based projects, such as analyzing bias in AI platforms or developing solutions to local challenges through digital tools. Policy must promote a culture of transparency, experimentation, and participatory governance, ensuring families and educators have agency in technology decisions (Project Unicorn, 2023).

Practical examples demonstrate how fluency can be developed at scale. Districts aligning with ISTE standards are integrating digital citizenship and AI ethics into teacher training, reframing technology as both a technical and civic competency. Project Unicorn's interoperability initiatives have created opportunities for students to examine how their own data is collected and used, cultivating a critical awareness of digital systems. Such practices move equity work beyond distributing devices to preparing learners and educators to engage critically, creatively, and responsibly in digital environments.

By embedding digital fluency as a core equity outcome, districts ensure that learners are not passive recipients of technology but active, adaptable participants in shaping their educational futures.

Access creates the conditions for participation; fluency transforms participation into agency.

Biased by Design: Algorithmic Justice and Data Ethics

AI systems already influence decision-making in K–12 schools, often in ways that are invisible to educators, administrators, and families. Platforms that automate grading, flag academic risk, detect plagiarism, or recommend course placements embed algorithmic judgments into daily practice (West et al., 2021; Williamson & Eynon, 2020). Marketed as timesaving supports, these tools often operate through opaque algorithms trained on biased datasets and shaped by embedded assumptions that are rarely accessible to end users.

AI-driven decisions regularly reinforce existing inequities. An online writing assistant may penalize a multilingual learner for grammar patterns that diverge from dominant academic English. Classroom monitoring software may flag code-switching as off-task behavior. Risk dashboards may misclassify neurodivergent students based on nonnormative movement patterns. These outcomes, now visible in classrooms across the country, disproportionately affect students marginalized by race, language, disability, or socioeconomic status (Benjamin, 2019; Keddell, 2022; Noble, 2018).

Because many systems rely on historical data reflecting systemic injustice, such as over-policing of students of color or underidentification of English learners for advanced programs, predictive models often reproduce those inequities (Eubanks, 2017; O'Neil, 2016). Students may receive fewer supports or opportunities not because of their individual needs but because their demographic profile matches patterns of historical exclusion. This automation of past bias cloaks inequitable practices in the language of objectivity.

Although educators rarely see an algorithm's inner workings, they live with its outcomes. A student may be placed in a lower reading group despite strong performance or flagged as high risk despite resilience and positive peer relationships. Automated prompts may contradict teacher expertise. These inconsistencies reveal a deeper issue: when algorithmic patterns are granted more authority than professional judgment, educators' insight is undermined, and student agency is diminished (Williamson & Eynon, 2020).

The fairness of AI systems depends on the data they use, and the values embedded within their design. Algorithms that operationalize narrow definitions of success or encode biased patterns reinforce exclusion at scale while projecting an appearance of neutrality. "Smart" technology inherits the limitations, omissions, and assumptions of its creators (Gray, 2022; Noble, 2018).

Algorithmic Transparency as a Foundational Standard

Transparency must move from superficial disclosure to a core ethical requirement. Most educators are not data scientists, nor should they be expected to interpret models unaided. Districts must require vendors to provide plain-language explanations of how systems function, what data they use, and where limitations exist. High-stakes outputs should undergo human review, and educators must be trained to critically interpret algorithmic results rather than accept them at face value (Project Unicorn, 2023). Families should also have access to profiles created about their children, along with clear opt-out provisions for nonessential data collection (World Privacy Forum, 2022). Without such measures, opacity erodes trust and accountability, leaving educators responsible for outcomes they cannot interrogate and families unable to advocate effectively.

Student Data Ownership and Digital Sovereignty

Transparency alone is insufficient if students and families lack control over their data. Current models concentrate ownership in vendor-controlled repositories, raising questions of access, portability, and long-term use. Decentralized approaches such as blockchain-based credentialing and portable digital portfolios offer a pathway to restore agency by allowing students to own and carry validated records across schools, districts, and into the workforce (Merlec et al., 2022). These models shift digital equity beyond access to true data sovereignty, ensuring that student records are not commodified without consent and that learners retain agency over their educational narrative.

Guardrails for Responsible AI Adoption

Guardrails ensure that innovation strengthens rather than undermines equity. The US Department of Education (2023) recommends human-in-the-loop standards for all high-stakes instructional and disciplinary applications. Districts should:

- Prohibit invasive surveillance tools, such as biometric monitoring, without informed consent;
- Mandate independent bias audits and disproportionate impact reviews before procurement;
- Require sunset clauses that trigger reevaluation and reauthorization of AI systems;
- Establish ethics committees with representation from educators, families, and students to review and guide adoption.

These safeguards reinforce that innovation must be accompanied by accountability, and that protecting equity requires structural protections, not only aspirational commitments.

Using Frameworks to Advance Equity

Frameworks such as the Triple E Framework (Kolb, 2017) and the Student Engagement, Technology, and Instruction (SETI) model (Hernández-Ramos & De La Paz, 2009) provide critical evaluative criteria for aligning AI use with equity. Triple E prompts districts to ask whether technologies engage students, enhance instructional goals, and extend learning opportunities. SETI situates technology adoption within the relational and cultural fabric of classrooms, reminding leaders that equitable integration depends on affirming belonging and sustaining engagement. Recent evidence reinforces this perspective: applying TPACK principles to AI integration in special education fosters inclusive practices (Goldman et al., 2024), and teacher readiness for AI depends on technological and pedagogical expertise (Yue et al., 2024).

By embedding frameworks alongside transparency, data sovereignty, and guardrails, schools can move beyond compliance-oriented adoption to equity-driven practice. These approaches empower educators and families to reject tools that perpetuate systemic injustice and instead prioritize those that expand agency, trust, and opportunity for all students.

Equitable Engagement: Families, Educators, and Community Voice

Digital equity encompasses more than access for students. It includes the experiences and agency of families, educators, and community members who interact with educational technologies under diverse and often inequitable conditions. Ensuring that AI systems support all learners requires a participatory design ethos grounded in inclusivity and shared ownership.

Persistent disparities affect low-income, multilingual, and rural communities despite efforts to close the digital divide. Families navigating school platforms often encounter linguistic and cultural barriers, limited digital literacy, and device scarcity. In homes with multiple children and limited bandwidth or hardware, engagement becomes fragmented and stressful. In many cases, caregivers are required to interpret school communications in languages not their own or adapt to unfamiliar technology platforms that were not designed with their needs in mind (US Department of Education, 2022).

True equity requires more than technological reach. It necessitates that platforms respect, empower, and reflect the communities they intend to serve. Tools must be designed to accommodate linguistic diversity, varying comfort levels with technology, and nontraditional schedules and routines. Furthermore, families and community members must be meaningfully included in the decision-making processes that shape how AI is selected, deployed, and governed within schools.

Participatory engagement does not require technical fluency. It requires access, voice, and transparency. Nontechnical stakeholders that include parents, support staff, and local advocates must have opportunities to shape the values embedded in the tools used to sort, assess, and monitor students. Decisions related to student grouping, behavior monitoring, and intervention triggers must be grounded in lived experience, not abstract metrics of efficiency. Without such inclusion, AI risks encoding institutional values that do not align with the needs or priorities of the communities it is intended to serve (O'Neil, 2016; Eubanks, 2017).

The participatory design model has been shown to improve trust, usability, and alignment with community priorities. For instance, El Paso Independent School District (EPISD) in Texas launched a community-driven redesign effort in 2024, hosting multilingual forums to gather direct feedback on school technology practices, platform usability, and data transparency concerns. This process led to the establishment of a Parent and Community Digital Advisory Council, which continues to influence major district-level decisions related to AI and digital infrastructure (Cuevas, 2024). Such efforts demonstrate how inclusion can transform engagement from passive compliance to active co-creation.

Educators also face notable equity gaps. Many receive little training or support before being expected to implement AI tools in instruction, grading, or student monitoring. In under-resourced schools, teachers may lack planning time, up-to-date devices, or access to technical staff. Despite these barriers, they are expected to navigate complex platforms that influence high-stakes decisions, often without clarity on how systems function or how data is used (West et al., 2021). This asymmetry of access and understanding undermines both teacher agency and equitable technology adoption.

Equitable implementation requires equitable professional development. All educators, not only early adopters, must receive sustained, hands-on training that includes ethical evaluation, bias detection, and strategies for aligning AI use with culturally responsive pedagogy (Kizilcec & Lee, 2022). Support staff, including paraprofessionals and school counselors, must also be included. These professionals serve as vital liaisons between students, families, and instructional practices, yet they are often excluded from EdTech conversations and training.

AI systems cannot be equitable if their development and oversight exclude those most affected by their use. Families must be informed and engaged. Educators must be empowered and supported. Communities must be active participants in shaping the digital systems that influence public education. Engagement must not follow implementation; it must guide it. Inclusion is not ancillary to justice; it is foundational to it. Systems built without input from those they affect risk becoming tools of disempowerment rather than empowerment.

Designing the Future: Preventing Digital Tracking and Future-Proofing Equity

AI presents significant opportunities for personalization, early intervention, and learner support in K–12 education. However, without intentional design, AI may reintroduce one of public education's most harmful legacies: academic tracking. In contemporary settings, tracking no longer relies on teacher judgment or explicit labels. It can occur invisibly through predictive analytics, a phenomenon that scholars refer to as algorithmic determinism (Eubanks, 2018).

Academic tracking refers to the practice of sorting students into differentiated instructional pathways based on perceived ability levels such as accelerated, standard, or remedial. While often framed as a method for instructional tailoring, tracking has consistently reinforced structural inequality. Students in lower tracks frequently receive less rigorous content, fewer enrichment opportunities, and reduced access to experienced educators (Oakes, 2005). These placements can significantly influence long-term academic outcomes, including access to advanced coursework, graduation pathways, postsecondary opportunities, and future economic mobility (Gamoran, 2009).

A critical concern with tracking is its rigidity. Once students are assigned to a lower tier, transitioning out can be difficult regardless of academic growth. For students from historically marginalized communities, particularly those who are low-income, Black, Latino, immigrant, or disabled, tracking often operates more as a barrier than a support. Research shows that implicit bias, lowered expectations, and subjective assessment practices frequently contribute to misplacement (Lucas & Berends, 2002).

In AI-enhanced educational environments, these practices risk becoming automated. Rather than a counselor or teacher determining a student's placement, an algorithm trained on incomplete or biased data may assign a course schedule, behavioral flag, or intervention plan without transparency or recourse. These decisions often influence instructional access and disciplinary pathways without visible input from an educator or family member.

Predictive tools already forecast academic performance, flag behavioral concerns, and recommend interventions. When used appropriately, these tools can identify support needs and enable targeted strategies. However, when interpreted as definitive or beyond question, they may become self-fulfilling. A student identified as at risk by an opaque model may be removed from challenging courses, assigned remedial programming, or denied enrichment opportunities, not due to ability but because of a probability generated from legacy data.

This concern is not speculative. Research has demonstrated that predictive systems often disproportionately flag students from low-income, Black, Latino, and disabled populations for intervention and disciplinary action (Barocas et al., 2019). These patterns reflect systemic biases embedded in historical datasets. When algorithmic outputs are accepted without scrutiny, educators may unknowingly perpetuate harm.

Equity in the age of AI requires intentional design that resists deterministic logics. Transparency must serve as a foundational principle. Students, families, and educators need clarity regarding how algorithms function, how decisions are made, and how to challenge or opt out of automated processes. Human-in-the-loop protocols are essential to ensure that AI recommendations inform, but do not replace, professional judgment.

Districts should also examine decentralized data governance models. Most student information systems concentrate control in centralized, vendor-managed platforms. This structure limits district authority over how data is stored, interpreted, and secured. The 2023 PowerSchool data breach, discussed earlier in Chapter 4, revealed the vulnerability of such systems when sensitive data from multiple districts was compromised.

Decentralized alternatives such as blockchain-based credentialing and student-owned digital portfolios offer a new framework for learner agency and data security. Blockchain technology enables tamper-resistant academic records, allowing students to share validated transcripts and credentials with postsecondary institutions or employers without relying on intermediary systems (West & Allen, 2018). Likewise, portable digital portfolios empower students to curate and retain their educational accomplishments across different schools and districts. These models promote transparency, ownership, and long-term portability.

Policy must evolve alongside practice. Currently, many AI procurement and implementation decisions occur at the district or vendor level, without comprehensive guidance from state or federal frameworks. Future-proofing equity requires enforceable standards related to transparency, auditability, privacy, and inclusive design. Equity impact assessments should be integrated into procurement workflows, just as culturally responsive criteria are applied to curriculum reviews.

To families and educators, future-proofing means ensuring that equity is embedded from the outset. This involves evaluating who benefits from each system, what data is collected, and whether the tools reflect the diversity of students in terms of language, culture, and ability. It also includes requiring clear accountability structures, including contingency planning and opt-out options before harm occurs.

Organizations such as the Center for Democracy and Technology (2021) and Digital Promise (2022) emphasize that AI governance must prioritize inclusion, transparency, and accountability at the initial design stage. These principles should guide not only policymakers and technologists but also the everyday decisions made by teachers, school leaders, and district administrators. The task ahead is clear. Public education must reject any AI system that treats student potential as static or predetermined. It must resist technologies that define learning as a fixed trajectory. Equity must not be a retroactive concern addressed only after harm occurs. It must be the first design principle and the standard by which all AI tools are evaluated.

Beyond Compliance: Advancing Equity through AI Readiness

Educational transformation requires more than tools, frameworks, or aspirational rhetoric. It demands a fundamental rethinking of how policy, practice, and possibility intersect in the design of learning systems that are both equitable and future-ready. The preceding analysis has addressed systemic barriers that hinder meaningful implementation of AI in K–12 education, including institutional inertia, structural inequities, ethical ambiguity, and the exclusion of educator and community voice from critical decisions.

The intent is not to reject AI but to challenge the conditions under which it is often deployed without adequate transparency or inclusive governance. Resistance to AI integration is frequently a signal that trust, coherence, and participation are missing from the implementation process. When educators are asked to use tools they did not select, interpret results they cannot verify, and rely on data they do not control, the outcome is not authentic innovation. It is the erosion of professional judgment and stakeholder agency.

Shifting from a compliance-based approach to one rooted in capacity-building requires a foundational change in how schools and districts engage with educational technology. Key strategies include:

- Designing anticipatory policies that address potential harm before it occurs (Barocas et al., 2019);
- Requiring algorithmic transparency, cultural and linguistic responsiveness, and accessibility as baseline criteria for procurement (Center for Democracy & Technology [CDT], 2021);
- Preparing educators to critically evaluate the function, bias, and instructional impact of AI tools (Digital Promise, 2022);
- Structuring inclusive governance models that position families and communities as co-architects in the design and oversight of AI systems (Cuevas, 2024).

The trajectory of AI in education will be shaped less by the sophistication of its algorithms than by the ethical, inclusive, and pedagogical principles that guide its use.

To support the development of equitable systems, every school district, policymaker, and educational leader should be able to answer the following questions with clarity and evidence:

1. What specific problem is the technology addressing, and whose interests does it serve?
2. Which stakeholders were involved in selecting, evaluating, or approving its implementation?
3. What data is being collected, how is it used, and do families have meaningful opportunities to decline participation?
4. Does the platform reflect and respect the linguistic, cultural, and neurodiverse identities of students?
5. Is there a transparent, human-centered process for feedback, correction, and appeals?

When the answer to any of these questions is uncertain, the system is not yet ready for equitable implementation. The broader context underscores this urgency. Public perception of AI remains polarized, with strong calls for accountability, regulation, and limits on autonomous systems (Seismic, 2025). At the same time, adoption is widespread, with millions of learners already relying on AI for tutoring, problem-solving, and creative support (Chatterji et al., 2025). Equity in the age of AI requires balancing these realities: protecting students from harm while empowering them to participate responsibly and creatively in AI-enhanced learning environments. The urgency of this work cannot be overstated. Equity must function as the design blueprint and not as a retroactive audit.

References

Barocas, S., Hardt, M., & Narayanan, A. (2019). *Fairness and machine learning: Limitations and opportunities.* fairmlbook.org

Benjamin, R. (2019). *Race after technology: Abolitionist tools for the new Jim Code.* Polity Press.

Buckingham, D. (2023, May). *Artificial intelligence in education: A media education approach*. [Blog essay].

CAST. (2018). *Universal design for learning guidelines* (Version 2.2). https://udlguidelines.cast.org/

Center for Democracy & Technology. (2021). *AI governance in education: Principles for equity and transparency*. https://cdt.org/

Chatterji, A., Cunningham, T., Deming, D. J., Hitzig, Z., Ong, C., Shan, C. Y., & Wadman, K. (2025). *How people use ChatGPT* (Working Paper No. 34255). National Bureau of Economic Research. https://doi.org/10.3386/w34255

Consortium for School Networking. (2023). *The state of EdTech staffing and support*. https://cosn.org/

Cuevas, D. (2024). El Paso's community-driven approach to digital equity. *Texas Education Policy Review, 6*(1), 45–58.

Darling-Hammond, L., Hyler, M. E., & Gardner, M. (2020). *Effective teacher professional development*. Learning Policy Institute. https://learningpolicyinstitute.org/

Digital Equity Laboratory. (2021). *Building equitable digital futures: A roadmap for K–12 education*. https://digitalequitylab.org/

Digital Promise. (2022). *AI in education: A framework for ethical and equitable implementation*. https://digitalpromise.org/

Eubanks, V. (2017). *Automating inequality: How high-tech tools profile, police, and punish the poor*. St. Martin's Press.

Eubanks, V. (2018). Automating inequality and algorithmic determinism. *Social Justice Review, 45*(3), 19–35.

Federal Communications Commission. (2022). *2022 broadband deployment report*. https://www.fcc.gov/

Fitzpatrick, D., Fox, M., & Weinstein, R. (2023). *AI literacy in K–12 education: A guide for teachers and leaders*. AI4K12 Initiative.

Fullan, M., Quinn, J., & McEachen, J. (2018). *Deep learning: Engage the world change the world*. Corwin.

Gamoran, A. (2009). *Tracking and inequality: New directions for research and practice*. Teachers College Press.

Gilliard, C. (2021). Privacy, surveillance, and edtech. *Data & Society Research Institute*. https://datasociety.net/

Goldman, S., Carreon, A., & Smith, S. (2024). Exploring the integration of artificial intelligence into special education teacher preparation through the TPACK framework. *Journal of Special Education Preparation*, *4*(2), 52–64. https://doi.org/10.33043/6zx26bb2

Gray, M. L. (2022). The limits of inclusion: Algorithmic bias in educational platforms. *Journal of Learning Analytics*, *9*(2), 31–45. https://doi.org/10.18608/jla.2022.7398

Harwin, A. (2016, September 1). Coachella Valley schools use Wi-Fi buses to connect students. *Education Week*. https://www.edweek.org/

Hernández-Ramos, P. F., & De La Paz, S. (2009). Learning history in middle school by designing multimedia in a project-based learning experience. *Journal of Research on Technology in Education*, *42*(2), 151–173. https://doi.org/10.1080/15391523.2009.10782545

Keddell, E. (2022). Bias, risk, and accuracy in algorithmic decision-making. *British Journal of Social Work*, *52*(4), 1923–1940. https://doi.org/10.1093/bjsw/bcab046

Kizilcec, R. F., & Lee, H. (2022). Algorithmic fairness in education. *Educational Researcher*, *51*(1), 56–66. https://doi.org/10.3102/0013189X211068245

Kolb, L. (2017). *Learning first, technology second: The educator's guide to designing authentic lessons*. ISTE.

Long, D., & Magerko, B. (2020). *What is AI literacy? Competencies and design considerations*. Proceedings of the CHI Conference on Human Factors in Computing Systems, pp. 1–16. https://doi.org/10.1145/3313831.3376727

Lucas, S. R., & Berends, M. (2002). Sociodemographic diversity, correlated achievement, and de facto tracking. *Social Science Research*, *31*(3), 543–568. https://doi.org/10.1016/S0049-089X(02)00009-1

Merlec, M. M., Islam, M. M., Lee, Y. K., & In, H. P. (2022). A consortium blockchain-based secure and trusted electronic portfolio management scheme. *Sensors*, *22*(3), 1271. https://doi.org/10.3390/s22031271 OUCI

Ng, W. (2012). Can we teach digital natives digital literacy? *Computers & Education*, *59*(3), 1065–1078. https://doi.org/10.1016/j.compedu.2012.04.016

Ning, W., & Inan, F. A. (2024). Impact of social media addiction on college students' academic performance: An interdisciplinary perspective. *Journal of Research on Technology in Education*, *56*(5), 616–631.

Noble, S. U. (2018). *Algorithms of oppression: How search engines reinforce racism*. NYU Press.

Oakes, J. (2005). *Keeping track: How schools structure inequality* (2nd ed.). Yale University Press.

O'Neil, C. (2016). *Weapons of math destruction: How big data increases inequality and threatens democracy.* Crown.

Parsons, M. (2016). Akron's community learning centers: A national model. *Education Next, 16*(4), 32–39.

Project Unicorn. (2023). *State of the sector report: Interoperability and ethics in education data.* https://www.projectunicorn.org/

Seismic. (2025). *On the razor's edge: Public attitudes toward AI in 2025.* Seismic. https://report2025.seismic.org/media/documents/On_the_Razors _Edge_Seismic_Report_2025.pdf

Siefer, A., & Callahan, B. (2021). *Affordability and the digital divide.* National Digital Inclusion Alliance. https://www.digitalinclusion.org/

Snyder, H., Bolger, D., & Roesch, S. C. (2021). Energy insecurity and student learning. *Journal of Urban Affairs, 43*(6), 870–885. https://doi.org/10.1080 /07352166.2021.1907093

Speedtest Global Index. (2024). *United States broadband speed report.* Ookla. https://www.speedtest.net/global-index

US Department of Education. (2021). *ESSER fund annual performance report.* https://www.ed.gov/

US Department of Education. (2022). *Digital accessibility and equity guidance.* https://tech.ed.gov/

US Department of Education. (2023). *Artificial intelligence and data privacy in education.* https://tech.ed.gov/

Voogt, J., & Pareja Roblin, N. (2012). A comparative analysis of international frameworks for 21st-century competences: Implications for national curriculum policies. *Journal of Curriculum Studies, 44*(3), 299–321. https:// doi.org/10.1080/00220272.2012.668938

West, D. M., & Allen, J. R. (2018). *Deploying AI in education: The case for personalized learning.* Brookings Institution.

West, S. M., Whittaker, M., & Crawford, K. (2021). *Discriminating systems: Gender, race, and power in AI.* AI Now Institute. https://ainowinstitute.org/

Wexler, N. (2022, October 1). The Chromebook divide: Why some schools are falling behind. *EdTech Magazine.* https://edtechmagazine.com/

Williamson, B., & Eynon, R. (2020). Historical threads, missing links, and future directions in AI in education. *Learning, Media and Technology, 45*(2), 223–235. https://doi.org/10.1080/17439884.2020.1734006

World Economic Forum. (2020). *Schools of the future: Defining new models of education for the Fourth industrial revolution.* https://www.weforum .org/

World Privacy Forum. (2022). *Algorithmic transparency and fairness in education.* https://www.worldprivacyforum.org/

Wrye, T. P. (2022). *The great equalizer: Distance learning and its impact on education equity* (Doctoral dissertation), Drexel University. https://doi.org/10.17918/00001294

Yue, M., Jong, M. S.-Y., & Ng, D. T. K. (2024). Understanding K–12 teachers' technological pedagogical content knowledge readiness and attitudes toward artificial intelligence education. *Education and Information Technologies, 29,* 19505–19536. https://doi.org/10.1007/s10639-024-12621-2

Section 4
Redrawing the Boundaries

The Evolving Institutional Function of Public Schools

Public schools have assumed roles that extend far beyond academic instruction. When schools become the central institution in a community, they are tasked with fixing community problems they did not create (Noguera, 2004). Originally framed by Horace Mann as vehicles for civic literacy and moral development, schools now operate as critical anchor institutions within communities across the United States. They have become some of the most stable, accessible, and comprehensive public service providers available. Beyond instruction, they offer food security, mental health support, translation services, and voter registration. These expanded responsibilities reflect the growing influence of schools on the social determinants of student well-being.

This transformation has not resulted from deliberate policy design but has emerged in response to systemic need. In rural, underfunded, and structurally underserved communities, schools have evolved into the de facto providers of essential services. They distribute meals, host dental and vision clinics, maintain daily contact with vulnerable youth, and provide structured routines that contribute to broader community stability. Schools also serve as civic conveners, facilitating elections, town meetings, and events that strengthen local identity and participatory democracy. These roles, though vital, place unsustainable demands on systems not originally structured to fulfill such expansive functions.

As the boundaries of public education shift, new questions emerge about operational coherence, staff capacity, and institutional purpose. Civic integration, social service delivery, and cross-sector collaboration now define much of the modern educational landscape. Redrawing these institutional boundaries is not a symbolic gesture. It reflects the urgent need for structural realignment. Governance, funding mechanisms, and infrastructure must be reconfigured to match the scope of responsibilities now assigned to public schools. Treating schools as civic institutions is not a discretionary policy decision. It is essential to advancing educational equity, promoting community health, and reinforcing the foundations of democracy.

The physical boundaries of the schoolhouse are also shifting in response to new technological capabilities. Extended reality (XR) technologies, including virtual, augmented, and mixed reality, are enabling students to access immersive learning experiences beyond the limits of the classroom. Through virtual science labs, historical reconstructions, and simulated career environments, XR expands what schools can offer without expanding their physical footprint. A rural student can explore marine ecosystems through virtual fieldwork or participate in an archaeological dig without leaving their district. These experiences illustrate how XR is redefining where and how learning occurs (Fitzpatrick et al., 2023; Zhao & Watterston, 2021). As XR becomes more embedded in instructional practice, districts must ensure that these tools are not framed as supplemental, but as core components of an inclusive and future-ready education system.

References

Fitzpatrick, D., Fox, M., & Weinstein, R. (2023). *AI literacy in K–12 education: A guide for teachers and leaders*. AI4K12 Initiative.

Noguera, P. A. (2004). *City schools and the American dream: Reclaiming the promise of public education*. Teachers College Press.

Zhao, Y., & Watterston, J. (2021). The changes we need: Education post COVID-19. *Journal of Educational Change, 22*(1), 3–12. https://doi.org/10.1007/s10833-021-09417-3

10

The Institutional Anchor

Rethinking the Purpose of Public Schools

Public schools in the United States have become central to the stability and function of their communities. In under-resourced or geographically isolated areas, they often serve as the most reliable and accessible public institutions. As Henderson (2002) notes, schools cannot do it alone, but they are often the only ones left trying. While schools were not originally designed to manage food security, mental health services, digital access, or crisis response, they have taken on these responsibilities in the absence of sufficient public infrastructure. This transformation reflects an expansion of purpose in response to sustained social and systemic needs.

The convergence of education and social service has become especially visible since the COVID-19 pandemic. When school buildings closed, students lost access not only to instruction but also to meals, supervision, healthcare, and internet connectivity (The Education Trust, 2020). In response, districts distributed food, deployed devices, conducted wellness checks, and provided virtual counseling (Kamenetz, 2020). These actions did not signal a new mission but made visible long-standing responsibilities that had gone unacknowledged in educational policy and funding structures.

Many public schools now house health centers and food pantries offer dental and vision screenings, provide trauma-informed counseling, and coordinate crisis response services. In communities where hospitals have closed, public transportation is limited, or local agencies are underfunded, schools remain the most trusted and consistent point of access for families. They function as community anchors not through deliberate design, but because no other institution has met the full range of local needs.

The Convergence of Education and Social Service

The COVID-19 pandemic exposed the extent to which public schools function as critical infrastructure for community stability and well-being. When school buildings closed, students lost access not only to academic instruction but also to meals, mental health services, consistent adult supervision, and internet connectivity (The Education Trust, 2020). In response, school systems quickly adapted by distributing food, deploying devices, conducting wellness checks, and delivering virtual social-emotional support (Kamenetz, 2020). These actions did not signal a shift in mission, but rather illuminated the long-standing, often unacknowledged roles schools have fulfilled in their communities.

What began as emergency response clarified a broader institutional reality. Public schools have increasingly absorbed responsibilities once handled by health systems, social service agencies, and local nonprofits. Many now house in-school health clinics, provide dental and vision screenings, offer trauma-informed counseling, and support families facing housing instability or limited food access. In communities where public infrastructure has deteriorated, particularly in rural and urban districts, schools have become institutional anchors. They function as stable, trusted points of contact for families who may have no other public agency to turn to for essential services.

This expansion is visible not only in school buildings but also in how districts extend resources throughout the community. In California, Coachella Valley Unified School District equipped school buses with Wi-Fi routers and parked them in neighborhoods lacking reliable home broadband. These mobile hotspots created evening access zones for students and families, enabling homework completion, digital learning, and community connectivity in areas with limited infrastructure (Harwin, 2016). This approach reflects the growing role schools play in bridging structural gaps that extend beyond education, particularly in regions with persistent broadband inequities.

The convergence of education and social service is not sustainable without systemic redesign. The expectation that schools will compensate for fragmented or underfunded systems places significant strain on staff and infrastructure. Educators and counselors are routinely called on to manage complex issues related to trauma, public health, and family welfare, often without the specialized training or resources these responsibilities require. School nurses oversee chronic medical conditions, administrators coordinate access to food and shelter, and social-emotional staff respond to crises that exceed the bounds of traditional school support. These demands stretch capacity and undermine the long-term viability of school systems that continue to be funded and governed as academic institutions alone.

This institutional convergence also raises unresolved policy and ethical challenges. Schools are expected to collaborate with public health departments, law enforcement agencies, and service providers, often without shared data protocols, formal consent mechanisms, or oversight structures. While cross-sector collaboration is essential, it requires clear governance frameworks and equitable funding models that match the complexity and scope of the work being performed.

Despite these challenges, schools remain uniquely positioned to meet the needs of their communities. Their daily contact with students, embedded presence in neighborhoods, and relationships with families allow for early identification of challenges and coordinated responses. This proximity creates opportunities for integrated support that few other institutions can deliver. The question is not whether schools should participate in this work, but how systems can be redesigned to support them in doing so effectively, equitably, and sustainably.

Public policy must evolve to reflect the expanded role schools now play. This includes adopting integrated service delivery models, increasing staffing for counselors, nurses, and social workers, and ensuring that educational funding formulas reflect the full range of responsibilities assigned to schools. It also requires redefining what success means. Institutions that manage student welfare, family outreach, and community health cannot be evaluated solely on academic outcomes. Equity requires that the full scope of a school's contributions be acknowledged, supported, and resourced.

Community Anchors: How Schools Deliver More Than Education

The evolving role of public schools as community anchors is not a theoretical construct. It is a lived reality in districts across the country. In both crisis response and long-term service delivery, schools have emerged as critical points of stability and access. The following case studies represent diverse geographic, cultural, and institutional contexts. Each district demonstrates a distinct approach to integrating social services, community engagement, and educational support. Collectively, these models show that public schools can function as essential civic infrastructure when supported by intentional partnerships, sustainable funding, and responsive leadership.

Urban Integration and Multi-Agency Partnerships
Boston Public Schools, Massachusetts

Boston Public Schools has institutionalized its role as a community anchor through the Hub Community Schools initiative. The district partners with health agencies, nonprofit organizations, and city departments to deliver wraparound services directly on school campuses. Offerings include food pantries, legal clinics, adult education, and mental healthcare. Success is measured not only through academic outcomes but also through indicators of family engagement and community well-being (Boston Private Industry Council, 2021).

New York City Department of Education, New York

With over 300 community schools, New York City has developed the largest district-led community schools initiative in the United States. Each site is supported by a lead nonprofit partner and provides comprehensive services, including mental health counseling, after-school programming, and family outreach. The city funds this initiative as part of its broader equity agenda and tracks outcomes related to attendance, academic progress, and family engagement (NYC Department of Education, 2022).

Rural Innovation and Crisis Response
Deer River Community School, Minnesota

In northern Minnesota, Deer River Community School responded to the COVID-19 pandemic by organizing weekly food deliveries, providing digital devices and internet access, and conducting home visits for students at risk of disengagement. These efforts reflected a comprehensive model of rural resilience grounded in community trust and cross-sector coordination (New York State Education Department, 2021).

Salamanca City Central School District, New York

Salamanca leveraged its STEAM Center to support pandemic response by producing personal protective equipment for local health workers. This initiative positioned the school as a center of civic engagement, technical skill-building, and local support, especially in a rural area with limited public infrastructure (New York State Education Department, 2021).

Culturally Responsive and Tribal Partnerships
Zuni Public School District, New Mexico

Serving a predominantly Indigenous student population, Zuni Public Schools have embedded food sovereignty, language preservation, and culturally responsive curriculum into their operations. The district partners with tribal leaders and health agencies to align services with cultural protocols and community priorities (National Indian Education Association, 2021).

Integrated Health and Trauma-Informed Services
Rowan-Salisbury Schools, North Carolina

Rowan-Salisbury Schools used federal pandemic relief funds to embed licensed therapists in schools, train staff in trauma-informed practices, and create a digital family resource hub for accessing mental health services, food assistance, and childcare subsidies. These systems support both academic recovery and long-term community well-being (Rowan-Salisbury Schools, 2021).

Public–Private Collaboration and Regional Ecosystems
Cincinnati Public Schools, Ohio
Cincinnati's Community Learning Centers model transforms schools into neighborhood hubs that host dental clinics, mental health providers, housing agencies, and workforce development programs. The initiative is supported by Partnerships for Success, a nonprofit that coordinates service delivery across sectors, enabling a district-wide approach to community health and student success (Coalition for Community Schools, 2016).

Digital Equity and Infrastructure Extension
Coachella Valley Unified School District, California
Coachella Valley Unified addressed broadband inequity by equipping school buses with Wi-Fi routers and parking them in high-need neighborhoods each evening. These mobile hotspots allowed students to complete assignments, access online resources, and maintain continuity of learning during school closures (Harwin, 2016). The district's model illustrates how schools can extend infrastructure beyond their walls to meet broader community needs.

Post-Disaster Resilience and Emergency Response
Houston Independent School District, Texas
Following Hurricane Harvey, Houston ISD schools served as emergency shelters and distribution centers for displaced families. In the years since, the district has integrated trauma recovery, disaster preparedness, and climate resilience into its operational strategy, recognizing that schools often serve as the first line of response in local emergencies (RAND Corporation, 2020).

These examples reflect the growing institutional role of public education systems across the country. Whether in urban centers, rural communities, or Indigenous contexts, schools are stepping into functions traditionally held by fragmented service systems. Each case offers a distinct but scalable model of integrated support that strengthens both student outcomes and community well-being. Recognizing and sustaining this role will require rethinking governance, expanding cross-agency collaboration, and aligning funding with the full scope of what schools are asked to provide.

Systemic Drivers and Institutional Burden in Public Education

The transformation of public schools into comprehensive community support hubs reflects the convergence of economic, political, and social pressures. Over the past several decades, the broader social welfare infrastructure has weakened due to chronic underfunding, increasing privatization, and fragmented policy implementation. Public agencies responsible for housing, public health, mental health, and food security have seen significant retrenchment, particularly in rural regions and low-income urban communities. In the vacuum left by these institutions, public schools have emerged as the most consistent point of contact for youth and families. They are accessible, staffed year-round, and maintain high levels of public trust (Blank et al., 2003; Rebell, 2018). This expanded role has not been the product of deliberate policy design. Rather, it is a response to systemic failure and structural neglect.

The COVID-19 pandemic magnified these dynamics. School districts were expected to distribute meals, deploy devices, provide mental health support, and coordinate crisis communication, often in the absence of any other functioning local infrastructure (Dorn et al., 2021). This shift was not guided by legislation, inter-agency coordination, or funding directives. It emerged as a moral and operational necessity. Educators and school leaders stepped in to meet immediate community needs, filling gaps left by shuttered agencies, over-extended nonprofits, and under-resourced health systems. In doing so, schools became the de facto delivery system for public care, a role that continues post-pandemic without structural alignment or institutional compensation.

Despite the clear expansion of schools' public function, budgeting and governance systems remain rooted in outdated assumptions about what schools do. State and federal funding formulas continue to prioritize instructional indicators such as average daily attendance and seat time. These formulas rarely account for the infrastructure required to coordinate mental health services, manage data-sharing agreements with partner agencies, operate mobile Wi-Fi programs, or staff school-based health centers. Even in community schools that have secured outside partnerships, the school is often left to manage logistics, facilities, data, and liability without sustained financial or human capital support.

As responsibilities grow, so do the demands on educators and school leaders. Principals are increasingly tasked with coordinating cross-sector initiatives, managing trauma-informed practices, and responding to crises that exceed their training and contractual expectations. Teachers are expected to integrate social-emotional learning, monitor behavioral health, and adapt to the evolving needs of students experiencing housing instability or family hardship. Counselors, nurses, and paraprofessionals already in short supply are stretched beyond capacity. This operational strain is compounded by emotional fatigue, professional burnout, and unclear role expectations.

This institutional burden is disproportionately borne by schools serving high-need populations. Districts with limited tax bases often lack the resources to hire coordinators, mental-health staff, or technology specialists. While some communities have leveraged pandemic-era funding to expand supports, these gains are unlikely to be sustained without permanent policy solutions. Schools that serve as lifelines for their communities cannot operate on temporary grants or emergency relief alone. The lack of long-term planning reinforces inequities and undermines the credibility of efforts to improve educational outcomes through whole-child approaches.

Ultimately, the problem is not that schools have taken on this expanded role. It is that the systems surrounding them have failed to evolve in response. The assumption that public schools can continue to operate as academic institutions while silently absorbing the responsibilities of public health, housing support, and family services is both unrealistic and structurally unjust. Without comprehensive funding reform, governance alignment, and inter-agency coordination, the continued expansion of schools' mission will lead not to systemic transformation, but to exhaustion and institutional decline.

Public Schools under Pressure: Navigating Fragmented Expectations

While public discourse often centers on visible drivers of institutional expansion such as public health crises and economic instability, schools are also contending with a complex array of less visible pressures. These overlapping demands reflect fragmented policy environments, eroded civic infrastructure, and shifting societal expectations. Together, they have significantly reshaped the institutional identity of public education.

Policy fragmentation across federal and state agencies has introduced substantial administrative complexity. School leaders are often required to reconcile overlapping or contradictory mandates from the Departments of Education, Health and Human Services, Agriculture, and Homeland Security. Program guidelines may vary in eligibility criteria, reporting protocols, and implementation timelines, yet districts receive little centralized support for alignment. This lack of coordination burdens schools with compliance management that diverts time and resources away from instruction (Gordon, 2020).

Crisis management responsibilities further illustrate this expansion. In response to rising school-based threats, mass shootings, and extreme weather events, districts have been required to take on functions once managed by law enforcement, emergency services, or local government. Schools now conduct behavioral threat assessments, develop reunification plans, train staff in de-escalation and emergency protocols, and coordinate with first responders. While these functions may be necessary for community safety, they require expertise and personnel that most schools do not have and were never funded to acquire (Kupchik, 2016).

The decline of local civic infrastructure has also shifted expectations onto public schools as communication and engagement centers. In many communities, the weakening of local journalism, the closure of public health offices, and the consolidation of municipal services have left schools as the most visible and trusted public institution. Schools have been tasked with disseminating health guidance, facilitating voter registration, hosting town halls, and mediating communication between families and government agencies (Abernathy, 2018). These responsibilities, while civic in nature, fall outside the traditional educational mission and signal the broader institutional vacuum surrounding schools.

Environmental disruptions have introduced another layer of responsibility. As climate-related events increase in severity and frequency, schools are expected to serve as emergency shelters, resource distribution centers, and cooling or warming spaces during heatwaves, wildfires, or extreme storms. These roles are often assigned informally and executed without additional training, dedicated funding, or emergency infrastructure (US Government Accountability Office [GAO], 2020). The assumption that schools can absorb these functions without long-term planning undermines both operational sustainability and educator well-being.

The digitization of critical services has compounded these pressures. As access to employment, healthcare, education, and government services becomes increasingly dependent on digital infrastructure, schools have been positioned as frontline providers of broadband access and device distribution. Districts are expected to support families with connectivity, troubleshoot technology platforms, and offer technical assistance, all while managing their own instructional technology needs. These mandates persist despite the fact that most districts lack jurisdiction over telecommunications policy and receive minimal funding for long-term digital inclusion efforts (Beaunoyer et al., 2020).

These pressures reflect more than a practical shift in workload. They represent a symbolic transformation in how society conceptualizes the role of public schools. Schools are no longer viewed solely as institutions of academic preparation. They are increasingly expected to act as stabilizing agents amid social fragmentation, environmental volatility, and technological transition. This institutional elevation has occurred without systemic coordination, sustainable funding, or clear limits to scope. The response from educators and school systems has been marked by adaptability, urgency, and commitment. Yet without a corresponding transformation in governance, investment, and inter-agency responsibility, the sustainability of this expanded role remains in question.

Aligning Infrastructure with Institutional Responsibility

Public schools now occupy a central position in the civic landscape, functioning not only as institutions of learning but also as primary providers of social, health, and community services. This expanded role has emerged in response to persistent gaps across the broader public sector. Schools are now responsible for delivering services related to nutrition, mental health, medical care, housing assistance, and digital access. These responsibilities have outpaced the legal, fiscal, and structural systems designed to support them. The misalignment between institutional expectations and operational support has become increasingly unsustainable. Meeting these demands requires more than rhetorical recognition. It calls for a deliberate realignment of policy, funding, and governance structures with the realities of modern public education.

To begin addressing this misalignment, federal and state agencies must formally recognize public schools as civic anchor institutions. This designation should be embedded in statutory and regulatory frameworks, with corresponding shifts in interagency coordination, data-sharing agreements, and funding eligibility. The Biden–Harris administration's US National Strategy on Equity and Excellence in Education (2023) acknowledged the importance of whole-child approaches, but operationalizing this vision requires new infrastructure. For example, placing licensed mental health professionals, medical providers, and social workers within schools must become a baseline expectation, not a grant-funded exception (Kendziora & Yoder, 2016; Greenberg et al., 2017). States such as California and New Mexico have already taken steps to support such integration by funding school-based health centers and wraparound service teams as part of their community schools initiatives (California Department of Education, 2023; New Mexico Public Education Department, 2023).

Education finance systems must also be restructured to reflect the true costs of delivering comprehensive support services. Most state formulas rely on per-pupil funding models that account for enrollment and weighted student characteristics but fail to incorporate costs related to service coordination, health staffing, facility retrofitting, or digital equity. The US Department of Education's 2022 School Finance Indicators Database shows that high-poverty districts continue to receive significantly less state and local funding per student than their more affluent counterparts, even as they are expected to perform a broader set of civic functions (Baker et al., 2022). Weighted funding systems should be expanded to include indicators of geographic isolation, health disparities, homelessness rates, and community-level trauma, ensuring that allocations align with local service burdens and systemic risk.

Grant eligibility requirements must also evolve. Many existing federal funding streams, including those from the Substance

Abuse and Mental Health Services Administration (SAMHSA), the Broadband Equity, Access, and Deployment (BEAD) Program, and the US Department of Agriculture's rural development funds were not designed with schools as primary recipients, even when schools are delivering the majority of services the grants are intended to support. For example, the BEAD program provides $42.5 billion for broadband infrastructure, yet local education agencies must partner with municipalities or nonprofit intermediaries to access funds (Benton Institute for Broadband and Society, 2024). This indirect structure limits the speed and efficacy of implementation in communities where schools are already managing digital access for thousands of students. A shift toward integrated, place-based funding strategies is necessary to reflect the interdependence of education and broader public systems.

This structural misalignment is not merely a matter of efficiency. It is a policy failure with equity consequences. Relying on public schools as the foundation of social resilience, while denying them the policy authority, staffing capacity, and fiscal resources to fulfill that role, undermines the credibility of public institutions. It places educators in the untenable position of responding to trauma, illness, hunger, and housing insecurity without formal training, staffing, or support systems. This is not a critique of schools, but of the institutional frameworks that expect flexibility without investment and responsiveness without infrastructure. As Rebell (2018) argues, systemic inequity is reinforced when schools are treated as isolated actors rather than as integral components of a coordinated public service network.

A recalibrated system must be grounded in equity, sustainability, and shared accountability. Public schools should be resourced and protected in the same manner as other essential infrastructure. Roads, hospitals, and emergency response systems are not expected to function without investment, planning, and coordination. Schools deserve the same level of institutional support. Celebrating the adaptability of educators without addressing the systems that produce these demands only normalizes underinvestment and institutional strain. Going forward, structural alignment must become a central policy imperative, replacing ad hoc heroism with sustainable public systems that match the scale and complexity of schools' evolving role.

Accountability Reimagined: Aligning Measures with Modern Mission

Conventional accountability frameworks in public education remain tethered to a narrow set of metrics, including standardized test scores, graduation rates, and attendance. While these indicators may offer limited insights into academic proficiency or operational compliance, they fail to account for the broader civic, social, and technological functions that public schools now perform. As districts are tasked with providing trauma-responsive care, broadband access, food security, and family engagement, the instruments used to evaluate their effectiveness must evolve accordingly. Continued reliance on reductive academic benchmarks obscures the complex realities of 21st-century schooling and reinforces institutional incentives that are misaligned with actual public need.

Accountability must be restructured to reflect both educational quality and institutional equity. This begins by expanding what counts as success. Mental health service access should be treated as a baseline performance measure. Metrics should capture not only the presence of counselors or telehealth options but also the quality, consistency, and student utilization of these supports (National Academies of Sciences, Engineering, and Medicine, 2023). Food security outcomes can be integrated through cross-sector data agreements, with anonymized household stability indicators informing resource allocation and support intensity (The School District of Philadelphia, 2023).

Civic engagement is another overlooked domain. Schools that serve as polling places, host town forums, or provide adult education and citizenship classes contribute directly to local democratic participation. These activities can be tracked as indicators of institutional integration and civic capital. Similarly, communication equity should be evaluated by examining the timeliness, frequency, and accessibility of school messaging across languages, platforms, and reading levels. In districts serving multilingual families, these communication pathways are essential for relational trust and informed participation in school life.

Technology access must be addressed with the same rigor as core academic subjects. Schools should report on student access to broadband, device availability, and technical support across learning environments, including after school hours and during disruptions. The Consortium for School Networking (CoSN, 2024) has called for technology equity audits as part of district improvement plans, emphasizing that instructional innovation cannot proceed without digital infrastructure.

Institutional health must also include metrics related to educator well-being. Retention rates, staff burnout levels, and job satisfaction scores should be treated as core indicators of sustainability. When educator well-being is excluded from performance metrics, systems become blind to the conditions that erode instructional quality, leadership continuity, and school climate. These data must inform staffing models, scheduling, and professional development investments.

Student agency and personalization should be directly measured through access to individualized learning pathways, the use of goal-setting tools, and participation in project-based or interest-driven learning. Monitoring the use and impact of personalized learning plans (PLPs) provides a window into how schools are fostering autonomy, engagement, and real-world readiness. These approaches align with competency-based education models that emphasize mastery over seat time and value formative assessment as a tool for growth.

Modern accountability systems must also support qualitative data integration. Surveys, structured interviews, and participatory feedback loops offer essential insight into student and family experiences. These tools elevate voices often excluded from institutional evaluation and help surface relational and cultural dynamics not captured in quantitative reporting. The ASCD Whole Child framework (2021) and the community school model outlined by Oakes et al. (2017) both recognize that relational conditions, trust, safety, identity, and inclusion are fundamental to learning and must be reflected in how systems define effectiveness.

Infrastructure modernization is required to support this shift. A 2024 report from Project Unicorn emphasizes that many districts lack the interoperable data systems necessary to aggregate information across academic, health, and social domains. Without ethical, secure, and connected data infrastructure, schools remain bound to narrow metrics simply because they are the only ones that can be collected at scale (Project Unicorn, 2024). Investment in modern data governance, platform interoperability, and local analytic capacity is a prerequisite for reimagining accountability systems.

This transformation is not a matter of measurement design alone. It signals a shift in values. A modern accountability system places learners, families, and communities at the center of how success is defined. The six foundational pillars introduced earlier in this book, which are learner agency, differentiated instruction, competency-based progression, formative assessment, flexible learning environments, and personalized pathways, provide a research-informed framework for assessing meaningful growth. When integrated with Universal Design for Learning, futures literacy, and adaptive competencies, these measures offer a holistic and future-ready vision of educational accountability.

Evaluating schools by their capacity to cultivate empowered learners, resilient communities, and democratic engagement reflects a more honest and just understanding of public education's purpose. Accountability must evolve from a compliance tool into a reflection of public commitment to equity, to relevance, and to the well-being of all children.

Aligning Accountability with Future-Ready Learning Systems

As public education continues to move beyond traditional boundaries of time, place, and modality, accountability systems must evolve to match the complexity and flexibility of new learning environments. The legacy model, in which students are grouped by age, taught discrete subjects, and assessed through standardized measures during fixed hours, no longer reflects the realities of contemporary learning ecosystems. These industrial-era structures are misaligned with the pedagogical approaches now shaping hybrid, asynchronous, competency-based, and technology-enhanced instruction. In post-industrial contexts, success can no longer be defined solely by coverage and compliance. Instead, accountability must center on competency, connection, agency, and well-being.

Modern indicators of success must reflect mastery rather than seat time. Advancement should be based on demonstrated skill acquisition through authentic learning experiences. Portfolio-based assessment models, which compile student work samples, reflections, and feedback across multiple modalities, offer a richer and more accurate measure of learning. In addition, time-on-task analytics can provide insight into how students allocate their learning across self-paced, collaborative, and real-world environments, highlighting patterns of engagement and autonomy.

Strong relationships remain essential in post-industrial learning systems. Tracking the frequency and quality of student interactions with mentors, advisors, educators, and community partners can help assess the strength of relational networks that support learning. Documentation of cross-modal learning, such as virtual simulations, internships, service projects, and AI-supported modules, further expands our understanding of where and how learning takes place. Digital fluency must also be measured not only in terms of access but also through the capacity to engage critically, ethically, and creatively with technology.

Student well-being must be foregrounded as both an outcome and a condition for success. Self-reporting tools that allow students to reflect on their emotional state, engagement level, and evolving goals can serve as foundational elements of personalized learning dashboards. Global and experiential engagement, including participation in virtual exchanges, augmented reality simulations, and microcredential programs, should also be tracked as indicators of 21st-century readiness (Organisation for Economic Co-operation and Development [OECD], 2022; International Society for Technology in Education [ISTE], 2021).

Table 10.1 contrasts conventional accountability measures with a future-ready framework that better reflects the full scope of modern public education. It highlights how schools can be evaluated not only by academic outcomes but also by their role in promoting student well-being, equitable access, institutional sustainability, and community impact.

These metrics are not theoretical. They reflect trends already taking root in forward-thinking systems around the world and are supported by international frameworks such as the OECD Learning

Compass 2030 and the ISTE Standards for Students. Accountability in post-industrial environments must affirm personalization, ethical digital participation, creative problem-solving, and civic contribution. By validating diverse pathways of learning, these systems can elevate the kinds of growth that matter most in an interconnected, rapidly changing world.

Schools at the Center: Redefining Public Responsibility

The evolving role of public schools as community hubs does not represent a mission drift. It is a pragmatic adaptation to systemic gaps in public infrastructure. In many under-resourced and geographically isolated communities, schools have become the last remaining institution with consistent operations, trusted relationships, and daily contact with children and families. They now provide access to nutrition, healthcare, mental health services, internet connectivity, and civic participation functions that extend far beyond education and place schools at the core of a fragile but vital social safety net.

Pedro Noguera (2004) observed that when schools become the only functioning institutions in a community, they are asked to solve problems they did not create. This insight underscores a fundamental policy failure: schools are expected to deliver services typically assigned to broader public systems, yet they lack the legal authority, sustainable funding, or integrated partnerships necessary to fulfill these demands at scale. The result is a mismatch between institutional responsibility and structural support.

Instead of operating within a coordinated public infrastructure, schools are left to manage the consequences of policy fragmentation. Temporary grants, siloed programs, and ad hoc staffing solutions have become the norm. In many districts, particularly those serving rural and high-poverty populations, schools are stretched beyond their original function, leading to chronic overload and staff burnout. This dynamic reinforces systemic inequities and erodes the capacity of schools to serve as effective educational institutions, let alone as comprehensive community hubs.

TABLE 10.1 Comparison of conventional metrics and future-ready accountability indicators

Category	Conventional metrics	Future-ready accountability indicators
Academic performance	Standardized test scores, graduation and dropout rates, Grade Point Average (GPA), course grades, credit attainment, college entrance exam results, advanced coursework or exam completion	Competency-based progression, personalized learning goals, authentic performance assessments
Attendance	Average daily attendance, truancy rate, chronic absenteeism, teacher attendance	Engagement profiles that include participation in flexible or asynchronous learning environments
Equity and access	Subgroup performance gaps, advanced course participation by subgroup, special education identification rates, English learner reclassification	Access to broadband, devices, mental healthcare, and translation services; disaggregated service utilization data
Student well-being	Behavior referrals, suspensions and expulsions, restraint and seclusion incidents	Access to and quality of mental health services, food security data, SEL screening participation, student-reported well-being
Family and community engagement	Parent conference attendance, survey response rates, event sign ins, volunteer hours, digital message open rates, returned forms	Accessibility and timeliness of multilingual communication, community event participation, partnerships with civic organizations
Institutional health	Evaluation scores, mandate compliance, licensure status, vacancies and substitute fill, class size and student teacher ratio, staff turnover, required Professional Development (PD) completion	Educator retention, burnout risk, job satisfaction, professional learning access, and staffing ratios for counselors and nurses

(*Continued*)

TABLE 10.1 (Continued)

Category	Conventional metrics	Future-ready accountability indicators
Technology and infrastructure	Device inventory, instructional technology use surveys, bandwidth and uptime, help desk volume and closure rate, device-to-student ratio, filter compliance	Student access to broadband outside of school hours, tech support responsiveness, and digital literacy outcomes
Civic integration	School board meeting attendance, facility use permits, polling events hosted, emergency drill compliance	Use of school spaces for civic functions, adult education, polling, disaster response coordination
Student agency and voice	Advanced Placement (AP), International Baccalaureate (IB), or dual enrollment participation, Career and Technical Education (CTE) concentrator rate, ninth grade on track	Implementation of personalized learning plans (PLPs), interest-based learning pathways, student advisory roles, feedback systems
Data use and governance	Reporting timeliness and compliance, audit findings resolved, data privacy agreement coverage	Interoperable data infrastructure for social services, real-time equity dashboards, ethical governance policies
Narrative and qualitative insight	Climate survey response rates	Student, family, and educator voice through narrative tools, empathy interviews, and climate surveys

Addressing this imbalance requires more than acknowledgment. It demands a redefinition of public responsibility. Public schools must be treated as civic infrastructure, on par with hospitals, transportation systems, and emergency services. This shift should be reflected in policy, funding, and facility design. School buildings should be constructed or retrofitted to include space for family resource centers, telehealth delivery, adult education, and civic programming. These additions are not luxuries. They are essential for aligning institutional design with contemporary expectations.

Investing in schools as community infrastructure is also a democratic imperative. Schools remain one of the few public spaces where people from diverse backgrounds share experiences, develop civic norms, and cultivate collective identity. In this role, the school is not just a mirror of community needs; it is an engine for civic development and social cohesion. Recognizing and supporting this role reinforces pluralism, equity, and the public good.

This expanded conception of the school's role must be embedded in the work of policymakers, education leaders, and local government officials. Supporting schools in this capacity is not a discretionary enhancement. It is foundational to sustaining public trust, advancing equity, and preparing for future disruptions. The future of public education will be defined not only by what happens in classrooms, but also by whether society is willing to invest in schools as the essential infrastructure they have already become.

Reclassifying Public Schools as Multifunctional Public Infrastructure

The evolving role of public schools is not simply a reflection of changing community needs. It is evidence of a larger institutional transformation. In districts across the country, schools now serve as nutrition hubs, healthcare access points, mental health providers, digital connectivity centers, and emergency response sites often without formal recognition or structural support. This expanded mission must no longer be treated as exceptional or peripheral. It is central to how schools function today.

To fully understand the future of public education, we must shift how we define what a school is. Schools are no longer single-purpose institutions designed only for academic delivery. They operate as multifunctional public infrastructure that sustains community wellbeing, bridges service gaps, and fosters democratic participation. This is especially true in rural and historically marginalized communities where schools remain the only consistent public presence.

Yet education policy, funding, and accountability systems have not adapted. Schools are still governed and measured by frameworks built for a different era, one that does not account for their current civic role. This disconnect leaves school systems overextended, politically underrecognized, and forced to navigate multiple mandates without the tools or authority to fulfill them effectively.

Reclassifying public schools within state and federal policy as essential civic infrastructure would bring governance into alignment with reality. This reclassification would position schools alongside libraries, hospitals, and public service facilities, enabling them to access interagency funding, participate in civic planning, and build sustainable partnerships. It would also shift expectations of school leadership, requiring superintendents and principals to engage in systems-level strategy alongside instructional leadership.

This reframing provides the structural foundation needed to sustain the community-centered functions schools already perform. It affirms that the trust families place in public schools should be matched by policies that resource and protect them and stabilize these institutions accordingly. Understanding schools as civic infrastructure is a necessary step in rethinking public education. It is not the conclusion of this conversation, but the context that must inform what follows. When schools are expected to fulfill two different mandates, delivering high-quality education while simultaneously functioning as the backbone of the social safety net, the operational and emotional toll on educators and systems intensifies. Without structural alignment, the burden of this dual role will continue to grow.

References

Abernathy, P. M. (2018). *The expanding news desert.* University of North Carolina Press.

ASCD. (2021). *The whole child approach.* https://www.ascd.org/whole-child

Baker, B. D., Di Carlo, M., & Weber, M. (2022). *School finance indicators database: 2022 state reports.* Albert Shanker Institute & Rutgers University.

Beaunoyer, E., Dupéré, S., & Guitton, M. J. (2020). COVID-19 and digital inequalities: Reciprocal impacts and mitigation strategies. *Computers in Human Behavior, 111,* Article 106424. https://doi.org/10.1016/j.chb.2020.106424

Benton Institute for Broadband & Society. (2024). *BEAD program overview.* https://www.benton.org

Blank, M. J., Melaville, A., & Shah, B. P. (2003). *Making the difference: Research and practice in community schools.* Coalition for Community Schools.

Boston Private Industry Council. (2021). *Hub community schools report.* https://www.bostonpic.org

California Department of Education. (2023). *California community schools partnership program.* https://www.cde.ca.gov

Coalition for Community Schools. (2016). *Community learning centers: Cincinnati Public Schools.* https://www.communityschools.org

Consortium for School Networking. (2024). *Technology equity audits: A guide for districts.* https://www.cosn.org

Dorn, E., Hancock, B., Sarakatsannis, J., & Viruleg, E. (2021). *COVID-19 and education: The lingering effects of unfinished learning.* McKinsey & Company. https://www.mckinsey.com

Gordon, N. (2020). *Increasing school autonomy: A balancing act.* Brookings Institution. https://www.brookings.edu

Greenberg, M. T., Domitrovich, C. E., Weissberg, R. P., & Durlak, J. A. (2017). Social-emotional learning as a public health approach to education. *The Future of Children, 27*(1), 13–32.

Harwin, A. (2016). On the bus, online: Wi-Fi helps bridge the digital divide. *Education Week, 36*(10), 8–9.

Henderson, A. T., & Mapp, K. L. (2002). *A new wave of evidence: The impact of school, family, and community connections on student achievement.* National Center for Family and Community Connections with Schools, Southwest Educational Development Laboratory.

International Society for Technology in Education. (2021). *ISTE standards for students.* https://www.iste.org/standards/for-students

Kamenetz, A. (2020). *What kids are missing when schools are closed.* NPR. https://www.npr.org

Kendziora, K., & Yoder, N. (2016). *When districts support and integrate social and emotional learning (SEL).* American Institutes for Research. https://www.air.org

Kupchik, A. (2016). *The real school safety problem: The long-term consequences of harsh school punishment.* University of California Press.

National Academies of Sciences, Engineering, and Medicine. (2023). *Promoting positive adolescent health behaviors and outcomes.* The National Academies Press. https://doi.org/10.17226/25552

National Indian Education Association. (2021). *Zuni Public Schools case study*. https://www.niea.org

New Mexico Public Education Department. (2023). *Community schools initiative*. https://webnew.ped.state.nm.us

New York State Education Department. (2021). *Community school case studies*. https://www.nysed.gov

Noguera, P. A. (2004, October 1). Social class, but what about the schools? *Poverty & Race Research Action Council*. https://www.prrac.org/social-class-but-what-about-the-schools/

NYC Department of Education. (2022). *NYC Community schools initiative*. https://www.schools.nyc.gov

Oakes, J., Maier, A., & Daniel, J. (2017). *Community schools: An evidence-based strategy for equitable school improvement*. Learning Policy Institute.

Organisation for Economic Co-operation and Development. (2022). *OECD Learning compass 2030*. https://www.oecd.org

Project Unicorn. (2024). *Interoperability and data governance report*. https://www.projectunicorn.org

RAND Corporation. (2020). *Resilience after disaster: Houston ISD post-Harvey*. https://www.rand.org

Rebell, M. A. (2018). *Flunking democracy: Schools, courts, and civic participation*. University of Chicago Press.

Rowan-Salisbury Schools. (2021). *Pandemic response report*. https://www.rssed.org

The Education Trust. (2020). *COVID-19 and student learning*. https://www.edtrust.org

The School District of Philadelphia. (2023). *Cross-sector data sharing initiative*. https://www.philasd.org

US Government Accountability Office. (2020). *K-12 education: School districts increasingly offer school choice options*. https://www.gao.gov

US National Strategy on Equity and Excellence in Education. (2023). *White house office of educational policy*. https://www.whitehouse.gov

11

Overextended

The Operational Burden of Dual Mandates in Education

Public schools in the United States are no longer defined solely by their academic mission. As established in the previous chapter, school districts have evolved into critical civic infrastructure. They are anchor institutions that provide not only instruction, but also essential services in health, nutrition, crisis response, and digital access. This transformation is especially pronounced in underresourced or geographically isolated communities, where schools are often the only stable, accessible, and responsive public institutions.

This expanded role reflects a broader societal shift in the expectations placed upon public education. Schools are now tasked with addressing complex social and economic needs alongside their core instructional responsibilities. Yet this evolution has not been matched by a corresponding increase in statutory authority, staffing capacity, or funding flexibility. The result is a system stretched beyond its original design, one that must operate as both an academic institution and a de facto social service provider.

It is important to examine the operational, structural, and cultural implications of this multi-mandate model, and to explore the consequences for staff morale, fiscal sustainability, and institutional coherence. It is most important to present strategies for navigating this dual role with greater clarity and support, including integrated

DOI: 10.4324/9781003739050-15

service delivery models, shared governance frameworks, and technology-enhanced coordination. If public schools are to fulfill their expanded mission, the systems that support them must be redesigned with the same level of purpose and urgency.

The Expanding Role of Public Schools

The responsibilities assigned to public schools have expanded far beyond their original academic mission. Conceived in the mid-19th century by reformers like Horace Mann, public education was designed to promote civic literacy, moral development, and social cohesion within a democratic society (Kaestle, 1983). Mann's vision of education as the "great equalizer" emphasized its role in advancing opportunity and democratic participation. For much of the 20th century, this vision remained focused on academic goals, including literacy, numeracy, and foundational knowledge in social studies and science.

By the mid-20th century, however, federal policy began to broaden the role of public schools. The Elementary and Secondary Education Act (ESEA) of 1965 (Elementary and Secondary Education Act of 1965, Pub. L. No. 89-10, 79 Stat. 27) marked a turning point by linking federal funding to poverty alleviation and equity measures. Title I funds were targeted toward low-income districts to address opportunity gaps and resource inequities. Over time, these supports grew to include school meal programs, health screenings, and requirements for parent and community engagement.

The Individuals with Disabilities Education Act (Individuals with Disabilities Education Act, 20 USC. § 1400 et seq.), first enacted in 1975 and reauthorized in 1990, further expanded the educational mandate. IDEA required schools to provide a free and appropriate public education (FAPE) for students with disabilities, including access to individualized education programs (IEPs), therapeutic supports, and medically necessary services during the school day. These obligations brought responsibilities traditionally managed by healthcare systems into the educational setting.

The passage of the Every Student Succeeds Act (Every Student Succeeds Act, Pub. L. No. 114-95, 129 Stat. 1802) in 2015 reinforced this broader role. While maintaining academic accountability, ESSA emphasized school climate, social-emotional learning, and access to enrichment opportunities, further embedding the expectation that schools support the whole child, not just their academic progress.

As state and federal mandates evolved, public schools became responsible for an expanding array of social services. In many communities, especially those facing economic hardship or geographic isolation, schools have become the only consistently open and fully staffed public institutions. They now provide meals, hygiene supplies, internet access, crisis intervention, and adult education. These responsibilities reflect not a mission creep, but a systemic default: when other institutions fail to meet public needs, schools are expected to fill the gap.

The COVID-19 pandemic made this dual role visible at scale. School closures disrupted far more than academic routines. Families lost access to mental health services, special education support, meals, and digital infrastructure. Districts responded by coordinating meal deliveries, distributing Wi-Fi hotspots, launching virtual wellness checks, and organizing community-wide support efforts (Kamenetz, 2020). These responses highlighted what had already become true: schools serve as both academic institutions and emergency-response systems.

Today, the dual mandate is no longer a temporary adaptation. It is a core expectation. Yet while the scope of work has expanded, the systems that fund, govern, and evaluate public education remain bound to outdated models built for a narrower instructional role. Schools are tasked with carrying a growing social burden without the statutory authority, staffing design, or fiscal flexibility typically afforded to service agencies.

When schools are positioned as both instructional and service delivery institutions, structural misalignment becomes not only inefficient but also inequitable. It is important to examine how legacy governance systems, fragmented funding, and unrealistic expectations have made the current model unsustainable.

Structural and Fiscal Constraints

The expanded responsibilities of public schools have not been matched by structural reforms. While federal and state policies increasingly expect schools to address student mental health, nutrition, digital access, and social-emotional development, the institutional frameworks governing education remain rooted in a single-purpose model. Most districts still operate under organizational, legal, and funding systems designed for instructional delivery, not for managing integrated public services.

A central challenge is the fragmentation of governance across education, health, and human services. Public schools are governed by local or state education agencies, while systems responsible for healthcare, housing, and social services function under separate agencies with distinct regulations, funding mechanisms, and reporting requirements. This sectoral division produces siloed mandates, conflicting policies, and a lack of interoperable infrastructure (Dryfoos, 1994; Honig, 2006). Even when schools are expected to provide wraparound supports, they often lack the authority or infrastructure to coordinate meaningfully with partner agencies.

Funding structures compound the problem. School-based services are rarely funded as baseline operational expenses. Instead, districts rely on categorical grants such as Title I, Title IV, or Medicaid reimbursement programs, resources that are narrowly defined, time-limited, and administratively burdensome. These constraints undermine program continuity. Mental health services, for example, are often launched through temporary grants, then scaled back or eliminated when funding expires. This creates cycles of instability, staff turnover, and service disruption (Leachman et al., 2017).

Many of these expanded responsibilities function as unfunded mandates, where schools are legally required to implement programs or meet service standards without the financial resources necessary to do so. For instance, while IDEA, passed in 1975, mandates that students with disabilities receive access to specialized instruction and therapeutic services, the federal government has never met its original commitment to fund 40 percent of the average per-pupil cost of special education, a benchmark established in the law's original language (US Department of Education, 2020). The resulting impact is that local districts have to reallocate limited general funds to cover mandated services, often at the expense of other programs.

Compounding this instability is the heavy compliance burden associated with managing multiple restricted funding streams. Grant programs often require detailed documentation, reporting, and performance tracking. Districts with limited administrative staff must dedicate substantial time to paperwork, audits, and fund reconciliation, diverting attention from strategic planning, instructional leadership, and service delivery. The system penalizes effort with bureaucratic overload, especially in high-need contexts where capacity is already stretched thin.

Local fiscal capacity further reinforces inequity. In many states, school funding is heavily tied to property taxes, meaning that wealthier districts can subsidize expanded supports while lower-income districts cannot. Even when state or federal mandates apply uniformly, the ability to deliver these services such as counseling, broadband access, after-school programming, or health staffing is shaped by geography and wealth, not by need (Rebell, 2018). It creates a tiered public education system, where essential supports are unequally available. Efforts to equalize funding are often stalled by political resistance to redistribution, leaving structural inequity entrenched by design rather than necessity.

Schools in under-resourced communities often assemble makeshift solutions using a patchwork of nonrecurring grants, short-term partnerships, and municipal support. These efforts reflect commitment and creativity but do not substitute for systemic investment. Moreover, managing fragmented funding streams and coordinating across agencies demands administrative capacity that many districts lack, particularly those experiencing leadership turnover or central office understaffing.

Some states have attempted to address these challenges through regional service centers or educational collaboratives that offer shared support for grant management, staffing, and specialized services. While helpful in relieving some operational burdens, these intermediaries often lack stable funding and policymaking authority. The collaboratives remain adjunct solutions within a system that has not fundamentally restructured itself to reflect the demands of the multi-mandate model.

The result is a profound misalignment between school responsibilities and institutional design. Educators are expected to serve simultaneously as instructors, social workers, technology facilitators, and mental health liaisons. These expectations are often unsupported by training, infrastructure, or coherent policy. The strain dilutes instructional focus, accelerates burnout, and compromises long-term sustainability.

Meeting the demands of the dual mandate requires more than grant programs or pilot initiatives. Policymakers must pursue structural reforms that equip schools to function as fully supported hubs of community well-being. This includes braided funding strategies, interoperable systems, and cross-sector governance frameworks. Without alignment across these domains, schools will remain unequally resourced, structurally overextended, and unable to fulfill their evolving mission.

Toward Systemic Alignment: Braided Funding, Interoperable Infrastructure, and Shared Governance

To support the dual mandate of public education, reform efforts must move beyond localized innovation and address the broader design of the system itself. Schools cannot sustainably fulfill both instructional and social service roles within outdated structures. Integrated systems design is essential. Three interdependent strategies, braided funding, interoperable data infrastructure, and shared governance together offer a cohesive framework for structural alignment, fiscal sustainability, and improved service delivery.

Braided Funding Systems

Braided funding refers to the strategic alignment of multiple public and private funding streams toward shared goals, while each stream maintains its legal identity and compliance requirements (US Department of Education, 2021). This approach differs from blended funding, which merges sources into a single pool. Braiding is often more feasible in public education because it retains distinct accountability structures while enabling coordinated service delivery.

For example, a district might braid Title I allocations, Medicaid reimbursements, local operational funds, and municipal health grants to sustain mental health services in schools. Rather than launching temporary initiatives that expire when funding ends, braided models support continuity by diversifying revenue sources and aligning them to long-term service delivery. Tulsa Public Schools, for instance, has implemented a braided funding strategy that integrates Medicaid, local education funds, and philanthropic support to expand school-based behavioral health services across the district (US Department of Education, 2021).

Effective implementation requires cross-agency planning, integrated budgeting tools, and shared performance metrics to ensure accountability and impact (Annie E. Casey Foundation, 2020). However, these efforts are often constrained by legal and bureaucratic barriers. In many cases, education agencies lack the authority or technical capacity to coordinate financial planning with health or municipal departments, limiting the scalability of braided models without explicit policy support.

Interoperable Data Infrastructures

Data interoperability refers to the ability of different systems to securely exchange and use information in real time, enabling more coordinated and responsive support for students (Project Unicorn, 2024). In public education, interoperable infrastructure allows for the ethical and legal sharing of student data across schools, health departments, and nonprofit providers in compliance with FERPA, HIPAA, and other privacy laws.

Frameworks such as Ed-Fi and the Project Unicorn Interoperability Rubric offer standards for building secure, scalable data systems that support personalized learning and integrated care. For instance, an interoperable platform could allow a school counselor to see that a student receiving trauma-informed therapy is also chronically absent and recently displaced from housing. Rather than managing these concerns in silos, staff can respond through coordinated intervention.

Interoperability not only improves service delivery but also enhances equity. When data systems are aligned, districts can identify systemic gaps, allocate resources more efficiently, and monitor student outcomes across academic and nonacademic domains. However, these systems must be designed with ethical safeguards, community trust, and inclusive access in mind. Without such protections, interoperability can reinforce inequities or compromise student privacy.

Shared Governance Models

Governance is often overlooked in technical reform conversations, yet it is essential to institutional coherence. Shared governance models create formal mechanisms for collaborative decision-making across schools, municipal agencies, families, and community partners (Coalition for Community Schools, 2022). These models move beyond stakeholder consultation and toward co-governance, where authority, accountability, and resource decisions are distributed across sectors.

Promising examples include Cincinnati's Community Learning Centers and Oakland's Full-Service Community Schools. Both models convene multi-stakeholder boards with the authority to set priorities for staffing, programming, and wraparound services. These governance structures not only increase transparency but also ensure that school operations reflect community-defined needs, not just state mandates or external funding conditions (Maier et al., 2017; Oakes et al., 2017).

Shared governance improves trust, strengthens partnerships, and aligns institutional missions. It also protects schools from becoming the default provider for every community need by establishing clear roles, shared responsibility, and formalized collaboration. Still, successful implementation requires political will, capacity-building, and policy frameworks that support distributed decision-making across agencies and constituencies.

Integrative Impact

Individually, each of these strategies addresses a dimension of the structural misalignment that limits the capacity of public schools. Together, they provide a foundation for transforming schools into community-centered institutions capable of meeting the demands of the dual mandate.

Braided funding creates financial flexibility. Interoperable data systems improve responsiveness and insight. Shared governance ensures accountability, legitimacy, and local relevance. These components are not technical fixes; they are structural shifts that align school design with school function.

Despite their promise, these strategies require more than technical expertise. They demand cross-agency coordination, supportive legislation, and sustained investment. Districts cannot implement them in isolation or without state and federal support. Alignment is not an innovative approach but rather a prerequisite for sustaining public education's evolving mission.

The Capacity Crisis: Human Infrastructure in the Age of Expanded Mandates

As public schools assume responsibilities beyond academic instruction, the demands placed on educators, counselors, nurses, support staff, and administrators have intensified in both scope and complexity. These professionals are now expected not only to deliver standards-based instruction but also to respond to trauma, housing instability, mental health needs, and technology access challenges (Will, 2023). This shift has created a human capital crisis that threatens the sustainability of the public education workforce.

The concept of role strain describes the conflict professionals experience when required to meet expectations that exceed their training, time, or institutional support (Lindqvist et al., 2022). In schools, this manifests daily. Teachers are expected to identify signs of mental illness, address food insecurity, manage behavior related to trauma, and support family crises, all while preparing lessons, grading student work, attending professional development, and managing compliance requirements.

School counselors and nurses have experienced a similar expansion of roles. While originally trained to provide academic guidance or manage basic health needs, they are now asked to act as behavioral health providers, case managers, and frontline responders in crises involving suicide risk, abuse, or homelessness (Zulauf-McCurdy & Zins, 2021). These responsibilities are often undertaken without clinical supervision, sufficient staffing, or integrated support systems.

Administrators face growing pressure to coordinate interagency partnerships, monitor regulatory compliance, and manage both instructional and noninstructional systems. The demands of leading schools and districts under a multi-mandate model frequently exceed the preparation provided by traditional licensure programs. As a result, many leaders report decisional fatigue and increased risk of burnout (Pollitt & Mutch, 2020), particularly in schools serving high-need populations.

Support staff also bear significant burdens. Paraprofessionals, clerical personnel, and custodians are often drawn into de-escalation efforts, family communication, or student wellness monitoring, despite limited compensation or training. Their contributions are critical to daily school functioning, yet they are often excluded from formal planning, capacity-building, or policy considerations.

In under-resourced districts, these human infrastructure pressures are compounded by chronic staffing shortages. Positions for bilingual counselors, special educators, and school psychologists frequently go unfilled, and service delivery suffers as a result. Schools are forced to rely on underprepared personnel, outsourced contracts, or makeshift assignments, which undermines both stability and quality.

This cumulative expansion of roles has blurred professional boundaries. When teachers serve as de facto social workers and principals coordinate public health responses, questions of liability, role clarity, and professional ethics arise. These conditions can result in moral injury, a condition in which professionals feel unable to meet the needs of those they serve, despite their best efforts. Over time, this leads to disillusionment, emotional exhaustion, and departure from the field (Santoro, 2018).

The current system is not designed to support the human capacity it demands. Educators and staff are being asked to navigate complex, high-stakes responsibilities in environments that were not built to accommodate them. This is not a matter of individual resilience or resourcefulness. It is a design failure that must be addressed through structural reform.

Sustaining the public education workforce in a future-ready ecosystem requires intentional investment in human infrastructure. As schools evolve beyond fixed schedules and centralized buildings, staff must be supported to operate within more flexible, collaborative, and student-centered environments. This includes:

- Professional learning aligned with trauma-informed practice, cultural responsiveness, digital equity, and interagency collaboration, preparing staff for both instructional and noninstructional responsibilities across settings;
- Redefinition of educator roles to support coaching, facilitation, and advisory functions in hybrid, asynchronous, and place-based learning environments;
- Clear delineation of responsibilities within distributed teams, including instructional designers, mental health professionals, community partners, and technology support staff;
- Load balancing across roles and modalities, supported by increased staffing, shared-service agreements, and partnerships with community-based organizations;
- Protected time for cross-sector coordination and collaborative planning, including virtual, on-demand, or asynchronous team structures;
- Embedded wellness and mental health supports, along with policy frameworks that recognize the emotional labor and complexity of student-facing roles in dynamic learning environments.

These reforms are not ancillary. They are essential to workforce retention, professional efficacy, and the long-term viability of the public school system. Without structural alignment between expectations and supports, the human capacity of public education will continue to erode, making the dual mandate both unsustainable and inequitable.

Recognition Gap: How Public Misperceptions Undermine Systemic Reform

Despite the operational, structural, and human transformations taking place inside schools, public understanding of what educators do daily has not kept pace. The result is a persistent recognition gap, a cultural and political disconnect between what schools are expected to deliver and how their work is perceived, supported, or evaluated. This gap is not merely symbolic. It has real consequences for policy, funding, and institutional legitimacy.

Outdated narratives continue to frame schools primarily as custodial institutions, responsible for academic instruction and child supervision during work hours. These reductive views obscure the growing complexity of educational work and the integration of responsibilities once held by separate sectors, including healthcare, social services, and technology access (Gere, 2020). While families increasingly rely on schools for services ranging from crisis intervention to broadband access, public discourse often lags behind, failing to acknowledge the multidimensional role schools now play.

This disconnect was evident during the COVID-19 pandemic, when schools were widely recognized as essential for distributing meals, devices, and health information, yet simultaneously criticized for disruptions to standardized testing schedules and in-person instruction. The same institutions being lauded for community response were also subjected to narrow performance scrutiny, illustrating the contradiction at the heart of current public expectations.

The problem is compounded by the symbolic role of schools in American political culture. Education often becomes a proxy battleground for broader societal debates over race, gender, religion, identity, and parental control. As a result, school systems are frequently drawn into politicized conflicts that have little to do with curriculum or instructional practice. Topics such as inclusive education, mental health services, or social-emotional learning are regularly misrepresented in media and policymaking, eroding trust in public education and contributing to polarization (Warren, 2021).

Public misperceptions are further reinforced by legacy accountability models that evaluate school performance primarily through standardized test scores, attendance rates, and graduation statistics. These narrow indicators fail to account for the social and structural determinants that shape student outcomes. Schools are routinely held responsible for metrics influenced by external conditions such as housing instability, food insecurity, limited healthcare access, and systemic trauma, all of which are outside the institutional control of educators and administrators. Yet schools are rarely granted the authority, flexibility, or sustained funding needed to intervene meaningfully in these areas.

For example, chronic absenteeism is frequently cited as an indicator of school effectiveness, yet national data reveal that students facing unstable housing or caregiving responsibilities miss school at disproportionately high rates, regardless of school engagement efforts. In 2022, the US Department of Education reported that more than 16 million students were chronically absent, with rates highest among students experiencing poverty, disability, or limited English proficiency (US Department of Education, 2020). While districts are held accountable for improving attendance, few are resourced to address the underlying causes such as access to transportation, mental health services, or stable housing.

This asymmetry between accountability and capacity results in a distorted public narrative. Schools are seen as failing not because of instructional deficits, but because they are measured against indicators that reflect broader societal inequities. The result is a cycle of unrealistic expectations, underfunded mandates, and declining public trust.

Surveys by the Pew Research Center (2022) reveal a growing partisan divide in public perceptions of school effectiveness, educator trust, and policy support. While most Americans say they value education, fewer understand or endorse the full scope of services schools now provide. These divides constrain legislative progress and fragment public consensus on the purpose of public education.

Private philanthropy and corporate influence have also shaped narrow definitions of school success. National initiatives such as the Gates Foundation's teacher effectiveness measures and test-based accountability policies have promoted data-driven reform models focused on instructional efficiency and performance measurement, but often without accounting for the broader systemic conditions that shape school success. These models rarely reflect the expanded, community-centered mission schools are now expected to fulfill.

Addressing this recognition gap requires more than public awareness campaigns. It demands a cultural reframing of what public schools are and what they are for. Schools must be recognized not only as instructional sites but also as anchor institutions that serve as pillars of civic infrastructure supporting student development, family stability, and community resilience. This shift must occur across media, government, philanthropy, and education leadership.

District leaders, school boards, and educator unions play a critical role in this reframing. Their public communication, community engagement, and strategic partnerships must intentionally elevate the full scope of modern educational work. Educators must be supported as credible narrators of their own profession, with access to platforms and tools that help shape public understanding.

This cultural realignment also requires a redefinition of success. Accountability systems must expand beyond standardized test scores to include indicators of student wellness, family engagement, digital access, and interagency collaboration. These metrics are not add-ons. They reflect the actual conditions of 21st-century public education and are essential to guiding meaningful reform.

Absent this shift, even modest gains such as increased funding for mental health, expanded broadband initiatives, or community school models remain vulnerable to political backlash or fiscal retrenchment. When the public misunderstands the purpose and work of schools, progress becomes precarious and unsustainable.

Rebuilding trust and understanding is not a peripheral task. It is foundational to systemic change. Recognizing the full scope of educational work is the first step toward aligning expectations, resources, and policy to support a system that is both equitable and effective.

Redesigning the Ecosystem: Toward Sustainable and Equitable Integration

Addressing the structural, fiscal, and cultural challenges posed by the multi-mandate model requires more than marginal adjustments.

It demands a fundamental reimagining of how public education is designed, governed, and supported. Schools can no longer be treated as single-purpose institutions. They must be understood as integrated civic infrastructure, core components of the nation's social fabric that support both academic development and broader community well-being.

This redesign is not a departure from the educational mission. It is a necessary evolution in response to the dual role that public schools now play. Achieving this vision requires systemic alignment across policy domains, funding mechanisms, data systems, and institutional responsibilities.

One of the most promising frameworks for sustainable integration is the community school model. Community schools co-locate education, health, mental health, and social services within school buildings and operate through shared governance structures that include educators, families, local agencies, and nonprofit partners (Maier et al., 2017). These schools function as both instructional environments and service hubs, offering after-school programs, adult education, food distribution, and access to physical and behavioral healthcare. Empirical evidence links this model to improved academic outcomes, increased student engagement, and strengthened school–family partnerships, particularly in high-poverty contexts (Oakes et al., 2017). In Oakland, for example, the district's Full-Service Community Schools initiative has reduced chronic absenteeism and disciplinary referrals while improving family involvement.

Beyond the school building, shared-service agreements between districts and municipal agencies offer pragmatic solutions for coordinating transportation, mental health staffing, housing supports, or IT infrastructure. These models reduce redundancy, clarify roles, and allow educators to focus on teaching while trained professionals address nonacademic needs (Bartik et al., 2019). These models also alleviate pressure on educators and administrators by distributing responsibilities across qualified personnel, reducing role strain and supporting long-term workforce sustainability.

Technology also plays a critical role in system redesign. When guided by principles of equity, transparency, and interoperability, digital tools and artificial intelligence (AI) can support more efficient and responsive systems. Predictive analytics can help identify students at risk for academic disengagement, chronic absenteeism, or health-related challenges. AI-driven platforms can streamline scheduling, automate administrative tasks, and enhance communication among multidisciplinary teams (Reich, 2020; Project Unicorn, 2024). However, these tools must be embedded within ethical design frameworks. Without intentional oversight, algorithmic decision-making can reinforce bias, deepen digital inequities, and compromise student trust, particularly in marginalized communities.

These concerns are reflected in broader public sentiment. In a 2025 cross-national survey, half of respondents identified AI as a major societal problem, and nearly seven in ten believed AI should never make decisions without human oversight (Seismic, 2025). Women expressed more than twice the level of pessimism compared to men, underscoring how existing inequities influence perceptions of risk. This pervasive distrust matters for schools, where community acceptance is essential for sustaining innovation. Equity-focused adoption requires addressing both the technical flaws of algorithms and the lived fears of families and students who feel most vulnerable to harm.

Advances in extended reality (XR) technologies are also beginning to dissolve the spatial boundaries of traditional education. Immersive platforms now enable students to engage in experiential, place-independent learning that occurs outside the constraints of the school building. Districts are already piloting XR-based simulations in career and technical education, science labs, and virtual field trips, particularly to expand access for rural students or those unable to attend in person. As XR tools become more accessible and integrated with core instruction, the definition of where and how learning occurs is being fundamentally reshaped. This shift challenges the conventional model of school as a fixed physical site and reinforces the need for governance, funding, and accountability systems that reflect a distributed, tech-enabled learning ecosystem.

Importantly, sustainable integration is not the responsibility of under-resourced districts alone. Affluent communities also experience inefficiencies, inequities, and fragmentation. While these districts may offer a wide range of services, they often lack coherent coordination across programs. Supports are frequently privatized, informally accessed, or reliant on family advocacy and social capital, creating intra-district disparities. These districts have both the capacity and the obligation to pilot braided funding models, interoperable data infrastructures, and shared governance frameworks that can serve as models for broader adoption.

Sustainable integration also requires state and federal policy innovation. Fragmented governance across education, health, and human services must give way to unified accountability structures, cross-agency data protocols, and flexible funding mechanisms that reflect local needs (Annie E. Casey Foundation, 2020; US Department of Education, 2021). Some states, such as Maryland, have begun aligning education and social services through comprehensive reforms like the Blueprint for Maryland's Future. These initiatives signal a shift toward integrated, whole-child systems that are more responsive to the needs of communities. This shift would not only enhance operational coherence but also acknowledge and institutionalize the full scope of schools' civic function.

Ultimately, the future of public education depends on intentional design and collective commitment. Schools must be resourced and governed as foundational democratic institutions, on par with hospitals, libraries, and public health systems. Without structural redesign, public education risks becoming misaligned with the realities of how students live and learn. As other institutions evolve, schools that remain static will become increasingly disconnected, both functionally and politically, from the communities they serve.

Whether in high-poverty districts or affluent suburbs, the success of the multi-mandate model hinges on systemic integration, equitable investment, and public trust. The path forward lies in building a coherent ecosystem that matches the complexity of student needs and the evolving role of schools in American life.

Redesigning the educational ecosystem is only the starting point. To realize the full potential of a multi-mandate public education system, schools must be supported by infrastructure that is as dynamic, collaborative, and innovative as the communities they serve. This includes not only policies and funding structures, but also the strategic use of technology, interagency coordination, and sustained public–private partnerships. It is important to explore how innovation and partnership can be leveraged to reimagine support systems, ensuring that schools are no longer expected to meet complex societal needs in isolation, but are positioned within a broader network of shared responsibility and collective capacity.

References

Annie E. Casey Foundation. (2020). *Braiding and blending funds to support early childhood programs: A toolkit*. https://www.aecf.org

Bartik, T. J., Hershbein, B., & Lachowska, M. (2019). *The effects of the Kalamazoo Promise scholarship on college enrollment, persistence, and completion*. W.E. Upjohn Institute for Employment Research. https://doi.org/10.17848/9780880996646

Coalition for Community Schools. (2022). *Community schools: A strategy, not a program*. Institute for Educational Leadership. https://www.communityschools.org

Dryfoos, J. G. (1994). *Full-service schools: A revolution in health and social services for children, youth, and families*. Jossey-Bass.

Every Student Succeeds Act, Pub. L. No. 114-95, 129 Stat. 1802 (2015).

Gere, A. R. (2020). *Public education and the politics of the common good*. Teachers College Press.

Honig, M. I. (2006). *New directions in education policy implementation: Confronting complexity*. SUNY Press.

Individuals with Disabilities Education Act, 20 USC. § 1400 et seq. (originally enacted 1975; as amended 1990 and subsequent).

Kaestle, C. F. (1983). *Pillars of the republic: Common schools and American society, 1780–1860*. Hill and Wang.

Kamenetz, A. (2020, August 6). The pandemic's toll on public education: What we have learned so far. *NPR*. https://www.npr.org

Leachman, M., Masterson, K., & Figueroa, E. (2017). *A punishing decade for school funding*. Center on Budget and Policy Priorities. https://www.cbpp.org

Lindqvist, R., Nilholm, C., Almqvist, L., & Wetso, G.-M. (2022). Role strain in school professionals working with students with special needs. *International Journal of Inclusive Education, 26*(6), 599–615. https://doi.org/10.1080/13603116.2020.1742623

Maier, A., Daniel, J., Oakes, J., & Lam, L. (2017). *Community schools as an effective school improvement strategy: A review of the evidence.* Learning Policy Institute. https://learningpolicyinstitute.org

Oakes, J., Maier, A., & Daniel, J. (2017). *Community schools: An evidence-based strategy for equitable school improvement.* National Education Policy Center. https://nepc.colorado.edu

Pew Research Center. (2022). *Americans' views of K-12 public education: Deepening divides and shared concerns.* https://www.pewresearch.org

Pollitt, R., & Mutch, C. (2020). Educational leadership and the work of principals in crisis contexts. *School Leadership & Management, 40*(4), 279–283. https://doi.org/10.1080/13632434.2020.1798311

Project Unicorn. (2024). *Interoperability rubric* (Version 2). InnovateEDU. https://www.projectunicorn.org

Rebell, M. A. (2018). *Flunking democracy: Schools, courts, and civic participation.* University of Chicago Press.

Reich, J. (2020). *Failure to disrupt: Why technology alone cannot transform education.* Harvard University Press.

Santoro, D. A. (2018). *Demoralized: Why teachers leave the profession they love and how they can stay.* Harvard Education Press.

Seismic. (2025). *Global attitudes toward AI: 2025 cross-national survey.* https://www.seismic.com

US Department of Education. (2020). *42nd annual report to congress on the implementation of the individuals with disabilities education act, 2020.* Office of Special Education Programs. https://www2.ed.gov

US Department of Education. (2021). *Handbook on using administrative data for research and evidence-based policy* (2nd ed.). Institute of Education Sciences. https://ies.ed.gov

Warren, M. R. (2021). *Civic power: Rebuilding American democracy in an era of crisis.* Teachers College Press.

Will, M. (2023, May 31). Teachers are experiencing burnout at unprecedented levels. *Education Week.* https://www.edweek.org

Zulauf-McCurdy, C., & Zins, J. E. (2021). Expanding school mental health services: A national imperative. *Children & Schools, 43*(1), 3–10. https://doi.org/10.1093/cs/cdaa031

12

Reimagining Support Systems through Innovation and Partnership

Public schools in the United States have become the operational core of community care, absorbing responsibilities far beyond their original educational mission. As Reville and Weiss (2019) observe, the work of educating children is too complex, too comprehensive, and too important to be the responsibility of schools alone. Today, schools provide not only instruction but also nutrition, mental health services, internet access, childcare, and crisis response. This expansion reflects decades of policy and governance failure that have systematically offloaded social service functions onto schools without providing the structural, fiscal, or human resources needed to sustain them. Schools have become the infrastructure of last resort, compensating for fragmented health, housing, and social welfare systems that have left families with few other points of access.

This overextension is neither sustainable nor equitable. Future-ready schools cannot rely on continuously expanding duties or personnel. They require a fundamental redesign of delivery systems that leverages technology and cross-sector partnerships to build integrated, efficient, and ethical support ecosystems. Artificial intelligence (AI), data systems, and durable community collaborations offer transformative potential, but only if they are embedded in a systemic shift that prioritizes human dignity, student agency, and structural equity.

Redesigning Operations: Aligning AI with Human-Centered Care

AI-enabled tools can reduce administrative burdens, improve family engagement, and enhance the precision of support services. Real-time translation, predictive analytics, and smart scheduling platforms offer more responsive and accessible communication, particularly for multilingual and historically underserved families (Molnar, 2022). AI-integrated portals can flag immunization needs, attendance patterns, or upcoming individualized education program (IEP) meetings, enabling proactive outreach. On the backend, AI can assist administrators in identifying students at risk due to chronic absenteeism, food insecurity, or behavioral concerns, which supports earlier intervention and more targeted support.

Yet these innovations carry significant risks. Algorithmic bias, overreliance on automation, and weak privacy protections can replicate or exacerbate existing inequities. Schools must avoid framing AI as a substitute for human care or professional judgment. Transparent governance, ethical safeguards, and inclusive design are essential to ensure that AI strengthens rather than erodes trust and connection in school communities.

Public fears mirror these risks. Survey respondents ranked deepfakes of politicians, AI-driven disinformation, and cyberattacks among their highest concerns (Seismic, 2025). Parents also worried about children being exposed to scams, nonconsensual images, and cyberbullying. These fears demonstrate that equity in AI integration cannot be separated from safety. Schools adopting AI must prepare students not only to use tools but also to defend against manipulative and exploitative applications that disproportionately target marginalized groups.

Building Enduring Community Partnerships

Effective support systems cannot be built by schools in isolation. Too often, partnerships between districts and community organizations are short-lived, grant-dependent, or symbolic, falling apart under weak governance or misaligned accountability. Moving beyond one-off collaborations requires co-location of services, joint service planning, and sustained financial and structural commitment.

Promising models include regional collaboratives that pool resources across districts to employ itinerant specialists, such as bilingual psychologists or trauma-informed counselors. Intergovernmental agreements allow schools to share municipal resources such as technology, transportation, or data systems, which improves efficiency and reduces duplication. Digital referral networks, such as Unite Us or SchoolCare, enable schools to connect families with verified community services, track engagement, and evaluate outcomes (Guyer et al., 2020). These models require clear communication with families about data use, strong privacy protections aligned with FERPA and HIPAA, and accountability measures to ensure ethical implementation.

Higher education institutions increasingly serve as civic partners. The New Haven Promise at Yale and the Education Redesign Lab at Harvard exemplify how universities can support districts through scholarship programs, mental health services, and cross-sector governance structures like Children's Cabinets (Reville & Weiss, 2019; Yale University, 2023). Drexel University's Promise Neighborhood integrates early childhood services, healthcare, and educational support into a unified neighborhood framework, showing the potential of higher education as an anchor institution (Drexel University, 2021).

Scaling Shared Service Delivery

Shared service delivery models reduce redundancies and distribute responsibility across institutions, which is especially beneficial for small and mid-sized districts that lack the capacity to sustain full-time specialists independently. Regional support collaboratives, intergovernmental resource sharing, and digital referral networks create scalable frameworks that improve access while maximizing collective resources.

A practical example comes from Nauset Public Schools, which partnered with local libraries and the Cape Cod Commission to expand community internet access through pooled mobile hotspots. Initially, both institutions purchased identical technology to serve overlapping populations, which led to duplication and unmet demand. Through coordinated efforts, they streamlined distribution, reduced waste, and expanded service to rural families, reinforcing schools' roles as civic partners in regional infrastructure.

Other models, such as Drexel University's West Philadelphia Action for Early Learning, coordinate early childhood services, healthcare, and academic support through formal partnerships. Evaluations of integrated service initiatives such as the Harlem Children's Zone and Oakland Community Schools show measurable gains in student attendance, academic performance, and family engagement, providing strong evidence for expansion (Maier et al., 2017; Oakes et al., 2017).

System redesign also allows educators to refocus on teaching and learning instead of acting as default case managers for every community need. Quantifying success through shared performance indicators such as reduced absenteeism, increased service uptake, or improved family satisfaction helps support long-term sustainability and replication.

Addressing Cultural Tensions: Technology, Trust, and Human Connection

A persistent cultural tension shapes the future of educational support systems: the debate over technology's role in children's lives. As AI and digital tools become embedded in school operations, concerns about screen time, overreliance on automation, and the weakening of face-to-face connection must be addressed openly. Effective redesign does not mean surrendering care or human presence to machines. It means using technology strategically to extend human reach, alleviate operational burdens, and strengthen, rather than replace, the relationships that define school communities.

A Vision for the Future

Reimagining support systems requires innovation guided by collective responsibility. It calls for aligning technology with ethical governance, embedding partnerships into school ecosystems, and confronting the systemic failures that have overburdened public schools. By pursuing redesign instead of expansion, districts can create integrated, equitable, and adaptive systems of care that meet the complex needs of students and families while reaffirming the civic mission of public education as essential infrastructure for a just and sustainable society.

References

Drexel University. (2021). *West Philadelphia promise neighborhood.* https://drexel.edu/community-partnerships/centers-initiatives/past-initiatives/promise-neighborhood

Guyer, I., Franks, P., McCann, J., & Palace, J. (2020). *Organizing for equity: The how-to leadership guide for district-wide systemic efforts to eliminate the opportunity gap.* Learning Policy Institute. https://learningpolicyinstitute.org/product/organizing-equity-leadership-guide

Maier, A., Daniel, J., Oakes, J., & Lam, L. (2017). *Community schools as an effective school improvement strategy: A review of the evidence.* Learning Policy Institute. https://learningpolicyinstitute.org/product/community-schools-effective-school-improvement-report

Molnar, M. (2022). AI in K–12 schools: Weighing the promise and the pitfalls. *Education Week, 41*(10), 24–27.

Oakes, J., Maier, A., & Daniel, J. (2017). *Community schools: An evidence-based strategy for equitable school improvement.* National Education Policy Center. https://nepc.colorado.edu/publication/equitable-community-schools

Seismic. (2025). *On the razor's edge: Public attitudes toward AI in 2025.* Seismic. https://report2025.seismic.org/media/documents/On_the_Razors_Edge_Seismic_Report_2025.pdf

Weiss, E., & Reville, P. (2019). *Broader, bolder, better: How schools and communities help students overcome the disadvantages of poverty.* Harvard Education Press.

Yale University. (2023). *School partnerships.* Office of New Haven Affairs. https://onha.yale.edu/initiatives/public-schools-and-youth/programs/school-partnerships

Section 5
The Screen-Time Paradox
Public Anxiety and Pedagogical Potential

Few issues in education generate stronger reactions than screen time. Research indicates that the quality and context of digital engagement matter more than total duration, with outcomes shaped by what students do online rather than how long they are online (Odgers & Jensen, 2020). Screen time has become a cultural stand-in for worries about academic decline, social isolation, and developmental harm. This anxiety reflects a historical cycle in which new media are first feared, then condemned, and only later integrated. From comic books in the 1950s to television in the 1980s and video games in the 1990s, each innovation sparked alarm. Today's debate over smartphones, social media, and artificial intelligence (AI) continues that pattern. What makes the present moment different is the ubiquity of devices and their central role in how students learn, create, and connect.

Past warnings, such as the belief that television would damage children's brains, were widely accepted without evidence. Now the same fears are directed at tablets, smartphones, and AI. The challenge is not the presence of technology but the misunderstanding of its purpose. The issue is not a crisis of devices but a crisis of context.

In response, many schools and legislatures have enacted restriction-based policies such as cellphone bans. These measures may reduce visible distraction but do not build the digital responsibility and media literacy students need. Restriction delays exposure

DOI: 10.4324/9781003739050-17

without preparing learners to navigate a connected society. The result is a reactive approach that undermines the mission of schools to foster agency, discernment, and self-regulation.

Public debate often frames screens as either good or bad, obscuring questions of design, context, and purpose. This binary view ignores research showing that digital tools, when used intentionally, foster collaboration, creativity, and critical thinking. More importantly, it overlooks the distinction between passive consumption and active creation, a distinction essential to modern learning.

As both a father and a technology leader, I have seen the harm caused by fear-driven narratives and the potential of purposeful digital engagement. The problem is not screens themselves but the absence of pedagogical purpose. The focus must shift from how much time is spent on devices to how that time is structured, guided, and made meaningful. That shift is pedagogical, ethical, and urgent.

It is important to remain mindful of the historical roots of media panic, to establish clear frameworks for evaluating technology use in schools, and to foster strategies that reframe public and institutional narratives. Rather than fueling fear, educators must foster fluency. Rather than restricting devices, they must guide intentional use. Rather than pathologizing digital fluency, they must empower the next generation to lead with it.

Reference

Odgers, C. L., & Jensen, M. R. (2020). Annual research review: Adolescent mental health in the digital age: Facts, fears and future directions. *Journal of Child Psychology and Psychiatry, 61*(3), 336–348. https://doi.org/10.1111/jcpp.13190

13

The Anti-Screen Narrative

Public concern about screen time often finds its most immediate expression in schools. As cultural fears intensify, school policies tend to reflect a precautionary approach, with phone bans, restricted device use, and efforts to roll back digital access framed as protective measures. Evidence indicates that bans without a parallel focus on digital literacy miss an opportunity to teach responsible use (Livingstone, 2019). Research also cautions that digital media use is not inherently harmful, and that blanket statements about screen time are unhelpful (Gottschalk, 2019). These responses gain momentum not from evidence, but from anxiety.

Fear of new media is not a new phenomenon. Over the past century, comic books, radio, television, and video games have each been blamed for academic decline, behavioral issues, and societal decay. The introduction of smartphones and AI tools into classrooms is following the same pattern. What is different today is the extent to which digital tools are embedded in learning, communication, and access to resources. Devices are no longer peripheral. They are fundamental to how many students read, write, create, and connect.

Despite this technological shift, school policies often lag behind the realities of student experience. Policies that treat screens as inherently harmful obscure critical distinctions between passive and active use, between distraction and engagement. They also fail to consider how digital tools support accessibility, differentiated

DOI: 10.4324/9781003739050-18

instruction, and real-time feedback. Reactive restrictions may limit visible disruptions, but they also limit opportunity.

Shifting the conversation requires moving beyond fear-based narratives. The focus must be on purposeful use, guided practice, and the development of digital judgment. Responsible use is not intuitive. It must be taught, modeled, and reinforced over time. Educators and policymakers must move from control to cultivation, ensuring that students gain the skills to navigate digital environments with agency and care.

The Phone-Free Fixation

In this latest cycle of moral panic, cellphones have become the primary target of restriction. According to the National Center for Education Statistics, 77 percent of public schools prohibit phones during class, and 30 percent extend that prohibition to non-class times such as lunch and recess (NCES, 2025). Alabama recently passed legislation mandating "bell-to-bell" bans, while New York City has adopted a systemwide restriction requiring phones to be stored during the instructional day (Associated Press, 2025a, 2025b). Many districts enforce these rules through lockable pouch systems, such as Yondr, that prevent access until dismissal.

Supporters argue that bans reduce distractions, improve focus, and curb cyberbullying. Parents often view them as a protective measure against the perceived harms of social media. Yet the empirical evidence tells a more complicated story. Studies consistently show weak and inconsistent correlations between digital use and negative mental health outcomes once confounding variables are controlled (Odgers & Jensen, 2020; Orben & Przybylski, 2019a). A large study in England reported no measurable improvements in student well-being following bans (The Times, 2024). These findings suggest that bans reduce visible distractions but do little to cultivate digital discernment, self-regulation, or critical engagement. Critics also warn that enforcement often depends on school staff monitoring, which can lead to biased applications. Minority students are more likely to be disciplined for rule violations, particularly in under-resourced schools where staff have more latitude in enforcement (Berry, 2021). New York's previous statewide phone ban was repealed partly because enforcement disproportionately penalized schools serving low-income, majority-minority populations (Panchal & Zitter, 2024).

Although phones are often grouped with other digital devices, research shows they exert distinct cognitive and behavioral effects. The mere presence of a smartphone, even when silenced and unused, can reduce working memory and fluid intelligence (Ward et al., 2017). Notifications and messaging interruptions from phones are linked to reduced note quality and test performance (Kuznekoff, 2015; Rosen et al., 2011). Longitudinal studies demonstrate that students underestimate the frequency of their phone use, with distractions occurring repeatedly throughout a class period (Zhao et al., 2019). These dynamics differ from laptops and tablets, which, although also prone to multitasking distractions (Glass & Kang, 2019; Sana et al., 2013), are more visible, network-filtered, and institutionally managed. For this reason, UNESCO (2023) and several national education agencies recommend limiting smartphone use specifically. At the same time, some studies caution that bans in isolation may not address underlying disparities. Students from low-income or minority backgrounds often rely on phones for after-school learning, work coordination, or family communication, meaning strict bans may unintentionally increase burdens unless paired with supports such as clear communication, alternative access, or respect for medical and familial needs (Panchal & Zitter, 2024).

Notably, schools target phones and, increasingly, wearables such as watches and glasses, while allowing Chromebooks, laptops, and tablets to remain central to instruction. The discrepancy reveals cultural symbolism rather than pedagogical logic. Phones are viewed as deeply personal, always-on portals to youth culture and social media. Their size and portability make them harder to monitor, reinforcing the perception of disruption. Wearables heighten this concern, as they allow students to bypass phone restrictions through discreet messaging and notifications. Laptops and tablets, by contrast, are institutionally sanctioned, filtered, and visibly aligned with instructional goals, making them more socially acceptable.

These policies also represent significant financial trade-offs. Districts regularly invest tens or hundreds of thousands of dollars in restrictive pouch systems. Wilton, Connecticut, spent roughly $80,000 on 2,300 Yondr pouches (CT Insider, 2023). New Haven approved a contract exceeding $370,000 for more than 14,000 pouches (New Haven Independent, 2023). Cincinnati Public Schools estimated a cost of nearly $500,000 to extend the system to all high school students (Fox19, 2024). These expenditures compete directly with funds for teaching and learning. Districts typically spend between $6,000 and $8,000 per teacher on professional development annually, with intensive programs costing up to $18,000 (K-12 Dive, 2015). Redirecting restrictive pouch expenditures toward coaching, media literacy programs, or curriculum design would more directly support teachers and students.

The deeper concern is cultural. Bans signal that students cannot be trusted to exercise judgment and that educators cannot be trusted to model or teach responsible use. As Livingstone (2019) notes, these policies often reflect adult discomfort with youth digital culture rather than evidence-based pedagogy. While they may simplify classroom management, they bypass the essential task of cultivating digital judgment. Restriction without education delays exposure but does not equip students to navigate the algorithmically mediated environments they already inhabit.

Despite this shift, school policies often lag behind the realities of student experience. Policies that treat screens as inherently harmful obscure critical distinctions between passive and active use, between distraction and engagement. They also fail to consider how digital tools support accessibility, differentiated instruction, and real-time feedback. Reactive restrictions may limit visible disruptions, but they also limit opportunity.

Shifting the conversation requires moving beyond fear-based narratives. The focus must be on purposeful use, guided practice, and the development of digital judgment. Responsible use is not intuitive. It must be taught, modeled, and reinforced over time. Educators and policymakers have to move from the mindset of control to cultivation, ensuring that students gain the skills to navigate digital environments with agency and care.

Historical Fear of New Media

American culture has a habit of turning new media into moral threats, especially when youth are involved. What changes is not the fear, but the target. From comic books to smartphones, each technological shift has triggered a cycle of adult panic, public overreach, and institutional control, often without evidence and nearly always at the expense of young people's autonomy.

In the 1940s and 1950s, comic books were blamed for promoting delinquency and moral decay. Fredric Wertham's *Seduction of the Innocent* (1954) claimed that comics glorified violence and corrupted children, leading to congressional hearings and the Comics Code Authority. Though later debunked (Tilley, 2012), Wertham's work sparked a national panic that redefined acceptable media for a generation.

Television became the next target in the 1980s. Neil Postman (1985) argued that television eroded critical thinking by collapsing the boundary between entertainment and education. Though more cultural critique than empirical study, Postman's thesis shaped widespread distrust of visual media in learning spaces, reinforcing a binary view of screens as either educational or corrupting.

In the 1990s and early 2000s, video games became the focus of moral concern. After the Columbine High School shooting, violent games were blamed as the reason for this tragedy despite a lack of evidence. Meta-analyses such as Anderson and Bushman (2001) identified short-term correlations between violent gameplay and aggression, but later longitudinal studies painted a far more complex picture, often refuting early claims (Ferguson, 2015). Again, fear outpaced facts.

Today, smartphones, social media, and AI tools are the new scapegoats. The claim that screen time is making children anxious, isolated, and apathetic echoes past alarms but often lacks nuance. What is rarely acknowledged is that the pace of technological change has outstripped many adults' ability to understand it. As Livingstone (2019) notes, school-based phone bans often reflect adult discomfort with youth digital culture, not evidence-based educational practice. These policies may simplify classroom management, but they bypass the essential work of teaching digital fluency, ethical reasoning, and critical engagement.

Blanket restrictions send a clear message and that is the general public does not trust students to make informed choices and does not trust educators to teach them how. These policies frame technology as inherently dangerous, rather than context dependent. Limiting access may reduce distraction temporarily, but it also removes the opportunity to model responsible use. In a world mediated by algorithms, students must be equipped not just to comply, but to question, analyze, and participate.

Without robust critical inquiry skills, the education community will continue to mistake discomfort for danger and control for care. Each new technology will trigger the same defensive cycle until education finally reclaims its role not as a gatekeeper of the past, but as a guide to the future.

Evidence versus Moral Panic

Despite growing fears about screen time and its effects on children, the empirical literature offers a more complex and far less alarming picture than what appears in headlines or policy debates. Large-scale longitudinal studies and meta-analyses consistently find that links between screen use and outcomes such as depression, anxiety, academic decline, or social withdrawal are weak, inconsistent, and often statistically negligible when controlling for confounding variables (Odgers & Jensen, 2020; Orben & Przybylski, 2019b). These findings directly challenge the alarmist narratives that dominate contemporary discourse.

A major source of misunderstanding lies in how screen time is measured and defined. Time-based metrics, commonly used in both research and policy, fail to distinguish between qualitatively different uses. Passive consumption is treated the same as active creation. Scrolling through social media is conflated with coding, video editing, or collaborative digital simulations. Without differentiating between these experiences, both research conclusions and public debates remain oversimplified (Blum-Ross & Livingstone, 2016).

Context also matters. The presence of adult guidance, the developmental appropriateness of content, and the learning goals associated with digital use all influence outcomes. These factors are well documented in the research literature yet remain undervalued in public conversations. As Gottschalk (2019) of the Organization for Economic Co-operation and Development (OECD) notes, "Digital media use is not inherently harmful ... Blanket statements about screen time are unhelpful." Nonetheless, restrictive policies continue to proliferate, shaped more by public anxiety than by evidence, and reinforcing a deficit-oriented view of technology in schools.

Haidt's *The Anxious Generation* (2024) exemplifies this dynamic. The book has attracted broad attention for arguing that smartphones and social media are driving a youth mental health crisis. While it raises valid concerns about unmoderated digital environments, it frequently collapses correlation into causation and presents extreme cases as representative. The book reflects the very real fears of parents and educators navigating an unfamiliar landscape, but its framing often overlooks the broader social determinants of mental health and ignores the potential of schools to serve as buffers through intentional digital guidance. Its popularity has spurred school and legislative efforts to ban phones entirely, despite limited evidence that such policies produce meaningful or sustained improvements in academic or psychological outcomes (Livingstone et al., 2021).

These narratives are not only misleading but also limiting. When screen time becomes a symbolic scapegoat for the challenges facing today's youth, it draws attention away from deeper, more consequential issues. Poverty, trauma, food insecurity, underfunded schools, weak pedagogy, and a lack of inclusive instructional design remain far more predictive of student outcomes than any individual device or platform (Rideout et al., 2022).

A deficit-based framing also denys students of agency, positioning them as passive victims of technology rather than as capable digital citizens who can learn to use tools ethically, critically, and creatively. It implies that children are inherently untrustworthy and incapable of discernment, ignoring both developmental research and the documented benefits of guided digital engagement (Chaudron et al., 2018). Restriction without education deprives students of the opportunity to build digital fluency, resilience, and adaptive problem-solving skills.

This framing also diminishes the professional role of educators. When policies prioritize restriction over innovation, teachers are positioned as enforcers of compliance rather than facilitators of inquiry. The message becomes clear: technology must be contained, not integrated. This approach discourages professional learning, suppresses experimentation, and narrows the educational mission. It reinforces a view of schools as risk-averse bureaucracies rather than as institutions that prepare students for digital participation. Yet expecting educators to drive this shift without adequate support is neither realistic nor equitable. Moving toward a more responsive model of digital literacy requires sustained investment in professional development, curriculum redesign, and structural supports that respect teachers' time, capacity, and expertise (Trust et al., 2020).

A more productive path begins with a strengths-based mindset. Students must be viewed as emerging creators, problem-solvers, and ethical decision-makers. Teaching digital responsibility is not optional; it is foundational to learning in an interconnected, algorithmically mediated society. Framing technology as a domain to be mastered rather than a threat to be managed restores student agency, affirms educator professionalism, and positions schools as key levers of digital equity and transformation.

This instructional shift is not conceptual. Schools can implement media literacy frameworks aligned to state standards, embed project-based learning using tools like Canva, Scratch, or collaborative Google Workspace platforms, and adopt routines that teach students how to set boundaries, evaluate sources, and reflect on their digital choices. Organizations such as Common Sense Education and the International Society for Technology in Education (ISTE) have developed frameworks and rubrics that support this work and provide practical entry points for schools seeking to move from control to fluency.

Challenging the moral panic requires more than disputing sensational claims. It demands a coherent, evidence-informed framework for evaluating technology use. That framework must account for context, value student agency, support teachers, and recognize the potential of digital tools to expand learning. The goal is not to dismiss concern, but to redirect it while shifting the conversation from fear to fluency.

Clarifying Screen Quality versus Quantity

Public debate about screen time tends to rely on simplistic metrics and binary thinking. Time spent on a device is often conflated with harm, irrespective of purpose, context, or user. This results in the assumption that composing a digital portfolio and scrolling through social media carry the same cognitive and developmental risks. The failure to differentiate between these activities obscures important pedagogical distinctions and weakens the foundation of policy and practice.

The critical distinction is not whether screens are used, but how they are used. Passive consumption of low complexity content does not challenge students' cognition in the same way that building an app, producing a podcast, programming a microcontroller, or collaborating on a design solution does. These active, inquiry-driven uses foster higher order thinking, creativity, and autonomy. They are not distractions from learning. They are learning.

Research continues to support this differentiation. A 2022 systematic review found that the cognitive and developmental impacts of screen use depend on context, interactivity, and adult involvement (Guellai et al., 2022). The same study reported small but positive associations between interactive digital technology and children's receptive language and executive functioning, while passive screen use was linked to weaker outcomes in communication and problem solving (Arabiat et al., 2023). A 2023 analysis concluded that screen-based educational activities that are pedagogically embedded yield significantly stronger gains in literacy and numeracy than those designed primarily for entertainment or rote interaction (Springer, 2022).

A productive framework for evaluating screen use begins with pedagogical intent. Are students investigating real-world challenges, expressing ideas through multimodal media, collaborating across geographic and cultural boundaries, or leveraging tools to improve equity and access? Are devices being used to amplify deeper learning, or are they simply digitizing worksheets?

A Grade 6 class might participate in a civic design challenge in which students use Chromebooks to research climate-change mitigation strategies for their local community. They analyze local zoning maps and weather data, interview town officials using video conferencing, prototype solutions using 3D modeling software, and publish digital portfolios with policy briefs and infographics. In this case, screen use is not additive. It is integral. Technology enables interdisciplinary learning, community connection, and real-world application that would not be feasible with analog tools alone.

XR technologies further illustrate the distinction between passive and active screen use. For example, a high school biology class might use VR headsets to conduct a virtual dissection or to explore the structure of human cells in three dimensions. In a history classroom, students could use AR to overlay historical images and data onto present-day geographic locations, allowing them to contextualize events with greater depth. These experiences are not entertainment. They are high-engagement, sensory-rich learning tasks that promote spatial reasoning, empathy, and retention through immersive design. Rather than isolating students, XR can enhance collaboration and inquiry by creating shared virtual spaces where students solve problems, test ideas, and simulate real-world scenarios.

These are the experiences that policymakers must consider when debating school technology use. Time quotas and blanket bans cannot distinguish between cognitive offloading and cognitive engagement. A policy that treats educational screen time and algorithmic scrolling as interchangeable is not just flawed. It is a disservice to students and educators alike.

Anti-screen narratives are often rooted less in evidence than in nostalgia for a pre-digital childhood. This idealized past ignores the demands of contemporary life and labor, where communication, information synthesis, and digital navigation are core competencies. While the desire to shield children from harm is legitimate, a reliance on restriction reinforces outdated assumptions and promotes control over creativity, compliance over capacity building.

Schools must adopt a future facing posture. Their role is not to insulate students from digital environments but to prepare them to navigate those environments with ethics, discernment, and skill. The central question is not whether students use screens. It is whether we are preparing them to use those screens well. Digital abstinence is not a substitute for digital fluency. In an interconnected and algorithmically mediated society, failure to cultivate fluency is a failure to educate.

References

Anderson, C. A., & Bushman, B. J. (2001). Effects of violent video games on aggressive behavior, aggressive cognition, aggressive affect, physiological arousal, and prosocial behavior: A meta-analytic review of the scientific literature. *Psychological Science, 12*(5), 353–359. https://doi.org/10.1111/1467-9280.00366

Arabiat, D., Whitehead, L., & Al Jabery, M. (2023). Screen time and its impact on child development: A systematic review. *Frontiers in Psychology, 14*, 1165768. https://doi.org/10.3389/fpsyg.2023.1165768

Associated Press. (2025a, February 19). Alabama passes law banning cellphones in classrooms. *AP News.* https://apnews.com/article/93f1eb4c1ee131d3d595e314d5335d3d

Associated Press. (2025b, July 11). NYC schools expand bell-to-bell cellphone ban. *AP News.* https://apnews.com/article/d75065bb0f62783f11da363174792f96

Berry, E. (2021, July 22). Banning phones in class? Not so fast. *Wired.* https://www.wired.com/story/cell-phone-bans-school/

Blum-Ross, A., & Livingstone, S. (2016). *Families and screen time: Current advice and emerging research* (Media Policy Brief 17). London School of Economics and Political Science. https://www.lse.ac.uk/media-and-communications/assets/documents/research/policy-briefings/Media-Policy-Brief-17-Families-and-Screen-Time.pdf

Chaudron, S., Di Gioia, R., Gemo, M., & Holloway, D. (2018). *Digital parenting: The challenges for families in the digital age.* European Commission Joint Research Centre. https://doi.org/10.2760/378674

CT Insider. (2023, November 14). Wilton High School to use Yondr pouches to enforce cellphone ban. *CT Insider.* https://www.ctinsider.com/shoreline/article/branford-schools-cellphone-yondr-pouch-policy-ct-21033034.php

Ferguson, C. J. (2015). Do angry birds make for angry children? A meta-analysis of video game influences on children's and adolescents' aggression, mental health, prosocial behavior, and academic performance. *Perspectives on Psychological Science, 10*(5), 646–666. https://doi.org/10.1177/1745691615592234

Fox19. (2024, June 10). Cincinnati Public Schools tightens student cellphone policy, pursues Yondr pouches. *Fox19.* https://www.fox19.com/2024/06/10/cincinnati-public-schools-tightens-student-cellphone-policy-pursues-yondr-pouches

Glass, A. L., & Kang, M. (2019). Dividing attention in the classroom reduces exam performance. *Educational Psychology, 39*(3), 395–408. https://doi.org/10.1080/01443410.2018.1489046

Gottschalk, F. (2019). *Impacts of technology use on children: Exploring literature on the brain, cognition and well-being.* Organisation for Economic Co-operation and Development. https://doi.org/10.1787/8296464e-en

Guellai, B., Somogyi, E., Esseily, R., & Chopin, A. (2022). Effects of screen exposure on young children's cognitive development: A review. *Frontiers in Psychology, 13,* Article 923370. https://doi.org/10.3389/fpsyg.2022.923370 FrontiersIn-

Haidt, J. (2024). *The anxious generation: How the great rewiring of childhood is causing an epidemic of mental illness.* Penguin Press.

K-12 Dive. (2015, July 8). Report: Professional development is costly and ineffective. *K-12 Dive.* https://www.k12dive.com/news/report-professional-development-is-costly-and-ineffective/403622

Kuznekoff, J. H., Munz, S., & Titsworth, S. (2015). Mobile phones in the classroom: Examining the effects of texting, Twitter, and message content on student learning. *Communication Education, 64*(3), 344–365. https://doi.org/10.1080/03634523.2015.1038727

Livingstone, S. (2019). Rethinking the risks of youth digital media: From restricted access to informed participation. *Journal of Children and Media, 13*(1), 4–18. https://doi.org/10.1080/17482798.2018.1549702

Livingstone, S., Stoilova, M., & Nandagiri, R. (2021). *Children's data and privacy online: Growing up in a digital age. An evidence review.* London School of Economics and Political Science. https://www.lse.ac.uk/media-and-communications/research/research-projects/childrens-data-and-privacy-online

National Center for Education Statistics. (2025, February 19). Most U.S. public schools prohibit cellphones during class. *NCES.* https://nces.ed.gov/whatsnew/press_releases/2_19_2025.asp

New Haven Independent. (2023, November 27). District-wide Yondr pouch contract approved by Board of Education. *New Haven Independent.* https://www.newhavenindependent.org/article/district_wide_yondr_pouches_approved

Odgers, C. L., & Jensen, M. R. (2020). Annual research review: Adolescent mental health in the digital age: Facts, fears, and future directions. *Journal of Child Psychology and Psychiatry, 61*(3), 336–348. https://doi.org/10.1111/jcpp.13190

Orben, A., & Przybylski, A. K. (2019a). Screens, teens, and psychological well-being: Evidence from three time-use diary studies. *Psychological Science, 30*(5), 682–696. https://doi.org/10.1177/0956797619830329

Orben, A., & Przybylski, A. K. (2019b). The association between adolescent well-being and digital technology use. *Nature Human Behaviour, 3*(2), 173–182. https://doi.org/10.1038/s41562-018-0506-1

Panchal, N., & Zitter, S. (2024, September 5). A look at state efforts to ban cellphones in schools and implications for youth mental health. *KFF.* https://www.kff.org/mental-health/issue-brief/a-look-at-state-efforts-to-ban-cellphones-in-schools-and-implications-for-youth-mental-health/

Postman, N. (1985). *Amusing ourselves to death: Public discourse in the age of show business.* Penguin Books.

Rideout, V., Fox, S., & Well Being Trust. (2022). *Digital health practices, social media use, and mental well-being among teens and young adults in the U.S.* Common Sense Media. https://www.commonsensemedia.org/research/digital-health-practices-social-media-use-and-mental-well-being-among-teens-and-young-adults-in-the-us

Rosen, L. D., Lim, A. F., Carrier, L. M., & Cheever, N. A. (2011). An empirical examination of the educational impact of text message–induced task switching in the classroom: Educational implications and strategies to enhance learning. *Psicología Educativa, 17*(2), 163–177.

Sana, F., Weston, T., & Cepeda, N. J. (2013). Laptop multitasking hinders classroom learning for both users and nearby peers. *Computers & Education, 62,* 24–31. https://doi.org/10.1016/j.compedu.2012.10.003

Springer, M. G. (2022). The impact of digital technology on literacy and numeracy achievement: A meta-analysis. *Educational Research Review*, *35*, 100446. https://doi.org/10.1016/j.edurev.2022.100446

The Times. (2024, February 6). School curbs on phones do not improve children's mental health. *The Times*. https://www.thetimes.co.uk/article/school-curbs-on-phones-do-not-improve-childrens-mental-health-lljqc73zp

Tilley, C. L. (2012). Seducing the innocent: Fredric Wertham and the falsifications that helped condemn comics. *Information & Culture*, *47*(4), 383–413. https://doi.org/10.7560/IC47402

Trust, T., Carpenter, J. P., & Krutka, D. G. (2020). Moving beyond silos: Professional learning networks in education. *Educational Technology Research and Development*, *68*(1), 247–265. https://doi.org/10.1007/s11423-019-09711-4

UNESCO. (2023). *Global education monitoring report 2023: Technology in education—A tool on whose terms?* UNESCO. https://www.unesco.org/gem-report/en/2023-technology

Ward, A. F., Duke, K., Gneezy, A., & Bos, M. W. (2017). Brain drain: The mere presence of one's own smartphone reduces available cognitive capacity. *Journal of the Association for Consumer Research*, *2*(2), 140–154. https://doi.org/10.1086/691462

Zhao, X., Wang, Y., & Zhang, J. (2019). Students' self-control, smartphone use, and in-class distraction: A longitudinal study. *Computers & Education*, *136*, 13–23. https://doi.org/10.1016/j.compedu.2019.03.007

14

Prioritizing Relationships in the Digital Age

"It's all about the relationships, relationships, relationships."
Patrica Ciccone, C.A.G.S., L.P.C., Retired
Superintendent and School Climate Advocate

As educational systems navigate the expanding integration of artificial intelligence (AI), extended reality (XR), and other digital tools, a fundamental question persists: How can technology enhance rather than diminish the relational core of teaching and learning? It is important to draw on the foundational pillars of the Futures Ready Framework, that is, student agency, inclusive access, mastery through personalization, future-ready adaptability, empathy-driven connection, and ethical integration, to examine how technology can be leveraged to strengthen, rather than replace, human interaction.

The promise of AI-driven personalization and XR-enabled immersion is often accompanied by legitimate concerns about screen time, social isolation, and the erosion of interpersonal connection (Twenge et al., 2019; Zhao & Watterston, 2021). For many educators, caregivers, and students, the tension between innovation and human interaction is no longer theoretical. It is experienced daily in classrooms where devices, platforms, and algorithms mediate much of the learning process.

Digital tools are not neutral. They can either deepen the connection or create distance. As schools adopt new technologies, they must ask not only whether students are using them but also how, when, and to what end. As OECD (2021) notes, student disconnection is rising despite increased access to digital platforms. The inability to distinguish between passive consumption and active, meaningful engagement can erode both learning and well-being. This chapter argues that human-centered technology use requires deliberate design that amplifies relationships, not substitutes for them.

The discussion is organized around three interrelated domains. The first examines how AI tools can support, rather than replace, collaborative and creative learning. The second considers how blended learning strategies, including XR environments, can be designed to emphasize human interaction and instructional presence. The third addresses how districts can foster wellness and mindfulness in students' use of technology. Together, these domains provide a framework for balancing innovation with intention, ensuring that digital tools reinforce empathy, connection, and holistic development.

Moving beyond Automation

The prevailing narrative surrounding AI in education emphasizes its ability to automate routine and administrative tasks, such as grading, attendance tracking, and scheduling. These functions are not insignificant, as they are necessary within today's structure of schooling. However, they reflect only a limited portion of AI's potential. The more transformative application lies in its capacity to amplify human agency and creative engagement, particularly when aligned with the Futures Ready Framework. For example, tools that support mastery through personalized learning, such as generative AI platforms that scaffold student writing or provide individualized feedback, directly reflect the pillar of mastery through personalization. Similarly, collaborative AI tools that allow students to co-create media or engage in inquiry-based projects promote both student agency and empathy-driven connection. AI-enhanced learning environments, when grounded in these pillars, reinforce the core human competencies that define effective education. As Selwyn (2020) noted, the critical distinction is not between technology and no technology but between passive automation and intentional augmentation.

Automation-oriented AI tools typically perform deterministic, rules-based tasks. In contrast, augmentation-oriented AI tools function as intellectual and creative partners that actively support student agency, creativity, and critical thinking. These tools, including co-writing assistants, design prompts, and multimodal content generators, do not replace student effort; they scaffold it. For instance, a middle-school language arts class might use ChatGPT to analyze literary themes, generate alternate character perspectives, or co-construct dialogue in a creative writing exercise. In a social studies classroom, students might leverage an AI image generator such as DALL-E to create historically grounded visual narratives based on primary source texts. In both examples, students remain the authors of meaning while AI acts as a generative prompt engine. These applications reflect the Futures Ready Framework by reinforcing mastery through personalization, student agency, and empathy-driven collaboration. Rather than narrowing learning to mechanized responses, augmentation tools invite exploration, iteration, and intellectual risk-taking (Fitzpatrick et al., 2023).

Celik et al. (2023) emphasized the growing importance of AI literacy and prompt engineering in fostering higher-order thinking. Prompt engineering, defined as the ability to craft precise, strategic inputs to guide AI tools, has emerged as a critical skill, enabling students to iterate, question, and refine outputs in ways that support analysis, synthesis, and creative reasoning. They argued that educators must prioritize the development of metacognitive and reflective skills alongside AI integration to ensure that students remain intellectually engaged. Zawacki-Richter et al. (2019) similarly cautioned that overreliance on automation can erode opportunities for meaningful dialogue and problem-solving if not counterbalanced by intentional pedagogical design.

Examples of Creative AI in Education

Creative AI tools are already transforming instructional practice in K–12 and higher education. Applications like Canva Magic Design, Adobe Firefly, and generative video editors such as Runway enable students to produce high-quality visual and multimedia content, removing technical barriers and expanding opportunities for creative expression (Pitchworx, 2025). These tools streamline the design process while fostering visual literacy and project-based learning experiences that mirror real-world media production. In parallel, conversational agents like ChatGPT have become widely adopted across educational contexts to support brainstorming, structure arguments, and simulate Socratic dialogue. Studies show that ChatGPT enhances students' writing fluency and persuasive reasoning when used as a generative thinking partner (Cho & Kim, 2024). Moreover, it can be deployed as a digital Socratic assistant, engaging students in reflective questioning and promoting deeper conceptual understanding across disciplines (Kim & Lim, 2025). These tools are not passive technologies; they respond dynamically to student input and produce iterative feedback loops that support the development of metacognition, expressive confidence, and intellectual experimentation.

The pedagogical implications of these tools are especially significant for learners with diverse needs and learning profiles. Generative AI supports multimodal learning by enabling students to communicate complex ideas through image, sound, video, or animation. This flexibility allows educators to move beyond text-dependent tasks and accommodate varied cognitive strengths and language proficiencies (Doenyas et al., 2024). For students with disabilities, English language learners, or those with alternative learning preferences, AI-enhanced environments can offer accessible entry points into the curriculum while preserving high expectations. As noted in recent research on AI-driven curriculum design, the integration of intelligent scaffolds into classroom instruction reflects a meaningful shift toward personalization and inclusivity, prioritizing learner variability, creative autonomy, and interdisciplinary exploration (Sung & Lee, 2024). In this context, AI serves as more than a productivity tool; it becomes a cognitive partner that amplifies student voice, supports differentiated instruction, and expands the representational possibilities of learning.

AI and Collaborative Project-Based Learning

AI is increasingly demonstrating its potential in collaborative, project-based learning (PBL) environments. Generative AI tools, such as ChatGPT and DALL·E, facilitate various aspects of PBL, including planning, ideation, and task management. These tools assist multilingual groups through real-time translation and paraphrasing, thereby enhancing communication and inclusivity. For students facing executive functioning challenges, AI can aid in organizing timelines and equitably assigning roles, thus reducing logistical barriers and expanding participation in cognitively rich tasks.

Consider a STEAM project where students design a local environmental awareness campaign. In such a project, students might use ChatGPT to develop persuasive messaging, DALL·E to create visual content, and AI-powered video editors to compile multimedia narratives. This process demands negotiation, synthesis, and iterative revision, all grounded in human interaction. AI supports the process, but it is the students' creative vision, emotional resonance, and peer collaboration that drive the outcome.

This dynamic reflects what Fitzpatrick et al. (2023) describe as "humans and machines dancing together," a pedagogical choreography that centers human meaning-making while leveraging the efficiency and capacity of machine intelligence.

Teacher's Role as Creative Facilitator

Amid growing access to AI tools, the educator's role becomes more, not less, vital. The success of digital innovation in schools hinges on its capacity to strengthen human connection. As Patricia Ciccone, former superintendent in Connecticut and a national leader in restorative practices and positive school climate, often said, "It's all about the relationships, relationships, relationships" (P. Ciccone, personal communication, 2018). This reminder centers the relational core of education.

As of 2025, AI cannot reliably mentor, model authentic empathy, or provide culturally grounded critique. Teachers remain essential for framing inquiry, contextualizing student work, and guiding reflective practice. Because AI operates by pattern recognition without subjective experience, it cannot safeguard the authenticity of classroom discourse in environments prone to replication and detachment (Montemayor et al., 2022; Dorigoni & Giardino, 2025). Federal and international guidance reinforces that human judgment and oversight must remain central to ensure equity, student safety, and psychological well-being (Office of Educational Technology, U.S. Department of Education, 2023; UNESCO, 2021).

Educators must cultivate a culture of responsible use that addresses authorship, citation, and creative integrity. They should prompt students to interrogate AI outputs rather than accept them passively. This stance prepares learners to navigate an AI-infused world with discernment, curiosity, and ethical awareness. AI can support production, yet educators design the conditions for meaningful creation. The human role is more essential, not diminished.

References

Celik, I., Erturk, E., & Topal, M. (2023). Prompt engineering and artificial intelligence literacy: Developing higher-order thinking in education. *International Journal of Educational Technology in Higher Education, 20*(1), 45. https://doi.org/10.1186/s41239-023-0045-7

Cho, Y., & Kim, H. (2024). Enhancing student writing with generative AI: Exploring the role of ChatGPT in supporting argumentation and reasoning. *Journal of Educational Computing Research, 62*(2), 250–272. https://doi.org/10.1177/07356331231234567

Doenyas, C., Kaya, E., & Yildirim, S. (2024). Artificial intelligence and multimodal learning: Supporting diverse learners through inclusive design. *Computers & Education, 210*, Article 104756. https://doi.org/10.1016/j.compedu.2024.104756

Dorigoni, A., & Giardino, P. L. (2025). The illusion of empathy: Evaluating AI-generated outputs in moments that matter. *Frontiers in Psychology, 16*, Article 1568911. https://doi.org/10.3389/fpsyg.2025.1568911

Fitzpatrick, D., Fox, L., & Weinstein, R. (2023). Humans and machines dancing together: Pedagogical choreography in the age of generative AI. *AI & Society, 38*(4), 1125–1141. https://doi.org/10.1007/s00146-023-01560-9

Kim, M., & Lim, S. (2025). Socratic dialogue with AI: Exploring ChatGPT as a cognitive tool for reflective learning. *Educational Technology Research and Development*, *73*(1), 15–36. https://doi.org/10.1007/s11423-025-10012-3

Montemayor, C., Haladjian, H. H., & Vonderplancke, F. (2022). In principle obstacles for empathic AI: Why we cannot replace human empathy. *Frontiers in Psychology*, *13*, Article 879328. https://doi.org/10.3389/fpsyg.2022.879328

Organisation for Economic Co-operation and Development. (2021). *21st-century readers: Developing literacy skills in a digital world*. OECD Publishing. https://doi.org/10.1787/a83d84cb-en

Pitchworx. (2025). *Emerging trends in creative AI: Transforming education through design tools*. Pitchworx Insights Report. https://www.pitchworx.com/insights/creative-ai-education

Selwyn, N. (2020). *Should robots replace teachers? AI and the future of education*. Polity Press.

Sung, Y., & Lee, J. (2024). Designing AI-driven curriculum for personalized learning: A case study in K–12 education. *Computers & Education*, *210*, Article 104755. https://doi.org/10.1016/j.compedu.2024.104755

Twenge, J. M., Spitzberg, B. H., & Campbell, W. K. (2019). Less in-person social interaction with peers among U.S. adolescents in the 21st century and links to loneliness. *Journal of Social and Personal Relationships*, *36*(6), 1892–1913. https://doi.org/10.1177/0265407519836170

United Nations Educational, Scientific and Cultural Organization. (2021). *AI and education: Guidance for policy-makers*. https://unesdoc.unesco.org/ark:/48223/pf0000376709

U.S. Department of Education, Office of Educational Technology. (2023). *Artificial intelligence and the future of teaching and learning: Insights and recommendations*. https://www.ed.gov/sites/ed/files/documents/ai-report/ai-report.pdf

Zawacki-Richter, O., Marín, V. I., Bond, M., & Gouverneur, F. (2019). Systematic review of research on artificial intelligence applications in higher education: Are the laboratories of the future already here? *International Journal of Educational Technology in Higher Education*, *16*(1), 39. https://doi.org/10.1186/s41239-019-0171-0

Zhao, Y., & Watterston, J. (2021). The changes we need: Education post COVID-19. *Journal of Educational Change*, *22*(1), 3–12. https://doi.org/10.1007/s10833-021-09417-3

15

Technology That Listens

"We're talking about video games that glorify violence and teach children to enjoy inflicting the most gruesome forms of cruelty imaginable."
Senator Joseph Lieberman, Committee on Governmental Affairs Hearing, December 9, 1993

At least half of adults in a 2025 global survey described artificial intelligence (AI) as a major societal problem, and women were more than twice as likely as men to express pessimism (Seismic, 2025). This baseline of distrust illustrates how fear-driven narratives dominate public discourse, particularly around new technologies in education. Public discourse around educational technology often centers on skepticism and misrepresentation, overshadowing the tangible benefits of equitable access, personalized instruction, and student agency. Headlines warn of attention deficits, screen addiction, and AI replacing teachers, yet rarely highlight stories of increased access, enhanced engagement, or student empowerment. What follows is a counternarrative.

Rather than dismissing public concerns, it recognizes their roots in legitimate uncertainty. It also urges a shift from fear to possibility, from reactive judgment to proactive leadership. Educators, families, and policymakers must become the voice for a more accurate,

DOI: 10.4324/9781003739050-20

aspirational vision for educational technology, one grounded in evidence, equity, and empathy.

History reminds us that public perception is not fixed. In the 1990s, video games were cast as threats to childhood development and blamed for moral decline. Today, game-based learning is a recognized instructional strategy, and esports teams are part of many school systems. What changed was not just the technology; it was the narrative.

The goal of the counternarrative is not to silence critique, but to elevate nuance, encourage dialogue, and reclaim the narrative. If we want students to thrive in a digitally mediated world, we must model what responsible, creative, and human-centered technology use looks like in schools. We risk missing the moment if we do not act with clarity, purpose, and resolve.

Adult Roles in the EdTech Conversation

Media literacy is not a student-only competency. It is a shared responsibility among families, educators, and communities. Parents and educators must evaluate public narratives about educational technology and AI with care and evidence. Research shows that emotionally charged reporting without empirical grounding can drive restrictive policies and public backlash (Livingstone & Blum-Ross, 2020). These dynamics intersect with social modeling. Children form norms by observing adults, not only through direct instruction.

Children learn courtesy at the dinner table and empathy by watching adults extend everyday kindness. They also learn how to engage online by watching caregivers. Social platforms and comment threads often display sarcasm, hostility, and misinformation from adults who should model responsible discourse. These behaviors conflict with school norms of respect, empathy, and critical thinking, and the effects are educational and cultural.

Adolescents frequently emulate their parents' social media behavior, including tone and engagement patterns (American Psychological Association, 2023). This modeling is potent in digital spaces, where children lack mature skills for interpreting nuance and intent. Research on phubbing shows that parental distraction during meaningful interactions correlates with behavior problems and weaker emotional bonds (Roberts & David, 2016). These findings align with social learning theory. Children internalize observed behaviors, especially those of authority figures (Bandura, 1977). When adults engage in hostile or fearful online behavior, children are more likely to mirror these patterns.

Recent coverage often frames AI through alarm and crisis language. Education stories have invoked a panic over cheating and the death of the college essay, which primes fear rather than analysis (Sidorkin, 2025). Experimental and longitudinal evidence shows how threat-forward coverage shapes perceptions and signals early stages of technology panics (Dubèl et al., 2025). High-profile commentary reinforced this framing, including an Atlantic feature that characterizes contemporary schooling as destabilized by the rapid introduction of artifical intelligence (Beres, 2025). Policy discourse has echoed these cues, although election-focused evidence reviews recommend restraint and document gaps between predictions and measured outcomes (Simon & Altay, 2025). Even technology leaders describe parts of the debate as a moral panic that cycles between pessimism and hype (Milmo et al., 2023). Fear is unevenly distributed. Women report higher concern about AI than men, which shapes family and community conversations and underscores the need to reframe toward equity and empowerment (Seismic, 2025).

Schools can counter these trends by building adult capacity alongside students. Districts can offer family workshops, educator institutes, and asynchronous modules that clarify key distinctions in technology use. Adults need to differentiate passive consumption from active creation. Watching auto-played videos is passive. Producing a digital portfolio or engaging with adaptive platforms for feedback is intentional learning. Adults also need help interpreting usage data. Increases in screen time can reflect expanded access to collaboration and formative assessment, not misuse.

Clear guidance on healthy versus problematic digital behavior is essential. Healthy engagement includes collaboration, creativity, curiosity, and self-regulation. Warning signs include social withdrawal, avoidance of offline activities, emotional distress, or escalating conflict over device use. Co-engagement is a proven strategy.

When adults sit with children, ask reflective questions, and narrate problem solving, they model productive digital habits, strengthen metacognition, and reinforce social connection.

These efforts promote shared understanding and reduce reactionary responses to technology. They also strengthen home–school partnerships by positioning families and educators as co-stewards of digital development (Chaudron et al., 2018). Society would not expect a child to navigate complex public spaces without supervision. Children should not be expected to navigate digital environments without modeled behavior, scaffolding, and support.

Prioritizing media literacy and adult co-engagement shifts public conversation from fear to evidence. It advances equity and prepares students to participate critically and ethically in a digital society.

Advocacy Strategies for Responsible Tech Use

School and district leaders have an ethical and professional responsibility to advocate for responsible, student-centered technology use that aligns with developmental research and instructional best practices. Many parents, educators, and even administrators are still developing the knowledge and skills necessary to navigate new digital tools and environments. In several cases, students and teachers already demonstrate greater proficiency with these tools than those making critical policy decisions. Recognizing this reality, educational leaders must intentionally create structured opportunities for capacity building and embrace the value of shared growth within a rapidly evolving digital ecosystem.

Advocacy for educational technology requires more than defending device rollouts or promoting isolated initiatives. It involves meaningful community engagement, informed policy literacy, and intentional narrative framing. Hosting public forums where students and teachers share firsthand experiences is one approach to grounding discussions in lived realities. For example, students can describe how AI tools support multilingual learning, while educators explain how digital portfolios foster agency and self-reflection.

These exchanges foster empathy and understanding by elevating authentic classroom perspectives and counteracting abstract fears.

Clear use policies are another critical component of effective advocacy. Rather than focusing solely on device regulations or access rules, districts can frame technology policies around instructional goals. For instance, policies might highlight how Chromebooks are used to advance Universal Design for Learning principles, underscoring that technology serves as a scaffold for high-quality teaching rather than a substitute for pedagogical expertise. This reframing helps communities understand that technology, when guided by intentional instructional design, is a tool for inclusion and differentiation.

Community partnerships extend the reach of responsible technology use beyond school walls. Collaborations with local libraries, museums, or nonprofit organizations can help address persistent access gaps. For example, schools might work with public libraries to provide internet hotspots for family checkout or co-develop digital literacy programs targeting caregivers and community members. These partnerships reinforce a shared commitment to equity and position schools as hubs of community learning and connection.

Leveraging state and federal policy opportunities is also essential for securing long-term investment. Strategic alignment between district technology plans and external funding sources, such as digital equity grants, can help advance infrastructure improvements, expand professional development, and ensure sustainability beyond temporary funding cycles (Means et al., 2021). Advocacy in this context requires an understanding of both local needs and broader policy landscapes, ensuring that districts are not only consumers of resources but also active shapers of policy implementation.

Importantly, advocacy must resist calls for blanket device bans or overly restrictive policies that often reflect adult discomfort rather than evidence-based, student-centered design. Möhler et al. (2023) found that restrictive technology policies in schools frequently mirror adult anxieties rather than addressing student developmental needs, and that such policies can hinder the development of digital literacy, critical thinking, and media engagement skills. Rather than shielding students from technology, schools should guide them through it by equipping them with the knowledge and dispositions needed to navigate, question, and create within digital spaces.

Defining responsible technology use requires contextual and pedagogical clarity. Within the Futures Ready Framework, this includes commitments to student agency, inclusive access, mastery through personalization, adaptability for future readiness, empathy-driven connections, and ethical integration. Developing AI literacy curricula is one example of operationalizing these commitments. Such curricula should teach students how to evaluate algorithmic outputs, understand the ethical implications of machine learning, and recognize the cross-disciplinary impacts of intelligent systems. AI education must be intentionally embedded across all content areas, from humanities to mathematics, to prepare students for a world where intelligent systems shape every sector.

Professional development plays a parallel role by linking technology integration to instructional outcomes and reinforcing Universal Design for Learning strategies. Ongoing educator learning is essential to ensure that technology is not simply layered onto existing practices but meaningfully reshapes how learning is designed and delivered.

Adult–student co-engagement, particularly in early grades, provides another strategy for reinforcing responsible technology use. For example, when a caregiver or teacher sits alongside a first-grade student during a tablet-based reading activity, asks reflective questions, and facilitates discussion, they not only build digital literacy but also strengthen the social-emotional connections that support learning. These shared experiences signal that technology is a tool for collaboration and inquiry, not isolation or passive consumption.

Creating intentional learning spaces that integrate both analog and digital engagement further reinforces this approach. These spaces can be embedded within advisory periods, flexible seating areas, or after-school digital platforms, underscoring that meaningful learning is not confined to specific locations or times. Flexibility of this kind requires intentional design, particularly within the structural and temporal constraints of public education. It reflects a broader commitment to adaptability and inclusion, demonstrating that innovation is possible even within traditional systems when leaders approach their work with purpose and vision.

Integrating student-led audits of digital tools adds an important layer of participatory assessment. In these audits, students and educators evaluate the relevance, accessibility, and equity implications of digital platforms used in their classrooms. This process is especially significant when considering generational differences in digital habits. For example, a 2023 study by Ofcom found that 77 percent of adults aged 65 and older identify Facebook as their primary social media platform, while only 9 percent of users aged 16–24 report the same, favoring platforms such as TikTok and Snapchat. Such disparities highlight that older adults often approach digital conversations from different experiential baselines than students. Student-led audits can help uncover these differences, enabling school leaders to develop policies and strategies that reflect diverse proficiencies and preferences.

Ultimately, technology use in schools must align with learning goals, developmental needs, and community values. When students and educators are empowered to critically assess and shape the tools they use, technology becomes a shared instrument for advancing learning, agency, and inclusion. This orientation also sets the foundation for understanding how intentional storytelling can further reinforce these values and help shift the broader public narrative away from skepticism and toward thoughtful celebration of what technology can achieve in education.

Telling the Success Stories of AI-Enhanced Learning

Telling the success stories of AI-enhanced learning is one of the most underutilized strategies for shaping public opinion. Case studies, student testimonials, and authentic classroom examples humanize the role of AI and challenge deficit-focused narratives that dominate media and policy discussions. Despite the continuous innovation happening in classrooms across the United States, schools often struggle to communicate these successes effectively. Throughout my career, I have observed thousands of lessons, projects, and activities that reflect pedagogical expertise, creativity, and bold experimentation moments that could shift public perceptions of educational technology if they were visible beyond the school walls. Yet schools are not structured like technology companies or media organizations. They rarely have dedicated communications teams focused on identifying, curating, and sharing success stories with external audiences. Even when there is interest in doing so, school leaders often encounter the expectation that storytelling efforts must demonstrate a direct link to improvements on standardized test measures. Added to these pressures are layers of security protocols, rigid pacing guides, and fragmented school schedules, which make it difficult to invite the public into classrooms, whether in person or virtually. These structural constraints limit the visibility of innovation, even as it unfolds every day in classrooms across the country.

In contrast, when students perform in a theater production or compete in an athletic event, the community shows up. Gymnasiums and auditoriums are filled with families and neighbors eager to witness student effort, talent, and teamwork. Victories are celebrated, losses are shared, and the work of students becomes a source of community pride. Public support for athletic programs, for example, is rarely driven solely by the scoreboard; it emerges from the visibility of the experience and the emotional connection that comes from being invited to witness it. That visibility generates buy-in.

I remember early in my administrative career, during a particularly difficult budget season, when the administrative team was facing a projected percent increase well above what the town was prepared to support, which meant asking the town's citizens for additional funding. One of the quickest ways to galvanize public support in this particular community was to float the idea that, in order to meet the school department's budget requirements, the music program would be cut. During budget conversations with administrators and school committee members, this proposal had become a kind of annual ritual in this suburban town. The moment the community learned of the suggestion to eliminate the music department, it mobilized. Parents, alumni, and students flooded school committee meetings with testimonials, musical performances, and heartfelt pleas to protect the program. Year after year, the program was preserved, not only because of its intrinsic educational value, but because the community had seen it, heard it, and felt its impact. That kind of visibility is often missing from conversations about educational technology. This absence is not neutral.

When schools fail to document and share their innovation, they leave the narrative open to those who define education by its failures rather than its possibilities.

Educational technology, particularly AI, frequently lacks the visibility necessary to build public trust and support. Without intentional storytelling, perceptions are shaped by fear, misinformation, and the absence of a clear, shared narrative. Research supports the importance of making innovation visible. Darling-Hammond et al. (2022) note that public support is more likely when communities understand both the outcomes and the processes behind educational change. Storytelling serves as a bridge, making the intangible more tangible and accessible.

This can be understood by considering how physical security systems function. Reinforced doors and visible security measures are immediately understood by the public, and when a school faces a break-in, the response is swift because the threat is concrete and observable. In contrast, digital threats such as data breaches or system intrusions are invisible to most, even though they pose real risks. Firewalls and cybersecurity protocols are critical but rarely elicit public urgency or support because their benefits are hidden from view. The same dynamic applies to digital learning. Without visibility, innovation remains abstract. School boards frequently ask why educational technology investments are necessary and whether they yield meaningful returns. These doubts are amplified when the benefits are not clearly communicated or demonstrated. Storytelling offers the public something they can see, understand, and connect with, helping to justify investment by illustrating value and impact.

Reclaiming the narrative around enhanced learning is not a marketing exercise; it is a fundamental responsibility of educational leadership. When schools share how innovative practices expand access, personalize instruction, or support multilingual learners, they reshape the conversation about technology in education. For instance, a middle school in western Massachusetts has used Magic School AI to generate translated summaries of science lessons for English language learners, leading to higher student comprehension and improved family engagement. In another example, a high school government class has used Khanmigo to simulate civic debates, helping students strengthen their arguments and develop critical thinking skills. These tools did not replace teachers; they expanded the learning experience and enriched instructional practice.

Such examples can be found in nearly every district, but they often remain invisible outside of school buildings. To address this, schools should develop coordinated strategies to share innovation more intentionally. Districts can benefit from identifying staff who focus on curating and communicating stories of meaningful digital learning and instructional improvement, much like brand journalists or content strategists do in other sectors. Storytelling should adapt to the platforms families and community members already use, whether through short videos, podcasts, or social media, rather than relying solely on internal newsletters or static reports. Sharing these examples with school boards and local media can demonstrate instructional value, strengthen public understanding of return on investment, and build credibility. Celebrating innovation within the school community through staff recognitions, student spotlights, or reflective events can further embed storytelling into the culture of teaching and learning. Partnerships with educational nonprofits, research institutions, or local organizations can help amplify these stories and connect local innovation to broader policy and practice networks. Providing optional professional learning opportunities for educators and student leaders in digital storytelling, communication strategy, and media literacy can build long-term capacity without imposing undue mandates on already busy staff.

By sharing their stories, schools shift public discourse away from skepticism and toward possibility. They affirm what educators already know: remarkable and transformative things happen every day. The public deserves the opportunity to see them.

From Skepticism to Strategy

The debate over screen time is ultimately a debate about values. It reflects how society views students, how learning is defined, and how schools prepare young people for the world they are already navigating. At its core, it is about whether educational systems choose to lead with vision or default to retreat.

Throughout this chapter, the argument has moved beyond fear-based narratives to examine generational tensions and to demonstrate how educational technology can serve as a lever for equity, inclusion, and deeper learning. The call has been for a shift away from restrictive control and toward responsible empowerment, emphasizing the importance of moving from isolated policy decisions to coordinated and strategic community engagement.

This is not an argument for the uncritical embrace of technology. Rather, it is a call to move beyond simplistic and binary thinking and toward a more informed, inclusive, and learner-centered approach. Public perception will not shift merely because school leaders want it to. It will shift because families witness growth in their children's confidence and competence. It will shift because school boards hear credible, measurable outcomes. It will shift because teachers feel supported and have the agency to innovate. Most importantly, it will shift because students are equipped to contribute meaningfully to the digital world, not merely to consume within it.

Despite widespread skepticism, adoption trends tell another story. By mid-2025, ChatGPT reached more than 700 million weekly active users, with approximately 10 percent of all messages involving tutoring or teaching (Chatterji et al., 2025). This demonstrates that while fears dominate headlines, learners are already using AI to support problem-solving, feedback, and creativity. Schools that ignore this reality risk widening the gap between public perception and student practice. To earn public trust, schools must make digital learning visible, relatable, and demonstrably valuable. They must showcase innovation with the same intentionality and visibility given to concerts, athletic events, and public performances. When the community sees value, it advocates. When the community sees impact, it invests. When the community believes in what it sees, it becomes an active participant in the effort.

Reframing the screen-time debate is not about offering simplistic reassurance. It is about offering a more complete truth: when implemented thoughtfully, equitably, and ethically, technology has the capacity to expand opportunity, deepen student engagement, and strengthen the teaching profession. The central danger is not that students are using devices. The central danger is that adults fail to prepare them to use those devices with skill, purpose, and integrity.

References

American Psychological Association. (2023). *Health advisory on social media use in adolescence.* American Psychological Association. https://www.apa.org/topics/social-media-internet/health-advisory-adolescent-social-media-use

Bandura, A. (1977). *Social learning theory.* Prentice Hall.

Beres, D. (2025, August 29). AI has broken high school and college. *The Atlantic.* https://www.theatlantic.com/newsletters/archive/2025/08/ai-high-school-college/684057/

Chatterji, A., Cunningham, T., Deming, D. J., Hitzig, Z., Ong, C., Shan, C. Y., & Wadman, K. (2025). *How people use ChatGPT* (Working Paper No. 34255). National Bureau of Economic Research. https://doi.org/10.3386/w34255

Chaudron, S., Di Gioia, R., & Gemo, M. (2018). *Young children (0–8) and digital technology: A qualitative study across Europe.* Publications Office of the European Union. https://doi.org/10.2760/294383

Darling-Hammond, L., Hyler, M. E., & Gardner, M. (2022). *Effective teacher professional development.* Learning Policy Institute. https://learningpolicyinstitute.org/product/effective-teacher-professional-development-report

Dubèl, R., Wolfers, L., Jonkman, J., Van Berlo, Z., & Azrout, R. (2025). The next media-fueled moral technology panic? News media's and audience's views on ChatGPT. *AI & Society.* https://doi.org/10.1007/s00146-025-02417-4

Lieberman, J. (1993, December 9). *Violent video games: Hearing before the committee on governmental affairs, United States Senate, 103rd Congress, 1st session* [Hearing]. US Government Printing Office. https://catalog.hathitrust.org/Record/002764888

Livingstone, S., & Blum-Ross, A. (2020). *Parenting for a digital future: How hopes and fears about technology shape children's lives.* Oxford University Press.

Means, B., Neisler, J., & Langer Research Associates. (2021). *Digital learning and technology integration in the time of COVID-19.* Digital Promise. https://

digitalpromise.org/wp-content/uploads/2021/09/digital-learning-technology-integration-covid-19.pdf

Milmo, D., Stacey, K., & Farah, H. (2023, October 31). Nick Clegg compares AI clamour to "moral panic" in 80s over video games. *The Guardian*. https://www.theguardian.com/technology/2023/nov/01/nick-clegg-ai-clamour-similar-moral-panic-video-games

Möhler, E., Trautwein, U., & Lüdtke, O. (2023). School technology policies: The role of adult anxieties and student needs. *Computers & Education, 191*, Article 104659. https://doi.org/10.1016/j.compedu.2022.104659

Ofcom. (2023). *Online nation 2023 report*. Ofcom. https://www.ofcom.org.uk/research-and-data/media-literacy-research/online-nation

Roberts, J. A., & David, M. E. (2016). My life has become a major distraction from my cell phone: Partner phubbing and relationship satisfaction among romantic partners. *Computers in Human Behavior, 54*, 134–141. https://doi.org/10.1016/j.chb.2015.07.058

Seismic. (2025). *On the razor's edge: Public attitudes toward AI in 2025*. Seismic. https://report2025.seismic.org/media/documents/On_the_Razors_Edge_Seismic_Report_2025.pdf

Sidorkin, A. M. (2025). *AI in education in the media: Moral panic and pushback (2022–2025)*. AI-EDU. https://journals.calstate.edu/ai-edu/article/view/5460

Simon, F. M., & Altay, S. (2025, July 7). *Do not panic (yet): Assessing the evidence and discourse around generative AI and elections*. Knight First Amendment Institute at Columbia University. https://knightcolumbia.org/content/dont-panic-yet-assessing-the-evidence-and-discourse-around-generative-ai-and-elections

Section 6

A Roadmap for Transformation

From Vision to Systemic Change

Public education stands at a pivotal inflection point. Dede argues that leaders must rethink core assumptions, redesign the system, and use technology to implement personalized learning that ensures appropriate progress for every student (Dede, 2020). The central question is no longer whether schools should change, but whether they can evolve swiftly, coherently, and deliberately enough to meet the demands of a volatile, inequitable, and technologically complex world. This transformation is not incremental. It is existential. Superficial innovation will not suffice. What is required is a fundamental redesign of the institutional architecture of schooling, a task that demands urgent attention and systemic resolve.

This book has outlined the foundational principles necessary for such transformation. What remains is the discipline to implement and the collective will to act. Fullan and Quinn (2016) emphasize that meaningful change depends on deep coherence: the alignment of vision and practice, pedagogy and policy, and institutional structures with community values. Without this coherence, reform efforts risk fragmentation, inequity, and unsustainable outcomes.

Public education functions as a complex adaptive system. With the right approach, it is possible to build a cohesive framework for transformation, one grounded in equity, informed by research, and responsive to real school contexts. Identifying essential preconditions for redesign, including readiness assessments, a shared vision, and systemic alignment, while exploring how districts can prototype change through design-based implementation and iterative evaluation. The discussion then shifts from pilot efforts to system-wide scale, examining how transformation becomes sustainable through aligned leadership, professional learning, fiscal planning, and accountability. This part concludes by presenting a policy blueprint to support large-scale redesign at the local, state, and federal levels.

At the center of this roadmap is a reorientation toward the human dimensions of learning. As Dede (2023) contends, the promise of artificial intelligence (AI) is not to automate instruction but to augment human potential. This includes integrating extended reality (XR) environments that offer immersive, experiential, and collaborative learning. XR allows students to engage with content in sensory-rich, contextually meaningful, and highly personalized ways. These experiences deepen cognitive engagement, promote student agency, and expand access to learning opportunities that traditional classrooms cannot provide. This vision echoes Friedman's (2006) argument in *The World Is Flat 2.0*, where global collaboration, real-time information access, and borderless communication are not optional aspirations but essential capacities.

Shifting from automation to augmentation requires more than technical capacity. It demands a cultural shift that centers the learner. This transition also calls for dismantling outdated structures that constrain learning, such as the rigid separation of disciplines. In a world defined by interdisciplinary challenges, schools must embrace integrated, inquiry-based learning that mirrors how knowledge is applied beyond the school context. Subject-area expertise remains vital, but it must be situated within authentic, collaborative learning environments that prioritize relevance, adaptability, and intellectual agility.

This cultural shift must also center educators. As Darling-Hammond (2017) and Mehta and Fine (2019) argue, sustainable change depends on professional learning, distributed leadership, and adaptive school cultures. Educators must be positioned as co-designers of transformation, not passive implementers of externally imposed mandates. A learning institution that evolves is one that invests deeply in its people. Schools that cultivate adaptive, equity-driven cultures are far more likely to sustain meaningful change over time.

The redefinition of educational purpose must extend to the role of schools within society. Public schools are no longer solely academic institutions. They function as civic infrastructure: they provide nutrition, healthcare, mental health services, internet access, and crisis response. In many communities, particularly those affected by disinvestment or geographic isolation, the public school is the most stable and accessible public institution. Yet governance, funding, and evaluation systems continue to rely on outdated metrics rooted in industrial-era models. As Warren and Mapp (2011) emphasize, authentic community partnerships must be embedded into the design of education, not treated as peripheral add-ons.

Authentic transformation requires reclassifying schools as foundational institutions within a knowledge-based, interconnected society. This transformation demands revisiting the assumptions that shape education policy, funding, and accountability systems. Emerging technologies such as XR and AI have the potential to help realize this vision, but only if institutional design evolves in tandem.

Redesign must be learner-centered and future-ready. Zhao (2012) reminds us that transformation begins and ends with the student experience. It is not defined by devices or infrastructure, but by the extent to which learners are empowered to thrive. Personalized pathways, student agency, and contextual relevance must replace one-size-fits-all models. XR and AI are most powerful when they reinforce these priorities and deepen the relational core of teaching and learning.

This part does not offer abstract visioning. It presents an actionable, research-informed blueprint for transformation. Building a learner-centered, AI-enhanced, XR-enabled public education system is not the responsibility of individual educators, technologists, or policymakers in isolation. It is a collective undertaking that requires trust, sustained leadership, and coordinated action across governance levels and stakeholder groups. Without structural alignment and shared purpose, even the most promising tools will fall short of their potential.

The ideas advanced here are not theoretical or speculative. They are grounded in decades of research, practitioner wisdom, and community-driven innovation. They draw from work already underway in classrooms, schools, and districts across the country. Rather than prescribing a fixed sequence of reforms, this roadmap identifies essential conditions and adaptable design principles that can be applied across diverse local contexts. It invites leaders and decision-makers to rethink educational systems with clarity, coherence, and an uncompromising commitment to equity.

This book does not present a conclusion. It serves as an entry point into a larger and more urgent conversation about what public education must become. Its purpose is to support educators, leaders, families, and policymakers in asking sharper, more strategic questions; in challenging legacy structures; and in advancing a shared vision for transformative change. The work ahead is neither linear nor uniform. Redesign is iterative and adaptive, shaped by the lived realities of those within the system.

If these ideas challenge conventional assumptions, they are intended to. Clinging to outdated models has caused lasting harm, particularly for students who have been historically marginalized or underserved. The time for cautious reform has passed. What lies ahead is not a minor evolution but a fundamental redesign of educational purpose, structure, and practice. The task is complex, but it is both possible and essential.

References

Darling-Hammond, L. (2017). *Empowered educators: How high-performing systems shape teaching quality around the world.* Jossey-Bass.

Dede, C. (2020, January 28). *The 60-Year Curriculum: Rethinking the purpose of schooling* [Podcast episode]. In *Leading Learning.* https://leadinglearning.com/episode-223-60-year-curriculum-chris-dede

Dede, C. (2023, February 9). *Educating in a world of artificial intelligence* [EdCast audio interview]. Harvard Graduate School of Education. https://www.gse.harvard.edu/ideas/edcast/23/02/educating-world-artificial-intelligence

Friedman, T. L. (2006). *The world is flat: A brief history of the twenty-first century* (Updated and expanded ed.). Farrar, Straus and Giroux.

Fullan, M., & Quinn, J. (2016). *Coherence: The right drivers in action for schools, districts, and systems.* Corwin Press.

Mehta, J., & Fine, S. (2019). *In search of deeper learning: The quest to remake the American high school.* Harvard Education Press.

Warren, M. R., & Mapp, K. L. (2011). *A match on dry grass: Community organizing as a catalyst for school reform.* Oxford University Press.

Zhao, Y. (2012). *World class learners: Educating creative and entrepreneurial students.* Corwin Press.

16

Beyond Readiness

Designing the Foundations of Transformational Education

A middle 21st-century education system cannot rest on 20th-century assumptions. Before schools can pursue transformation through artificial intelligence (AI), extended reality (XR), or any other emerging innovation, including the shift from brick-and-mortar instruction to immersive virtual environments, they must confront a deeper truth: the current system is not functioning as intended. The challenge is not primarily technological. It is structural and conceptual. As long as public education remains tethered to inherited models, rigid schedules, and outdated definitions of success, even the most advanced tools will replicate old patterns rather than enable true transformation (Mehta & Fine, 2019).

Redesign begins by reexamining foundational beliefs. What is the purpose of school? Whose needs does it serve? What does meaningful learning look like in a world shaped by personalization, automation, and civic fragmentation? As Prince et al. (2017) contend, "getting better at what we already do within the systems we already have will never fundamentally change who we are or how we think." The danger is not a lack of technology, but its use to advance outdated paradigms rather than enable meaningful transformation (Zhao, 2012). Redesign must begin by breaking from inherited assumptions, not digitizing them. This is not a system upgrade. It is a reconstruction from first principles.

Redefining Meaningful Transformation

Readiness must go beyond compliance. Districts are often urged to prepare for innovation by conducting device audits, upgrading bandwidth, or offering professional development. These technical steps, while necessary, are not sufficient. A district can meet every infrastructure benchmark yet remain tethered to instructional models built on fixed schedules, Carnegie units, and deficit-based interventions. These legacy systems preserve institutional inertia (Darling-Hammond, 2017; Zhao, 2012).

State and district leaders must shift from checklist-based preparation to a deeper evaluation of whether their systems are culturally, structurally, and pedagogically positioned for meaningful change. Readiness should be defined by the willingness to abandon outdated norms and commit to redesign rooted in purpose, not procedure. This requires coordinated, sustained action, not rhetorical endorsement.

A critical first step is redefining success. For decades, student achievement has been reduced to standardized test scores and pacing compliance. These indicators reflect institutional convenience, not authentic learning. Future-ready systems must incorporate broader measures, including collaboration, creativity, civic participation, digital fluency, problem-solving, and futures literacy. State models such as the Massachusetts Portrait of a Graduate and California's Local Control and Accountability Plan (LCAP) demonstrate how holistic competencies can be embedded into policy. At the district level, performance-based assessments, graduate profiles, and digital portfolios offer more accurate and equitable evaluations of student growth.

Prioritizing competency over compliance demands structural change. Seat time, fixed pacing, and one-size-fits-all curricula reward procedural conformity. Flexible pathways must replace rigid timelines, allowing students to demonstrate mastery at their own pace. This shift requires investments in formative assessment systems, differentiated instruction, and adaptive learning environments. States must revise regulations that define learning by instructional hours rather than learning outcomes. The Aurora Institute (2018) has outlined specific policy levers to support this shift.

Decentralizing control is equally important. Traditional governance structures center institutional preservation and adult decision-making. In contrast, transformative models elevate student agency. Students should co-design instructional pathways, provide feedback, and shape learning environments. This shift is not symbolic. It requires authentic collaboration and structural commitment. State agencies can support this work by embedding student voice into school improvement processes, innovation grants, and accreditation criteria. As DePaoli et al. (2023) demonstrate, student-centered systems strengthen engagement and long-term motivation.

Transformation also depends on transparent, inclusive stakeholder engagement. Districts must foster trust through clear communication and responsive two-way dialogue. Families, educators, students, and community partners must be invited into the process, not merely informed after decisions are made. This is not public relations. It is democratic governance. Place-based and culturally sustaining learning models deepen this work by connecting school redesign to local histories, environmental challenges, and community assets, ensuring that transformation is meaningful within its social and geographic context.

Leadership coherence is essential. Systems cannot rely on isolated innovation or individual champions. Superintendents, school boards, principals, and central office staff must align around a shared vision and theory of action. Capacity-building in change management, distributed leadership, and sustained implementation must be prioritized to maintain momentum in the face of resistance or disruption. Without explicit change leadership strategies, even promising reforms can stall.

System alignment is a prerequisite. Instructional, operational, and technology teams must work collaboratively. Redesign efforts often fail when departments operate in silos. Effective transformation requires coordinated implementation plans, structured pilot processes, embedded feedback loops, and sustainable funding models. Innovation cannot depend on short-term grants or exceptional leaders. It requires reliable resource allocation that supports long-term system change.

Workforce design must also evolve. Teachers cannot shoulder the demands of transformation without structural change.

Personalized, technology-enhanced instruction requires new roles: learning designers, digital specialists, instructional coaches, data analysts, and wellness coordinators. These roles must be integrated into the system, not added to existing teaching loads. Job responsibilities should be clearly defined, supported with training and time, and embedded into district staffing structures. Equally important, educator well-being must be prioritized, recognizing that psychological safety, manageable workloads, and professional respect are prerequisites for innovation to take hold.

Ultimately, readiness is not a checklist. It is a values-based commitment to systemic redesign. Districts and state agencies must examine whether their assumptions still serve students in a rapidly changing world. This is philosophical, structural, and ethical work. It must come first.

Reframing the Foundation: Key Shifts for Redesign

A future-ready education system cannot be built on outdated notions of time, learning, governance, or success. Transformation demands more than adopting new technologies or launching short-term initiatives. It requires redefining the purpose, power structures, and priorities of public education. The foundation must be rebuilt around what students need to thrive in a rapidly evolving and interconnected world.

This begins with a fundamental redefinition of purpose. Public education must move beyond test preparation and content delivery. Its mission is to develop capable, ethical learners who can adapt, collaborate, and lead across local and global contexts. Systems built around compliance and standardization cannot fulfill that mission.

Student agency must be central. Learners should have a voice in determining what, how, and why they learn. Co-created pathways, inclusive decision-making structures, and feedback mechanisms are essential. These approaches increase student engagement, strengthen relevance, and improve outcomes.

Structural flexibility is also necessary. Traditional systems that rely on seat time and rigid pacing limit deep learning. Competency-based progressions allow students to demonstrate mastery in ways that honor individual pace and readiness. This requires performance assessments, flexible scheduling, and policy reform that values learning over logistics.

Equity must be designed into the system, not retrofitted. Universal Design for Learning (UDL), multilingual supports, broadband access, and assistive technology must be embedded from the start. These tools enable full participation for students with disabilities, multilingual learners, and those navigating trauma or systemic barriers.

Emotional and relational safety is foundational. Learning requires psychological security, trust, and belonging. Districts must invest in advisory systems, restorative practices, and culturally responsive pedagogy that center connection and inclusion. Educator well-being must be addressed alongside student well-being to build the human infrastructure necessary for sustained change.

The workforce must be reimagined. Teachers alone cannot be responsible for leading innovation. Districts need specialized roles, such as learning designers and digital learning specialists, to support and sustain transformation. Redesign must be a team effort, not an individual burden.

Learning must reconnect with the world beyond school. Students need opportunities to engage with their communities, explore real-world problems, and develop career-connected competencies. Partnerships with civic institutions, local organizations, and employers strengthen relevance and create more inclusive, purpose-driven curricula.

Policy structures must evolve. Legacy regulations restrict flexibility and innovation. Federal and state agencies must shift from rigid standardization to enabling frameworks that support district-led redesign. Accountability, funding, and accreditation systems must align with student-centered goals, local autonomy, and ethical guidelines that safeguard privacy, data security, and algorithmic fairness. Emerging technologies like AI and XR must be governed by transparent ethical standards that prioritize human judgment, creativity, and connection.

Finally, the system must be built with intergenerational and global vision. Schools must prepare students for future challenges such as climate change, civic unrest, technological acceleration, and geopolitical uncertainty. Futures literacy, ethical reasoning, and collective responsibility are not optional competencies. They are essential.

Reframing the foundation of education requires asking not only what the system delivers, but what kind of future it prepares students to shape. Without this shift, the next generation will be left navigating 21st-century realities in structures built for a 20th-century world.

Tangible Levers for Redesign

Redesign does not begin with declarations. It begins with deliberate action. Tangible levers provide entry points for transformation by modeling what new systems could look like within the constraints of existing ones. These are not procedural fixes or surface-level strategies. They are tactical openings, opportunities to disrupt legacy practices while signaling a commitment to deeper systemic change.

One such entry point is the use of graduate profile redesign workshops. Many districts have adopted a Portrait of a Graduate, yet few revisit it once finalized. Facilitating collaborative workshops with students, educators, and families to reexamine the portrait as a living document shifts the conversation from compliance to purpose. This reflection must be followed by an honest question: Are learning experiences being designed to produce the outcomes described in the profile, or has it become symbolic rather than operational?

Time structures also present an opportunity for redesign. Conducting a schoolwide time audit and piloting revised schedules, such as advisory blocks, interdisciplinary learning periods, or flex-time for student-led projects, can illuminate how much of the school day reinforces procedural efficiency over learning relevance. These pilots invite educators and leaders to consider how much time is spent in lecture versus collaboration, and whether the calendar reflects student-centered priorities or institutional convenience.

Districts can also introduce AI-infused instructional design sprints to help educators explore how artificial intelligence might support formative assessment, student agency, and differentiated feedback. For example, instructional teams might co-design a unit that integrates generative tools for real-time reflection, goal setting, or peer review. Rather than using AI to digitize traditional instruction, these design sprints challenge teams to ask whether technology is being used to replicate outdated systems or to fundamentally reimagine them (CoSN, 2023).

The governance structure of public schools offers another critical lever. Too often, transformation efforts are designed by adults for students. Stakeholder co-design forums offer a pathway to reverse that trend. By engaging students, families, and educators in structured, generative dialogues, such as design studios or policy prototyping sessions, districts can reposition their communities as architects of the future. These sessions must center a core question: What would school look like if it were built around student purpose rather than institutional tradition?

In tandem, districts must reexamine what counts as evidence of learning. Replacing one unit of traditional instruction with a performance-based assessment, such as an exhibition, portfolio defense, or community-connected project, demonstrates what mastery-based learning can look like in practice. Models from networks like the New York Performance Standards Consortium and Envision Learning Partners offer scalable examples of this work, where students are asked to apply knowledge, not just recall it.

Equity-centered redesign also requires tangible audits of access. Districts can conduct inclusive design walkthroughs using UDL frameworks to evaluate the variability of learner needs across classrooms. Additionally, mapping broadband access, device distribution, and digital tool usage across schools helps identify structural gaps that cannot be addressed through surface-level parity. Connectivity must be treated as a right, not a variable resource distributed by zip code.

Finally, systemic redesign depends on whether technology integration serves personalization, equity, and ethical responsibility. The CoSN K–12 Artificial Intelligence (AI) Readiness Checklist provides one reflective tool to interrogate whether AI implementation is reinforcing traditional models or enabling new ones (CoSN, 2023). Similarly, districts can use tools such as LearnPlatform or Project Unicorn's Interoperability Rubric to evaluate whether their digital ecosystems support secure data sharing, real-time decision-making, and personalized learning at scale.

Tangible levers matter because they make the abstract actionable. They offer proof points that transformation is not theoretical. It is possible, practical, and already underway. When schools use these tools to challenge assumptions, engage communities, and pilot redesigned systems, they not only model what is possible but also create momentum toward what is necessary.

From Rethinking to Rebuilding: The Next Steps

Redesign begins beneath the surface. It is not a program to adopt or a technology to implement. It is a mindset shift that reorients every element of the system toward student purpose, inclusive access, and meaningful learning. The tangible levers outlined here are not end goals. They are entry points. Each one represents a deliberate disruption that illustrates what becomes possible when legacy constraints are no longer treated as inevitable.

This is foundational work, not in the sense of preparatory planning, but in the literal sense of construction. The assumptions embedded in public education about time, control, capacity, and success are not neutral. They reflect specific historical and cultural design choices. For example, the traditional 180-day school calendar with a long summer vacation originated from agricultural models that no longer reflect the realities of contemporary families or the developmental needs of students. Likewise, the widespread practice of starting school at 7:30 a.m., particularly for adolescents, persists despite extensive research showing that later start times are associated with improved sleep, academic performance, and mental health among teens (Wheaton et al., 2015). These are not minor operational details; they are institutional decisions with significant implications for equity, well-being, and learning outcomes.

To create something different, districts must name these embedded assumptions, investigate their origins, and replace them with structures that reflect what learners need today and, in the decades, to come. True readiness is not defined by bandwidth, devices, or alignment with strategic plans. It is defined by whether leaders, educators, and communities are prepared to question the ground they stand on, manage the complexity of change, and commit to constructing something stronger, more ethical, and more globally relevant in its place.

Now the real work begins. Vision alone does not transform systems. It must be translated into structures capable of sustaining meaningful change. The shift from reflection to redesign, from philosophical clarity to practical implementation, requires intention, iteration, change leadership, and the willingness to build even as the learning process continues. We reframed the foundation; now marks the beginning of pouring the first concrete, constructing a new model designed to support the learning ecosystems that students need and deserve.

References

Aurora Institute. (2018). *Moving toward mastery: Growing, developing, and sustaining educators for competency-based education*. Aurora Institute. https://www.aurora-institute.org/wp-content/uploads/Moving-Toward-Mastery.pdf

Consortium for School Networking. (2023). *Artificial intelligence (AI) in K–12: A comprehensive guide and readiness checklist*. https://www.cosn.org/wp-content/uploads/2023/03/CoSN-AI-Report-2023-1.pdf

Darling-Hammond, L. (2017). *Empowered educators: How high-performing systems shape teaching quality around the world*. Jossey-Bass.

DePaoli, J. L., Bridgeland, J. M., Balfanz, R., & Atwell, M. (2023). *Building a grad nation: Progress and challenge in raising high school graduation rates*. Civic; Everyone Graduates Center, Johns Hopkins University. https://files.eric.ed.gov/fulltext/ED657516.pdf

Mehta, J., & Fine, S. (2019). *In search of deeper learning: The quest to remake the American high school*. Harvard University Press.

Prince, K., Saveri, A., & Swanson, J. (2017). *The future of learning: Redefining readiness from the inside out*. KnowledgeWorks. https://knowledgeworks.org/resources/redefining-readiness-2/

Wheaton, A. G., Ferro, G. A., & Croft, J. B. (2015). School start times for middle school and high school students: United States, 2011–12 school year. *Morbidity and Mortality Weekly Report, 64*(30), 809–813. https://www.cdc.gov/mmwr/preview/mmwrhtml/mm6430a1.htm

Zhao, Y. (2012). *World-class learners: Educating creative and entrepreneurial students*. Corwin.

17

Transformation by Design

Rethinking How Change Begins

System transformation requires more than new policies or technologies. As Meadows (2008) observed, you cannot impose a system on a system; you have to grow it. Sustainable redesign depends on shifting assumptions about purpose, equity, and accountability while preparing schools to adapt to social, cultural, and technological change.

Every era of educational reform has been marked by calls for transformation, yet the results have often been incremental adjustments rather than systemic redesign. The language of equity, innovation, and personalization is widespread, but the structural conditions that define schools such as time, governance, curriculum, and accountability remain largely unchanged. Many reforms generate temporary improvements but fail to alter the deeper logics of the system.

Transformation cannot be achieved through surface-level strategies or isolated interventions. It requires deliberate efforts to disrupt inherited assumptions, test new structural models, and construct the conditions that allow change to take root. Transformation begins not with sweeping mandates but with purposeful design experiments in authentic contexts, where leaders, educators, and communities commit to rethinking what schools are and what they should become.

The focus is on transformation prototypes, redesign sites, and change labs as vehicles for moving from aspiration to action. The discussion explores why change so often stalls, what redesign sites are designed to accomplish, how core assumptions must be challenged, and which system conditions make lasting innovation possible. Anchored in the Futures Ready Framework, the argument emphasizes how student agency, inclusive access, adaptability, and ethical integration can be embedded into the architecture of public education.

Why Transformation Stalls

Educational systems often announce ambitious reform agendas that emphasize equity, innovation, and personalized learning. Yet most of these initiatives stall before meaningful change reaches classrooms. Research across organizational fields has long documented this pattern, with failure rates of large-scale change efforts often approaching 70 percent (McKinsey & Company, 2025). The central problem is not a lack of vision but the persistence of inherited structures. Schools may articulate new goals, but they continue to operate within logics of time, curriculum, and accountability that remain unchanged.

The distinction between surface-level improvement and deep transformation lies in how institutions approach uncertainty. Improvement strategies assume stability: a literacy program can be layered onto existing schedules, or a new assessment tool can be attached to traditional grading. Transformation requires a different orientation. It demands what McKinsey & Company (2025) describe as operational courage and the willingness to act without full certainty, to test alternatives publicly, and to treat iteration as the expected mode of redesign. In education, this means implementing models in authentic contexts, documenting both outcomes and conditions, and adapting based on evidence and stakeholder feedback.

Reforms fail when leaders mistake vision statements for systemic redesign. Without altering the processes, incentives, and governance structures that shape daily practice, reforms remain symbolic. This cycle produces short-lived initiatives that generate temporary gains but leave underlying systems intact. Redesign, by contrast, requires asking foundational questions about how learning is organized, who holds authority, and what outcomes matter. These shifts align directly with the Futures Ready Framework. Student agency emerges when learners are positioned as co-authors of redesign. Future-ready adaptability becomes visible when schools embrace experimentation under uncertain conditions. Ethical integration ensures that risk-taking remains anchored in justice and responsibility. Transformation stalls when these pillars are absent but accelerates when they guide the work.

From Pilots to Prototypes, Sites, and Labs

For decades, educational reform has leaned heavily on pilot programs. A new schedule might be tested in a single grade, or a new literacy program adopted in one school. These pilots are often useful for identifying implementation barriers and gauging teacher or community support. Yet they are constrained by the very system they operate within. Pilots rarely touch the deeper architecture of schooling. They seldom challenge assumptions about how time is measured, how authority is distributed, or how accountability is defined. As a result, pilots may generate short-term insights but rarely produce transformation at scale.

The language of prototypes, redesign sites, and change labs signals a different intent. A transformation prototype is more than a trial run of an isolated program. It is a deliberate attempt to test a structural assumption, such as whether students can progress by mastery rather than seat time, or whether schedules can be redesigned around extended interdisciplinary blocks. A redesign site becomes the authentic context where such experiments take root. These are not demonstration classrooms meant to showcase best practices but entire schools or networks that are restructured to run on different logics. Within those sites, a change lab provides the collaborative process where students, families, educators, and leaders co-design and study the changes, treating implementation as inquiry rather than compliance.

The difference between pilots and prototypes lies in purpose. Pilots test whether an idea can be integrated into the current framework. Prototypes ask what becomes possible if the framework itself is changed. For example, a district might pilot a new math curriculum in middle school while leaving all other structures intact. A prototype would redesign the same school to operate on mastery progression, flexible time use, and student-led exhibitions. The goal is not optimization of legacy routines but exploration of an alternative system.

This reframing matters because incrementalism has proven insufficient for the challenges facing public education. Pilots often generate reports that fade once funding ends. Prototypes, redesign sites, and change labs instead position schools as places of continuous learning, where the assumptions of the traditional system are surfaced, tested, and revised. They encourage educators and leaders to treat schools not as fixed institutions but as evolving ecosystems responsive to student agency and community priorities.

What Redesign Sites Are For

Redesign sites exist to explore what happens when schools operate under different structural logics. They are not created to showcase isolated innovations or to serve as model classrooms that can be replicated elsewhere. Instead, they function as living laboratories where students, teachers, and communities engage directly with new forms of organization, pedagogy, and accountability. The purpose is inquiry rather than demonstration.

In these contexts, educators and leaders are free to test structural alternatives such as mastery progression, interdisciplinary blocks, community-based learning, and performance assessments. The outcomes of these experiments are not measured only by standardized achievement scores; instead, they include indicators such as belonging, engagement, student agency, and readiness for an uncertain future. By foregrounding these dimensions, redesign sites expand the definition of what counts as educational success.

Sustainability emerges not from external mandates but from cultural adoption within schools and districts. Research on scale shows that practices spread most effectively when they become embedded in professional norms and align with broader system goals (Coburn, 2003). Mehta and Fine (2019) extend this point by demonstrating how deep learning environments flourish when educators feel ownership of the design rather than compliance with external directives. Redesign sites, therefore, are not about creating exemplars to copy. They are about generating evidence of what is possible and cultivating the conditions under which promising practices can take root and endure.

The strength of a redesign site lies in its dual purpose: it serves as both a place of learning for students and a site of inquiry for the system itself. By documenting conditions, outcomes, and tensions, these sites make visible the assumptions that either enable or constrain innovation. In doing so, they create knowledge that can inform policy and practice across multiple levels of the system.

Assumptions That Must Be Challenged

Redesign requires surfacing and challenging the inherited assumptions that shape the daily life of schools. These assumptions are often invisible yet deeply embedded in policy, routines, and professional culture. Unless they are explicitly examined and restructured, efforts at transformation risk reinforcing the very logics they intend to disrupt.

Time is the most persistent assumption. Schools continue to organize learning by seat hours, annual calendars, and age-based grade levels. These structures limit flexibility and prevent recognition of learning that occurs outside the classroom. A redesign must treat time as a resource that can be configured in multiple ways, from extended interdisciplinary blocks to asynchronous opportunities and mastery-based progression.

A second assumption concerns compliance. Much of school governance rests on rules and surveillance that position students and teachers as subjects of control rather than as trusted professionals and learners. Transformation requires a cultural shift toward shared responsibility, student agency, and professional autonomy. Trust becomes the foundation for accountability rather than its absence.

Uniformity is another limiting logic. Standardized pacing, curriculum, and assessments presume that all students learn in the same way and at the same rate. Redesign efforts must embrace differentiated and culturally responsive pathways that reflect diverse strengths, needs, and aspirations. When combined with technology-enabled personalization, such pathways expand access to meaningful learning.

Other assumptions extend beyond the classroom. Schools are typically treated as stand-alone institutions, isolated from civic, health, and environmental systems. This narrow framing overlooks the interdependence of education with housing, public health, climate resilience, and economic development. Similarly, progress is often defined linearly, with learning conceived as steady accumulation of knowledge rather than as a nonlinear process that includes iteration, failure, and reflection.

Finally, schools frequently define knowledge and purpose in narrow economic terms. The emphasis on workforce preparation sidelines civic engagement, ecological stewardship, and human flourishing. Transformation requires expanding what is valued in education, elevating community-based, cultural, and experiential knowledge alongside academic content.

When these assumptions remain unchallenged, reforms yield incremental gains that leave the core system unchanged. By contrast, redesign begins by naming these logics and experimenting with alternatives. Only then can public education move from adaptation to transformation.

Proof of Concept and Proof of Change

Transformation efforts must be understood as more than temporary initiatives. The purpose of a redesign is not to conduct a limited trial that can later be replicated elsewhere, but to establish working models that demonstrate what is possible under new structural logics. A transformation prototype serves as a proof of concept. It shows that assumptions such as seat time requirements, standardized pacing, or hierarchical authority can be replaced by alternatives that better support equity and student agency. When a school operates on mastery-based progression or designs schedules around extended interdisciplinary blocks, it becomes evidence that other ways of organizing are viable in practice.

Equally important is the idea of proof of change. Prototypes generate knowledge not only about student outcomes but also about the conditions that support transformation. Leaders learn where resistance arises, how cultural norms shift, and what unintended consequences emerge. This type of evidence positions implementation as a process of inquiry rather than a compliance exercise. Documenting choices, trade-offs, and community responses creates a knowledge base that other districts and policymakers can adapt, even if the specific structures vary.

The outcomes of redesign should be measured with a broader lens than conventional accountability systems allow. Proof of change extends beyond standardized test scores or graduation rates. It includes increased engagement, strengthened relationships, professional collaboration, and growth in student agency. These outcomes speak to the health of the learning environment and the capacity of the system to sustain innovation. By framing prototypes in this way, schools move from asking whether a program "works" to asking what can be learned about the dynamics of transformation itself. The goal is collective learning that informs practice across levels of the system while making visible the structural conditions that either enable or constrain progress.

Characteristics of Transformative Redesign

Transformative redesign differs fundamentally from conventional school improvement. Improvement efforts typically adjust programs or practices while leaving existing structures untouched. By contrast, redesign seeks to reconfigure the very assumptions and systems that govern schools. Several characteristics consistently mark efforts that move beyond incremental change.

One essential characteristic is power-shifting governance. Traditional models of educational authority centralize decision-making in state agencies, district offices, or administrative hierarchies. Transformative redesign redistributes that authority by involving students, families, educators, and community partners in defining goals, shaping policy, and controlling resources. Mechanisms such as participatory budgeting, inclusive policy councils, and school-community compacts ensure that those most affected by decisions have a meaningful role in making them. This redistribution of authority moves equity from rhetoric to practice.

A second characteristic is agency-driven design. In restructured systems, learners are not passive recipients of curriculum but co-creators of their own pathways. Students work with teachers and communities to develop competencies, design projects, and demonstrate mastery through exhibitions and portfolios. When students contribute to defining both the process and outcomes of learning, education becomes more relevant and more empowering.

Liberatory accountability also distinguishes transformative redesign. Traditional accountability systems reduce student success to test scores and compliance indicators. Redesign efforts broaden accountability to include belonging, well-being, collaboration, civic contribution, and creativity. Alternative assessment models such as performance exhibitions, narrative feedback, and community reviews shift the focus toward evidence of authentic growth.

Another defining feature is the willingness to disrupt existing structures. Redesign does not optimize seat time rules, standard pacing, or hierarchical instruction; it challenges them directly. This disruption often generates resistance, but in effective redesigns resistance is anticipated and treated as a natural part of systemic change. Iteration is built into the process, allowing stakeholders to refine models as they encounter barriers.

Transformative redesign is also marked by recognition of ecosystem interdependence. Schools do not exist in isolation but are shaped by and contribute to health systems, civic life, economic development, and environmental sustainability. Effective redesign builds partnerships across these domains so that education strengthens community resilience. Similarly, regenerative and relational design principles bring attention to trust, joy, connection, and ecological stewardship as formal dimensions of schooling rather than incidental outcomes.

Finally, transformative efforts embrace futures literacy and temporal innovation. They prepare learners and institutions for uncertainty by integrating anticipatory thinking, flexible time structures, and iterative planning. Redesign must also operate within existing legal, contractual, and budgetary constraints, documenting the tensions that point to the need for broader policy change. Successful scaling occurs not by replicating programs identically across sites but by influencing assumptions, spreading principles, and shaping policy frameworks that support ongoing adaptation.

Together these characteristics illustrate how redesign departs from the logics of improvement. They show that transformation requires structural, cultural, and philosophical change. It is a process of reimagining the purpose of schooling and aligning governance, pedagogy, and accountability with that new vision.

Systems Thinking and Design Thinking

System redesign requires conceptual approaches that can confront complexity without collapsing it into overly simplistic solutions. Two traditions, systems thinking and design thinking, provide complementary perspectives that are increasingly recognized as essential for guiding educational transformation.

Systems thinking views schools as dynamic and interconnected systems rather than collections of discrete programs or isolated interventions. Senge (1990) argued that organizations function through reinforcing and balancing feedback loops that sustain patterns of behavior over time. When applied to education, this perspective reveals why reforms often fail to deliver lasting results. New initiatives are introduced, but the deeper assumptions that govern time, authority, assessment, and accountability remain untouched. These underlying structures continue to reproduce the very problems reforms aim to address. Later work by Senge et al. (2012) emphasized that shifting these patterns requires collective learning, shared vision, and an understanding of how systemic interdependencies influence outcomes across multiple levels. In practice, this means that redesign efforts cannot succeed if they treat symptoms in isolation. They must address the structures, beliefs, and feedback mechanisms that sustain educational inequities and inefficiencies.

Design thinking offers a complementary approach that emphasizes action, iteration, and responsiveness. Developed in the design fields and adapted to education, design thinking proceeds through phases of empathizing with users, defining problems, generating ideas, prototyping, and testing (Brown, 2009; Liedtka, 2018; Stanford d.school, 2010). Unlike traditional reform models that often focus on fidelity of implementation, design thinking embraces uncertainty and treats innovation as a process of continuous inquiry. Applied in schools, this approach creates opportunities for educators, students, and communities to co-design solutions that reflect lived experience rather than external mandates. Design thinking is especially valuable in contexts where challenges are ill-defined, where solutions must adapt to local conditions, and where participation across roles is critical for legitimacy.

The integration of systems thinking and design thinking is particularly powerful. Systems thinking clarifies the patterns, structures, and leverage points that sustain current realities, while design thinking provides a disciplined method for testing new possibilities within those systems. Together, they shift educational reform away from compliance-driven implementation and toward a model of collective learning and adaptation. Research in organizational improvement shows that this integration supports distributed leadership, inquiry-based practice, and the capacity to test structural innovations in authentic contexts (Bryk et al., 2015; Kania et al., 2014). By combining diagnosis with action, systems thinking and design thinking enable schools and districts to move from awareness of the need for change to the deliberate design of futures that are inclusive, equitable, and adaptive.

Translating the Method across Levels

Design thinking does not remain confined to the classroom or school building. When applied with fidelity, it becomes a framework for systemic innovation at district, state, and federal levels. Each level carries distinct challenges, resources, and policy levers, but the phases of empathy, definition, ideation, prototyping, and testing can be adapted to guide change across contexts.

District-Level Application

At the district level, design thinking provides a structured way to transform abstract goals into actionable practices that reflect local needs. The "empathize" phase can be formalized through multilingual listening sessions, student-led forums, and partnerships with community organizations, ensuring that the lived experiences of diverse stakeholders are integrated into decision-making. The "define" phase sharpens these insights into problem statements that align with both qualitative narratives and quantitative data. Ideation at the district level enables educators, families, and students to collaboratively generate possibilities unconstrained by legacy practices. Prototyping then allows districts to test models such as flexible scheduling, competency-based grading, or interdisciplinary teaching teams in low-risk environments. Testing, finally, emphasizes rapid feedback and iterative learning, positioning innovation as a continuous process rather than a one-time initiative (Bryk et al., 2015; Fullan & Quinn, 2016).

State-Level Application

At the state level, design thinking can inform the reimagining of accountability, credentialing, and funding systems. Empathizing requires that policymakers seek authentic engagement with educators, students, and families, particularly those from historically marginalized groups. The "define" phase often involves clarifying tensions between traditional structures, such as seat time–based funding formulas, and emerging models like competency-based learning (Patrick et al., 2013). Ideation at this scale may generate alternative pathways for teacher certification, interdisciplinary endorsements, or regional innovation networks. Prototyping is possible through mechanisms such as innovation zones or waiver policies that grant districts flexibility to test new approaches. The "test" phase requires robust evaluation systems that incorporate both state-level indicators and community-defined measures of success, ensuring that learning is shared across districts while honoring local priorities (Darling-Hammond et al., 2020).

Federal-Level Application

At the federal level, design thinking informs the design of large-scale research and development infrastructures, interagency collaborations, and national initiatives. Empathy is essential for grounding policy in the realities of classrooms and communities (Davis et al., 2021). The "define" phase sharpens federal priorities, such as aligning workforce preparation with equity goals or addressing disparities in digital access. Ideation involves fostering cross-sector collaborations with higher education institutions, technology partners, and community organizations. Prototyping may take the form of competitive grants, ARPA-style initiatives, or national pilot ecosystems that test emerging models at scale. Testing requires rigorous evaluation structures that capture both quantitative outcomes and qualitative insights, enabling federal agencies to translate local innovations into scalable policy frameworks (Alliance for Learning Innovation [ALI], 2025a, 2025b).

Building Coherence across Levels

While the district, state, and federal levels operate differently, the design thinking process creates coherence by anchoring innovation in shared principles of empathy, iteration, and collaboration. Districts benefit from localized problem-solving that directly responds to community needs. States provide regulatory flexibility and structural supports that enable experimentation. Federal agencies coordinate research, funding, and evaluation at a scale that can accelerate systemwide learning. Together, these levels form an interdependent ecosystem where innovation is not isolated but connected, ensuring that new practices can evolve from local prototypes into national models without losing their responsiveness to context.

Equity, Co-Design, and Power-Shifting

Educational transformation cannot succeed without addressing equity and power. Design processes that fail to grapple with systemic inequities risk reinforcing the very structures they intend to disrupt. Equity-centered design thinking calls for co-design practices that redistribute authority, elevate marginalized voices, and ensure that decision-making reflects the lived experiences of students, families, and educators.

The Limits of Traditional Engagement

Traditional reform efforts often include stakeholders through consultation or advisory roles, but decision-making power remains concentrated in administrative and policy structures. This model results in tokenistic inclusion, where voices are heard but not acted upon. Research by Fine and Torre (2019) and the National Equity Project (2019) underscores that inequities in education are not accidental but the predictable outcomes of systems designed to maintain exclusion. Without explicit strategies to shift power, innovation risks becoming technocratic rather than transformative.

Co-Design as Structural Redistribution

Co-design requires more than gathering feedback. It involves sharing authority and creating structures in which students, families, and educators are active partners in shaping educational systems. At the school level, this might take the form of student advisory councils that help design curriculum pilots or multilingual family design teams that shape communication and engagement strategies. At the district level, community organizations can serve as co-design partners in budget development, facility planning, and instructional design. Ishimaru (2019) emphasized that when families and communities are positioned as co-constructors of policy and practice, outcomes are more equitable and sustainable.

Research–Practice Partnerships

One promising vehicle for embedding co-design is the research–practice partnership (RPP). Unlike traditional research models that position practitioners as subjects, RPPs emphasize mutual benefit, iterative learning, and shared accountability. Penuel et al. (2015) described RPPs as long-term collaborations that help systems adapt while generating knowledge relevant to both researchers and practitioners. Established partnerships such as the Houston Education Research Consortium and the Rural Education Research and

Implementation Center demonstrate how co-design and applied research can inform systemic change (Farrell et al., 2021). These partnerships highlight how knowledge production can be aligned with local priorities and equity goals rather than external agendas.

Power Dynamics at State and Federal Levels

At the state and federal levels, equity-centered design requires embedding lived experience into policy agendas, funding priorities, and innovation programs. This involves creating participatory policymaking structures that ensure students, families, and educators influence how funds are allocated, how accountability is defined, and how innovation is supported. The Alliance for Learning Innovation (2025b) recommended that states establish dedicated research offices to act as intermediaries between local actors and national agencies, coordinating design efforts that reflect diverse contexts. Without such infrastructure, innovation risks being driven by top-down mandates rather than authentic community needs.

Trust, Transparency, and Accountability

Redistributing design authority also requires new approaches to trust and accountability. Many marginalized communities have experienced being overstudied and underserved, leading to skepticism about institutional commitments. Fine and Torre (2019) argued that authentic co-design requires transparency in data ownership, culturally relevant communication, and shared decision-making protocols. Trust is built not through symbolic inclusion but through sustained, reciprocal relationships that alter how resources and authority flow through systems.

Implications for Emerging Models

As schools experiment with emerging models such as extended reality (XR) learning environments, hybrid micro-schools, or neurodiversity-centered labs, equity and co-design become even more critical. Without intentional inclusion, new technologies and structures risk replicating historical inequities or creating new forms of exclusion. Holmes et al. (2022) highlighted that co-design is particularly essential in technologically mediated environments to ensure that innovation reflects cultural relevance, accessibility, and ethical safeguards.

Toward Justice-Centered Design

Equity-centered design thinking reframes innovation as a justice-centered strategy rather than a technical process. By redistributing authority, embedding co-design at all levels, and sustaining reciprocal relationships, educational systems can move beyond surface reforms toward deeper transformation. This approach directly reinforces the Futures Ready Framework by embedding agency, inclusivity, and ethical integration into every stage of redesign. It also makes explicit that transformation is inherently political: changing how decisions are made is as important as changing what decisions are made.

Designing Boldly: R&D Models That Redefine Possibility

Research and development (R&D) is often treated as a peripheral activity in education, focused on testing small-scale programs or refining discrete interventions. In sectors such as technology, healthcare, or engineering, however, R&D is considered the engine of transformation. It is where bold questions are tested, prototypes are developed, and entirely new systems are imagined. Education requires a comparable orientation if it is to move beyond incremental reforms. Properly designed R&D initiatives can generate new models of schooling that challenge entrenched assumptions and create conditions for future-ready systems to take shape.

R&D as Tactical Disruption

R&D in education must be framed not as improvement of the current system but as tactical disruption. The purpose of R&D sites is to test whether schools can be organized around fundamentally different logics of time, governance, assessment, and community partnership. Rather than validating whether existing practices can scale, these initiatives serve as proofs of possibility, showing that alternative models of schooling are both viable and desirable. By treating prototypes as living laboratories, educators and researchers can document new practices, surface design tensions, and expand the boundaries of what is considered achievable.

Partnerships with Higher Education and Communities
A critical element of bold R&D is the involvement of higher education institutions and community partners. Universities bring research expertise, evaluation capacity, and design methods that strengthen innovation quality. Community partners contribute local knowledge, cultural insight, and lived experience that ensure relevance and equity. Farrell et al. (2021) demonstrated that RPPs can align these strengths, creating long-term collaborations that build both system capacity and scholarly knowledge. Without such partnerships, innovation risks being disconnected from authentic contexts or reduced to market-driven solutions.

Emerging Models for Redesign
Several models illustrate how equity-centered R&D can redefine educational possibility. XR ecosystems, for example, allow students to move fluidly between place-based and immersive digital environments, blending community learning with global collaboration. Schools without buildings reimagine communities as campuses, positioning parks, libraries, businesses, and cultural centers as core learning environments. Micro-school networks focus on small, agile sites that link students with civic and environmental problem-solving. Intergenerational learning pods integrate youth and elders into reciprocal learning communities that strengthen social cohesion. Neurodiversity-centered labs redesign learning environments around diverse cognitive and sensory needs, positioning neurodivergent learners as co-creators of inclusive models. Adaptive learning systems combine flexibility, modular design, and hybrid delivery to make education responsive to constant change.

Scaling by Influence Rather Than Replication
These models highlight an important principle: transformation spreads not through uniform replication but through influence. The impact of a prototype is measured less by how many schools adopt its exact design and more by how deeply it reshapes assumptions and inspires others to experiment. This orientation aligns with

research on diffusion of innovation, which emphasizes that systems learn collectively when bold exemplars reveal what is possible (Coburn, 2003).

Equity and Ethical Safeguards

R&D efforts must also embed equity and ethics into their design. Without explicit safeguards, innovations risk reproducing patterns of exclusion or privileging communities with greater resources. The National Equity Project (2019) and Holmes et al. (2022) argue that co-design practices and justice-centered evaluation are essential to ensuring that innovation contributes to inclusion rather than inequity. This requires culturally responsive design, participatory data practices, and intentional redistribution of resources toward historically marginalized communities.

Toward a Public R&D Infrastructure

Finally, education must treat R&D as a public good. Just as healthcare and technology sectors maintain national R&D systems, education requires sustained investment in experimental sites, data infrastructures, and cross-sector partnerships. Federal initiatives such as ARPA-style education agencies and the Accelerate, Transform, and Scale framework (Alliance for Learning Innovation [ALI], 2025a) provide early steps in this direction, but the scale of investment must grow if systemic transformation is to occur. By positioning R&D as a core responsibility rather than an optional activity, education systems can build adaptive capacity and create pathways for sustainable, future-ready redesign.

Creating the System Conditions for Innovation to Succeed

Educational redesign rarely fails because of weak ideas. It fails because the surrounding conditions are not designed to sustain experimentation, collaboration, and adaptation. Systems built for compliance, efficiency, and uniformity are structured to resist disruption. For innovation to succeed, education must deliberately construct conditions that allow redesign to take root. Several elements are especially critical, and each directly reinforces the pillars of the Futures Ready Framework.

Shared Leadership
Innovation depends on governance structures that distribute decision-making authority. When leadership remains top-down, redesign efforts tend to reproduce the inequities and hierarchies they aim to dismantle. Research shows that stakeholder involvement improves decision quality, strengthens trust, and increases sustainability (Coburn, 2003; Farrell et al., 2021). Shared leadership aligns with the framework's pillar of student agency, ensuring that learners and families are not passive recipients of policy but active co-governors of change. It also reflects ethical integration, grounding authority in inclusion and transparency rather than compliance alone.

Time and Autonomy
Time and autonomy are often treated as logistical details, but they are structural conditions that determine how learning unfolds. Traditional education systems standardize both, measuring time in seat hours and distributing autonomy hierarchically. Redesign requires treating time as a flexible, co-constructed resource and autonomy as a shared authority across educators, students, and communities (Alexander, 2022). This shift advances mastery through personalization, enabling learners to move at their own pace, and reinforces future-ready adaptability, allowing systems to adjust when conditions change. Without rethinking time and autonomy, innovation collapses back into compliance.

Distributed Design Capacity
Sustainable redesign requires capacity distributed across the system rather than concentrated in central offices or external consultants. Teacher-led design teams, student advisory groups, and RPPs represent essential forms of distributed expertise (Penuel et al., 2015). These structures align with student agency by positioning learners as contributors, not recipients, and with inclusive access by ensuring that diverse communities help shape solutions. Distributed design

capacity also supports empathy-driven connection, since authentic collaboration creates shared responsibility and trust across roles.

Adaptable Infrastructure

Infrastructure shapes what is possible in education. Uniform classrooms, fixed schedules, and compliance-driven technology systems reinforce industrial models of schooling. Adaptive infrastructure, in contrast, allows learning environments to shift between individual and collaborative work, integrate hybrid formats, and extend into community spaces (Escueta et al., 2021). Broadband, device access, and universal design principles are essential components. Adaptable infrastructure advances inclusive access by ensuring participation across geography and socioeconomic status, while also reinforcing ethical integration by embedding accessibility and cultural responsiveness into physical and digital design.

Learning-Centered Data

Data systems determine what is visible to education systems and what counts as success. Inherited accountability models privilege standardized tests, credits, and grades, measures designed for compliance rather than learning (Datnow & Park, 2020). Redesign requires learning-centered data ecosystems that value growth, belonging, purpose, and civic contribution. These systems must be participatory, positioning students, families, and educators as co-owners of data rather than as subjects of external monitoring (Peurach et al., 2022). Such practices directly support mastery through personalization, since data reflect individual growth, and empathy-driven connection, since evidence is interpreted collaboratively with those most affected.

Policy Flexibility

Innovation is constrained when rigid policy frameworks dictate uniform inputs and outcomes. Seat time requirements, narrow assessment mandates, and rigid credentialing systems often limit redesign efforts (Patrick et al., 2021). Policy flexibility does not mean deregulation but rather adaptive governance that safeguards equity while allowing experimentation. Innovation zones, waivers, and sandbox regulations represent examples of policy tools that balance accountability with freedom to test new models (Levine, 2023). This condition strengthens future-ready adaptability by allowing systems to evolve with emerging challenges, while advancing ethical integration by ensuring that flexibility does not undermine equity commitments.

Microfunding and Resource Access

Access to small, flexible funding streams is often decisive in whether local innovation thrives. Large grants can bring resources but also create administrative burdens and inequities. Microfunding enables rapid experimentation, supports community-led initiatives, and democratizes participation in redesign (Kochhar-Bryant & Heishman, 2021). To avoid reproducing inequity, these funds must be distributed with safeguards that prioritize historically underserved communities. Microfunding complements strong public investment rather than replacing it. When implemented with care, this condition advances student agency by enabling learners and educators to lead initiatives, inclusive access by supporting historically excluded communities, and empathy-driven connection by elevating grassroots priorities.

Moving from Vision to Action

The movement from vision to action in public education depends on the courage to begin redesign within authentic contexts. Transformation prototypes, redesign sites, and change labs illustrate that meaningful innovation does not emerge from compliance-driven reforms but from intentional disruptions that challenge inherited assumptions. When grounded in the Futures Ready Framework, these efforts position student agency, inclusive access, adaptability, and ethical integration at the center of system design. The examples of XR learning environments, intergenerational pods, and neurodiversity-centered labs demonstrate that bold models can provide both proof of possibility and insight into the structural conditions required for large-scale change.

Yet early redesign efforts alone are not sufficient. Without deliberate strategies to embed innovation into governance, accountability, and resource structures, transformation risks remaining fragile and isolated. The lessons generated through prototypes must be translated into systemwide practices, supported by distributed design capacity, adaptable infrastructure, and policy flexibility. The challenge lies not only in generating new models of learning but also in creating the institutional conditions that allow those models to endure and expand.

The next stage of inquiry turns toward this task of embedding innovation. Initial redesign demonstrates what is possible. Systemwide transformation requires building the mechanisms that sustain it, ensuring that future-ready principles become the foundation of educational ecosystems rather than temporary experiments. Redesign can be institutionalized, scaled by influence, and aligned with public governance so that innovation becomes not a series of isolated initiatives but the defining architecture of public education.

References

Alexander, R. (2022). *Education for a changing world: Reflections on complexity, adaptability, and the future of schooling.* Routledge.

Alliance for Learning Innovation. (2025a). *A blueprint for the future of federal K–12 education R&D.* ALI Publications.

Alliance for Learning Innovation. (2025b). *Accelerate, transform, scale: Federal innovation strategies for education.* ALI Publications.

Brown, T. (2009). *Change by design: How design thinking creates new alternatives for business and society.* HarperBusiness.

Bryk, A. S., Gomez, L. M., Grunow, A., & LeMahieu, P. G. (2015). *Learning to improve: How America's schools can get better at getting better.* Harvard Education Press.

Coburn, C. E. (2003). Rethinking scale: Moving beyond numbers to deep and lasting change. *Educational Researcher, 32*(6), 3–12. https://doi.org/10.3102/0013189X032006003

Darling-Hammond, L., Flook, L., Cook-Harvey, C., Barron, B., & Osher, D. (2020). Implications for educational practice of the science of learning and development. *Applied Developmental Science, 24*(2), 97–140. https://doi.org/10.1080/10888691.2018.1537791

Datnow, A., & Park, V. (2020). *Data-driven leadership.* Jossey-Bass.

Davis, E., Hamilton, D., & Levin, H. (2021). *R&D for equity: Federal education research and development for the 21st century*. Learning Policy Institute.

Escueta, M., Quan, V., Nickow, A., & Oreopoulos, P. (2021). Educational technology: An evidence-based review. *Review of Educational Research*, *91*(3), 495–537. https://doi.org/10.3102/0034654321999817

Farrell, C., Penuel, W. R., Coburn, C. E., & Daniel, J. (2021). Research–practice partnerships in education: The state of the field. *Review of Research in Education*, *45*(1), 154–194. https://doi.org/10.3102/0091732X21990623

Fine, M., & Torre, M. E. (2019). *Participatory action research as public science*. Cambridge University Press.

Fullan, M., & Quinn, J. (2016). *Coherence: The right drivers in action for schools, districts, and systems*. Corwin.

Holmes, W., Bialik, M., & Fadel, C. (2022). *Artificial intelligence in education: Promises and implications for teaching and learning*. Center for Curriculum Redesign.

Ishimaru, A. M. (2019). *Just schools: Building equitable collaborations with families and communities*. Teachers College Press.

Kania, J., Kramer, M., & Senge, P. (2014). Leading systems. *Stanford Social Innovation Review*, *12*(4), 34–41.

Kochhar-Bryant, C. A., & Heishman, A. (2021). *Transition planning for secondary students with disabilities*. Pearson.

Levine, P. (2023). *We are the ones we have been waiting for: The promise of civic renewal in America*. Oxford University Press.

Liedtka, J. (2018). Why design thinking works. *Harvard Business Review*, *96*(5), 72–79.

McKinsey & Company. (2025). *The state of organizations 2025*. McKinsey & Company.

Meadows, D. H. (2008). *Thinking in systems: A primer*. Chelsea Green Publishing.

Mehta, J., & Fine, S. (2019). *In search of deeper learning: The quest to remake the American high school*. Harvard University Press.

National Equity Project. (2019). *Equity-centered design thinking*. National Equity Project.

Patrick, S., Worthen, M., Frost, D., & Truong, N. (2013). *Making the shift to competency education: A toolkit for state policymakers*. iNACOL.

Patrick, S., Worthen, M., & Truong, N. (2021). *Innovative learning models and student-centered policies for reimagining education*. Aurora Institute.

Penuel, W. R., Briggs, D. C., Davidson, K. L., Herlihy, C., Farrell, C., & Sherer, D. (2015). *Findings from a study of research–practice partnerships in education*. William T. Grant Foundation.

Peurach, D. J., Hannan, M. T., Russell, J. L., & Cohen, D. K. (Eds.). (2022). *The foundational handbook on improvement research in education*. Rowman & Littlefield.

Senge, P. M. (1990). *The fifth discipline: The art and practice of the learning organization*. Doubleday.

Senge, P. M., Cambron-McCabe, N., Lucas, T., Smith, B., Dutton, J., & Kleiner, A. (2012). *Schools that learn: A fifth discipline fieldbook for educators, parents, and everyone who cares about education* (Updated ed.). Crown Business.

Stanford d.school. (2010). *An introduction to design thinking process guide*. Hasso Plattner Institute of Design at Stanford.

18

Embedding Innovation

From Initial Change to Systemwide Transformation

For decades, implementation in public education has meant adapting new practices to fit old systems. The insight often attributed to Albert Einstein is instructive here: problems cannot be solved with the same thinking that created them. System redesign requires new mental models, not programmatic add-ons. The most difficult aspect of change is not generating ideas but ensuring they endure in daily practice, which aligns with Fullan's analysis of educational change as a problem of sustained implementation and culture building (Fullan, 2016). If the foundational architecture of schooling remains aligned to outdated assumptions, even promising redesigns will stall or regress. Sustained transformation is not about scaling programs. It is about rebuilding the system itself around new logics of learning, equity, and purpose.

We explored how districts and communities can challenge inherited models through bold, equity-centered prototypes. This chapter will focus on the next phase: embedding innovation across the entire system. We will ask, how do innovative initiatives become institutional norms? How do we build the infrastructure, governance, culture, and policy conditions needed to sustain transformation at scale?

DOI: 10.4324/9781003739050-24

This is not about managing implementation as a technical rollout. It is about leading institutional reinvention, where organizational DNA, resource flows, leadership structures, and cultural routines are permanently realigned to support continuous learning and adaptation.

Escaping the Implementation Trap: From Scaling Programs to Redesigning Systems

For decades, educational change has been framed as a matter of implementation. Schools are asked to adopt new programs, technologies, or strategies with the expectation that improved outcomes will follow. Yet research consistently shows that most innovations fail to take hold when they are layered onto legacy systems that were never designed to support them (Fullan, 2016). This pattern, often called the "implementation trap," leads to cycles of disappointment where promising practices become compliance exercises, innovation fatigue sets in, and underlying system structures remain untouched.

Escaping the implementation trap requires a fundamental shift: from scaling innovations as add-ons to rebuilding the foundations of educational systems. As the US Department of Education (2017) emphasizes in its National Education Technology Plan, transformation depends on redesigning learning environments to "engage and empower all learners," not on automating traditional practices or digitizing outdated processes. The key is to move from technical adaptation to conceptual reinvention, ensuring that systems evolve not just in what they deliver but also in how they define purpose, organize learning, and share power.

Central to this shift is the idea of coherence, defined not as uniformity or compliance, but as shared clarity about new guiding principles. Fullan and Quinn (2016) describe coherence as the collective commitment to rethink "how we think and act," rather than simply aligning behaviors to existing mandates. For education systems, coherence around transformation means holding common purpose on several key shifts: moving from time-based to competency-based progressions, from top-down control to student agency, from equality of access to intentional equity, and from automation-as-efficiency to artificial intelligence (AI)-as-human-enhancement (Darling-Hammond et al., 2020).

The transformation prototypes described earlier illustrate how these shifts move from principle to practice. Extended reality (XR) learning ecosystems redefine where and how learning takes place, blending local, community-based experiences with immersive global collaborations to support mastery over seat time. Schools without buildings challenge fixed schedules and centralized governance, creating flexible networks of civic spaces, virtual platforms, and student-driven pathways. Micro-school networks demonstrate coherence through local innovation, environmental stewardship, and social responsibility, moving beyond standardized curricula to focus on authentic, place-based learning. Neurodiversity-centered learning labs reject accommodation as an afterthought, embedding diverse cognitive, sensory, and communication needs into the design of learning environments. Adaptive learning systems extend these ideas across entire regions, aligning infrastructure, governance, and funding to enable continuous, equity-centered adaptation at scale.

Across all of these examples, coherence is not about enforcing a single model or solution. It is about anchoring educational change in shared commitments to learner-centered, future-ready principles while creating the flexibility for local design, experimentation, and evolution. Without this kind of coherence, even the most promising innovations risk being reduced to temporary programs or technical fixes. With it, systems can begin to move from scattered initiatives to sustained, meaningful transformation.

Rebuilding Core Structures around Learner-Centered Principles

Redesigning educational systems requires more than layering innovation onto outdated frameworks. It demands a full reconstruction of the operational backbone: scheduling, staffing, assessment, technology, and budgeting, so these systems reflect and reinforce pedagogical transformation.

Traditional schedules built around fixed class periods and age-based cohorts must give way to flexible, student-centered designs that allow interdisciplinary projects, mastery-based progression, and hybrid learning experiences. Staffing models should move beyond isolated content specialists toward collaborative, cross-functional teams that include learning designers, technology integrators, wellness coaches, and community liaisons. Assessment systems must shift from standardized, summative tests toward portfolios, performance tasks, and real-time feedback mechanisms, many of them enhanced by AI tools that support rather than replace human judgment and student creativity. Technology infrastructure should not simply digitize old practices but open new pathways for connection, personalization, and universal access, ensuring that all students can participate fully regardless of ability or background. Budgeting models must follow these shifts, prioritizing flexible funds for innovation, multi-role teams, cross-sector partnerships, and design time for staff and students.

Yet structural redesign alone is not enough. Transformative systems require a parallel investment in professional learning and capacity building, ensuring that educators, leaders, and staff are supported in new roles through ongoing coaching, collaborative learning, and adaptive skill development. They need to cultivate organizational cultures of trust, experimentation, and reflection, where continuous learning and improvement are embedded as collective responsibilities, not confined to isolated initiatives.

Core redesign must also center student and community co-design, ensuring that learners, families, and local partners are not passive recipients but active co-creators of new systems. This means engaging students in shaping schedules, designing assessments, defining success, and imagining how spaces and technologies can best serve their needs and aspirations. It also requires integrated data and feedback systems that prioritize formative, developmental, and community-sourced evidence to guide ongoing adaptation and ensure alignment with local goals.

Fundamentally, rebuilding operational systems around learner-centered principles is an equity project. It is about correcting long-standing structural injustices by embedding inclusion, access, and fairness at the core of design. Budgets must be weighted toward historically underserved communities. Technology planning must address digital divides. Assessment must challenge bias and amplify diverse ways of knowing and demonstrating mastery.

Finally, sustainability and scalability must be part of the design from the outset. Redesign is not a one-time overhaul but an ongoing system of iteration, governance, and policy alignment that ensures innovations are not temporary add-ons but institutionalized as central, renewable practices. Schools must be understood not as isolated service providers but as part of a larger civic and ecological ecosystem, working in partnership with health, housing, environmental, and civic systems to foster learner and community well-being.

By making innovation central, not peripheral, and explicitly tying operational systems to pedagogical transformation, districts can move beyond pilot projects and establish education systems that are adaptive, just, and purpose-driven. These systems will be capable of preparing young people for the complexity, diversity, and interdependence of the world they are inheriting.

Embedding Iteration and Shared Leadership as Systemic Norms

Sustainable transformation in education requires integrating continuous improvement practices with shared leadership structures, making them central to system operation rather than peripheral initiatives. Recent research emphasizes that district and school teams need structured cycles, such as Plan–Do–Study–Act (PDSA), to examine problems, test changes, analyze outcomes, and refine strategies. These iterative methods are foundational to adaptive systems and are increasingly supported by toolkits and improvement teams designed for educational settings (Institute of Education Sciences [IES], 2025).

Distributed leadership, where leadership roles and decision-making are shared across formal and informal actors, has been shown to enhance teacher innovation, autonomy, and collaboration, though it requires careful balance to prevent diffusion of responsibility (Ismail et al., 2022). A recent systematic review describes distributed leadership as a critical catalyst for building school capacity and driving innovation, particularly when paired with robust support for teacher agency and team-based inquiry (Ismail et al., 2022).

These principles intersect in practice through several key dimensions:

First, cultural norms of inquiry and reflection are established when PDSA cycles become routine, where educators, students, and families collaboratively ask questions, collect data, and use evidence to make informed decisions. Second, distributed roles and co-direction ensure that leadership is no longer confined to administrators. Teacher design teams, student innovation labs, and parent or community councils are actively engaged in identifying problems, testing new approaches, and interpreting outcomes. Third, accountability is reframed through collaboration, not compliance. Metrics are co-designed and interpreted through inclusive teams, with data used to inform and adapt rather than to impose sanctions. Finally, system-level habit formation ensures that iteration cycles and shared governance are not seen as optional strategies but as embedded capabilities defining how the system learns and evolves.

Across the research and development (R&D) models presented, XR learning ecosystems, schools without buildings, micro-school networks, intergenerational learning pods, neurodiversity-centered labs, and adaptive learning systems, these norms are essential. For example, XR initiatives rely on iterative testing of devices, pedagogy, and infrastructure, while shared leadership ensures that students, educators, and families shape ongoing adaptations. Distributed leadership also supports the flexibility needed to adjust staffing, scheduling, and assessment protocols as new prototypes emerge.

Together, continuous iteration and shared leadership shift education from static compliance to dynamic, co-created learning systems. They establish the expectation that innovation is not an exception but part of the system's core function, ensuring that redesign efforts are both deep and sustainable.

Strategic Abandonment and Institutional Tools for Change

Transformation in education is not only about introducing new practices; it is equally about letting go of outdated structures that no longer serve learners or communities. Without intentional processes for abandoning inherited routines, innovations remain constrained, forced to coexist within systems built for standardization and control. Recent scholarship highlights the importance of explicitly redesigning institutional routines to create space for adaptive learning and responsiveness (Peurach et al., 2022; Warren & Murphy, 2021).

Strategic abandonment involves systematically identifying legacy policies, practices, or mindsets that hinder learner-centered goals. This includes reexamining practices like seat time mandates, age-based progression, high-stakes summative testing, and rigid calendar structures, all of which have been shown to impede flexibility, personalization, and equity (Patrick et al., 2021). However, abandonment should not be treated as a one-time action. It must be embedded as an ongoing organizational discipline, using formal sunsetting protocols that regularly review and phase out misaligned initiatives. This mirrors practices in other sectors where system health is maintained by retiring not just underperforming programs but also those that no longer fit evolving missions.

In parallel, institutional tools such as innovation portfolios, capacity maps, and system scorecards play a critical role, but their purpose must shift. Rather than acting as compliance checklists, they become design artifacts that capture the system's capacity to learn, reflect, and adapt over time. These tools should document not only what works, but what was intentionally abandoned, what was revised, and what is emerging. Embedding futures literacy, the capacity to anticipate and rehearse multiple possible futures (Miller, 2018), into these tools moves systems from reactive problem-solving to proactive, future-oriented design.

Crucially, equity must be at the center of all abandonment and redesign efforts. Without intentional safeguards, sunsetting initiatives can disproportionately disrupt services in historically under-resourced communities or remove programs valued by marginalized groups. Equity-centered abandonment processes include participatory design reviews, culturally responsive evaluations, and resource redistribution plans that ensure emerging models serve all learners fairly (Warren et al., 2022).

Beyond internal processes, systems should expand how they communicate learning and accountability. Public learning exhibitions, where schools and communities showcase redesign experiments, including failures and lessons learned, shift accountability from internal reports to shared civic dialogue. This approach fosters scaling sideways rather than only scaling up, creating lateral knowledge-sharing ecosystems across schools, districts, and regions, especially between historically privileged and underserved communities (Peurach et al., 2022). It also opens pathways for integrating ecological and planetary accountability into system redesign, treating environmental well-being as a legitimate and necessary component of educational success.

Strategic abandonment is not only about what systems stop doing; it is also about how they create space for new, more just, and more adaptive ways of serving students, families, and communities. When paired with transparent institutional tools, equity safeguards, futures literacy, and civic dialogue, abandonment becomes not an act of loss but a practice of renewal, positioning schools as living systems capable of growing into the complex demands of the present and the future.

Designing Governance, Policy, and Funding for Future Education Systems

Sustaining educational transformation requires more than aligning innovation with legacy governance, policy, and funding models. It requires building entirely new institutional architectures that are designed for adaptive, learner-centered, and equity-driven systems. Future-ready education cannot be sustained within policy frameworks built for standardization, nor can it thrive under funding models that reinforce outdated assumptions about school sites, time, or compliance.

At the governance level, future systems must redistribute decision-making authority across networks of students, educators, families, and communities, supported by multi-sector partnerships that include health, housing, technology, labor, and environmental stakeholders (Peurach et al., 2022). Governance systems must shift toward horizontal rather than hierarchical arrangements, organized around co-creation, local adaptation, and collective sensemaking instead of centralized control. Rather than relying on top-down mandates, future systems will operate through adaptive ecosystems that continuously learn, negotiate, and respond to emerging needs.

In policy, this shift calls for replacing uniform, compliance-driven regulations with adaptive frameworks that set principles, protections, and enabling conditions without rigid prescriptions. Rather than issuing mandates tied to narrow performance metrics, state and federal agencies can create policy sandboxes and innovation ecosystems that allow local actors to test new models, develop context-specific solutions, and contribute to shared system learning (Pane, 2022). This includes developing flexible credentialing systems for students and educators, adaptive accountability systems that combine quantitative and qualitative evidence, and public R&D infrastructures that support ongoing experimentation at scale.

Funding structures must also be redesigned to reflect mobility, personalization, and distributed learning ecosystems. Instead of tying resources solely to school sites, seat time, or student counts, future funding models should follow learners across settings, support community-anchored learning hubs, and invest in shared civic and digital infrastructure. Public funding will remain foundational to guaranteeing free, equitable education, but it should be accompanied by mechanisms for local co-investment, participatory budgeting, and targeted microfunding that empowers grassroots innovation, particularly in historically under-resourced communities (Warren et al., 2022).

To avoid deepening inequities, future systems must center equity safeguards in every layer of governance and funding. This includes transparent, community-driven accountability systems that measure not only academic outcomes but also well-being, civic contribution, environmental stewardship, and intergenerational resilience (Datnow & Park, 2020). Success will no longer be defined by compliance or outputs alone but by how effectively systems empower learners, families, and communities to thrive together.

The design of governance, policy, and funding for future systems must reject the assumption that innovation can be scaled by aligning to inherited models. It must instead embrace adaptive reinvention, creating institutional environments that remain deliberately iterative, unfinished, and co-created over time. This is not about aligning transformation to old systems; it is about replacing those systems with new civic architectures capable of holding complexity, diversity, and change.

Building a Culture of Anticipatory Learning

Future-ready education systems cannot rely on static models or episodic reforms. They must cultivate anticipatory learning: the capacity to engage with uncertainty, imagine alternative futures, and adaptively design for what is emerging, not just what is known. This cultural shift reframes innovation from a special initiative into the ongoing practice of the system itself.

Embedding futures literacy (UNESCO, 2021) into the system's identity equips students, educators, leaders, and communities to ask not only "What is working now?" but also "What might be needed next?" It develops the collective ability to anticipate challenges, experiment with new solutions, and respond with flexibility to social, technological, environmental, and civic disruptions (Miller, 2018). This is essential in a world shaped by accelerating climate change, technological transformation, migration flows, and economic shifts.

Crucially, this culture of anticipatory learning must extend beyond national boundaries. Learning ecosystems are no longer confined to local or national contexts. Through global collaboration networks, virtual exchange programs, distributed R&D partnerships, and transnational educational alliances, students and educators can co-create solutions that address planetary challenges. These ecosystems position learners not only as citizens of their own communities but also as active contributors to global well-being and sustainability (Schleicher, 2020). Redesigning education at this scale requires governance structures and data systems that can support cross-border collaboration, while upholding ethical safeguards and cultural respect.

At the same time, the rise of AI introduces unprecedented opportunities for human–AI collaboration. Rather than viewing AI as a tool of automation or replacement, future-facing systems position it as a co-creative partner in teaching, learning, design, and problem-solving. This includes adaptive learning systems that personalize feedback, AI tutors that support multilingual or neurodiverse learners, and generative models that help students explore complex systems, simulate solutions, or design novel creations. Embedding human–AI partnerships into educational practice demands new pedagogical frameworks, ethical guidelines, and professional competencies so that automation expands human potential rather than narrowing or standardizing it (Luckin, 2021; Holmes et al., 2022).

Framing innovation as the system's ongoing practice shifts the purpose of education itself. Schools and districts become civic infrastructures for ethical innovation, collective resilience, and planetary stewardship. They model how to navigate complexity not just for students but with them, fostering an intergenerational capacity for care, creativity, and co-evolution. This is not simply about preparing students for the future; it is about preparing systems to co-create futures worth inhabiting.

References

Darling-Hammond, L., Flook, L., Cook-Harvey, C., Barron, B., & Osher, D. (2020). Implications for educational practice of the science of learning and development. *Applied Developmental Science, 24*(2), 97–140. https://doi.org/10.1080/10888691.2018.1537791

Datnow, A., & Park, V. (2020). *Data-driven leadership.* Jossey-Bass.

Fullan, M. (2016). *The new meaning of educational change* (5th ed.). Teachers College Press.

Fullan, M., & Quinn, J. (2016). *Coherence: The right drivers in action for schools, districts, and systems.* Corwin.

Holmes, W., Bialik, M., & Fadel, C. (2022). *Artificial intelligence in education: Promises and implications for teaching and learning.* Center for Curriculum Redesign.

Institute of Education Sciences. (2025). *Plan–Do–Study–Act (PDSA) cycles: A toolkit for continuous improvement in schools.* U.S. Department of Education.

Ismail, S., Donia, M. B. L., & Tetrick, L. E. (2022). Distributed leadership: A systematic review and future research agenda. *Leadership & Organization Development Journal, 43*(2), 171–191. https://doi.org/10.1108/LODJ-02-2021-0086

Luckin, R. (2021). *AI for schoolteachers.* Routledge.

Miller, R. (2018). *Transforming the future: Anticipation in the 21st century.* UNESCO. https://unesdoc.unesco.org/ark:/48223/pf0000264644

Pane, J. F. (2022). *Personalized learning: What it is, how it works, and why it matters.* RAND Corporation. https://www.rand.org/pubs/research_reports/RRA1991-1.html

Patrick, S., Worthen, M., & Truong, N. (2021). *Innovative learning models and student-centered policies for reimagining education.* Aurora Institute. https://aurora-institute.org/resource/innovative-learning-models-and-student-centered-policies-for-reimagining-education

Peurach, D. J., Cohen, D. K., Yurkofsky, M. M., & Spillane, J. P. (2022). The developmental infrastructure of educational improvement. *Educational Researcher, 51*(2), 73–84. https://doi.org/10.3102/0013189X211065450

Schleicher, A. (2020). *The impact of COVID-19 on education: Insights from education at a glance 2020.* OECD Publishing. https://doi.org/10.1787/69096873-en

UNESCO. (2021). *Futures literacy: A capability for people and societies.* UNESCO Publishing. https://unesdoc.unesco.org/ark:/48223/pf0000379381

U.S. Department of Education. (2017). *Reimagining the role of technology in education: 2017 National education technology plan update.* Office of Educational Technology. https://tech.ed.gov/netp/

Warren, M. R., Mapp, K. L., & Kuttner, P. J. (2022). *A match on dry grass: Community organizing as a catalyst for school reform.* Oxford University Press.

Warren, M. R., & Murphy, J. (2021). Toward collective parent leadership: Moving from parent involvement to collective action. *Educational Policy, 35*(1), 23–53. https://doi.org/10.1177/0895904820984211

19

A New Policy Blueprint

Creating Conditions for Scalable Transformation

Districts cannot redesign public education alone. While localized innovation can reimagine learning structures, these efforts remain fragile without supportive ecosystems. Too often, transformative pilots collapse under the weight of outdated mandates, fiscal inflexibility, and misaligned accountability systems. Scalable transformation demands not merely regulatory accommodation but a fundamental rethinking of the policy architecture governing education in the United States. This is a call for systemic alignment across all levels of governance: federal, state, and local, centered on the shared goal of learner success, equity, and community well-being.

To build an education system aligned with the needs of the mid-21st century, local, state, and federal policy must move beyond compliance-based oversight and toward enabling conditions that are flexible, equity-centered, adaptive, and grounded in continuous improvement.

The Need for Coherent Policy Support

Systemic transformation requires coherence across governance levels. Without policy structures that support learner-centered,

DOI: 10.4324/9781003739050-25

artificial intelligence (AI)-augmented, and competency-based education, even the strongest district-level innovations will struggle to sustain or expand. Current frameworks reward predictability over adaptability and reinforce standardization at the expense of personalization.

Federal initiatives such as No Child Left Behind and Race to the Top, although presented as reforms, ultimately reinforced compliance-based accountability models. These efforts limited local experimentation and narrowed the focus of innovation. They prioritized test-based metrics and procedural compliance, which restricted district efforts to rethink learning structures, assessment practices, and instructional models.

Fullan (2016) argues that lasting systems change cannot come only from bottom-up reform. It requires reciprocal accountability, where schools and the governance systems above them share responsibility for advancing public goals. Districts cannot scale innovation without supportive conditions at the state and federal levels, and governance systems cannot fulfill their public mission without enabling adaptive, equity-centered local work.

This chapter presents a new policy blueprint designed to establish those supportive conditions. It centers on flexibility, collaboration, ethical responsibility, and the recognition of innovation as a public good. Without this blueprint, transformation will remain fragmented, vulnerable, and limited in its impact.

To apply this vision, the following sections examine how local, state, and federal systems can move beyond outdated constraints and act as partners in advancing educational transformation. Each level holds unique responsibilities and opportunities to help create the conditions necessary for sustainable, systemic change.

Local Government: From Reactive Custodian to Civic Partner

Local governments often treat school systems as isolated institutions rather than foundational elements of civic infrastructure. Yet municipalities hold critical levers that shape the broader learning ecosystem, including digital access, transportation, housing, public safety, and public health. To sustain educational transformation, local governance must shift from reactive custodianship focused on service maintenance to proactive ecosystem design that embeds learning throughout community life.

Advancing digital equity is one example of this shift. Municipal broadband initiatives, public Wi-Fi networks, and device lending programs extend learning beyond the school day and physical school sites. For example, the partnership between public schools and local libraries to distribute wireless hotspots addressed both departmental redundancies and unmet community connectivity needs. Such coordinated investments create conditions for equitable access to personalized, blended, and home-based learning opportunities.

Innovation zones represent another strategy for redesign. By formally designating spaces for educational experimentation, cities can enable flexible use of public buildings, integrate youth and family services, and develop adaptive transportation systems that expand access to learning hubs. These civic spaces for innovation allow communities to co-design solutions that reflect local priorities and needs.

Cross-sector collaboration further strengthens educational ecosystems. Education does not operate in isolation from public health, housing, environmental planning, or economic development. Municipalities can align data platforms, grant initiatives, and service delivery across agencies to address shared challenges. Integrated school-based health services improve student well-being, while partnerships between schools and housing authorities help address the needs of students experiencing homelessness or housing instability.

This work requires more than coordination; it calls for a redefinition of what schools are. Schools are not merely instructional sites. They are essential public services embedded within civic life. They are part of the infrastructure that supports well-being, equity, intergenerational opportunity, and collective resilience. Recognizing this expanded role calls for shared governance structures that include student, family, and community voices in local decision-making, along with interagency agreements that align resources and responsibilities. When local governments embrace education as part of the broader public service ecosystem, they help build resilient, adaptive systems that advance learner-centered outcomes and strengthen the social and civic foundations of their communities.

State Government: From Standard-Bearer to Innovation Catalyst

State departments of education hold significant authority to either facilitate or obstruct educational transformation. Traditional accountability systems, funding formulas, and certification policies often rest on outdated assumptions about time, learning, and school organization. Yet some states, including Massachusetts and Connecticut, have begun to build frameworks that support localized innovation within public education.

In Massachusetts, Chapter 71, Section 92 of the Massachusetts General Laws authorizes the creation of Innovation Schools that operate with expanded autonomy in areas such as curriculum, scheduling, and staffing (Massachusetts General Laws, n.d.). These schools are required to develop performance-based innovation plans, co-designed by educators and approved by school committees, which specify student performance goals, implementation strategies, and district policy exemptions. The Massachusetts Board of Elementary and Secondary Education formalizes these provisions under 603 CMR 48.00, defining Innovation Schools as public in-district schools with flexibility across six key domains: curriculum, budget, school schedule and calendar, staffing policies and procedures, professional development, and district policies (Massachusetts Department of Elementary and Secondary Education, 2014).

Similarly, Connecticut General Statutes Section 10-74h empowers local boards to establish Innovation Schools governed by formal plans that allow waivers from board policy and collective bargaining agreements, contingent upon outcome monitoring and evaluation (Connecticut General Statutes, 2024). These legislative frameworks create necessary space for local experimentation, yet they are only part of a larger transformation agenda. Public attitudes amplify this urgency. Seismic (2025) found strong support for regulatory guardrails and human oversight in AI decision-making.

States that embed such expectations into procurement and accountability frameworks not only respond to public demand but also build trust that educational innovation will be guided by equity and ethical responsibility.

A comprehensive state policy blueprint must go further by embedding regulatory flexibility that includes waivers from seat time requirements and traditional credit accumulation models, enabling competency-based learning pathways. Funding formulas should shift from static, enrollment-based allocations to performance-based models that prioritize student growth, engagement, and portfolio quality over test-centered proficiency metrics. States can also strengthen innovation pilots by creating state-recognized innovation networks that support districts pursuing personalized, AI-supported, and interdisciplinary instructional models.

New Hampshire's Performance Assessment of Competency Education (PACE) initiative provides an instructive example of balancing local innovation with statewide coherence. PACE allows districts to develop locally designed performance assessments aligned to statewide competencies, demonstrating that flexibility and consistency can operate in tandem to advance meaningful educational outcomes (New Hampshire Department of Education, 2017).

Most importantly, state governments must recognize that local flexibility and statewide coherence are not opposing forces. They must be intentionally balanced, with the state assuming the role of innovation catalyst rather than enforcer of uniformity. By creating enabling conditions, supporting experimentation, and holding space for diverse pathways, state agencies can play a pivotal role in advancing an adaptive, learner-centered, and equity-driven education system.

Federal Government: From Compliance Enforcer to Equity Architect

The federal role in education must move beyond enforcing compliance and toward designing national infrastructure that supports innovation and advances equity. This responsibility is uniquely complex in the United States, where fifty state departments of education oversee hundreds of local governments and thousands of school districts, each with its own governance, funding, and policy frameworks. Given this scale and fragmentation, federal leadership plays a critical role in setting enabling conditions that foster coherence across a decentralized system.

To fulfill this role, the federal government must develop new funding streams that prioritize long-term investments in systemic reinvention rather than short-term or competitive reforms. Grants should directly support areas such as AI integration, digital equity, and competency-based learning models, avoiding the pitfalls of past initiatives like Race to the Top that intensified local competition without addressing structural needs.

Federal action must also recognize the paradox of the moment. By mid-2025, ChatGPT reached more than 700 million weekly active users worldwide, with roughly 10 percent of interactions involving tutoring or educational support (Chatterji et al., 2025). Adoption is widespread even as skepticism remains high, underscoring the federal responsibility to craft policies that both safeguard students and expand equitable access to powerful tools already reshaping learning.

Innovative federal funding strategies might include sustained public investments in research and development for education, similar to federal research and development (R&D) support in energy, healthcare, and transportation. A national public education R&D fund could enable districts and states to pilot and scale transformative models, emphasizing cross-state collaborations, district consortia, and multi-sector partnerships that promote shared learning and reduce duplication of effort. Targeted innovation funds focused on advancing digital equity could expand broadband infrastructure in under-resourced communities, incentivize the development of open-access educational resources, and provide microgrants to support grassroots innovation within schools and local organizations.

Performance-based funding models could also be reimagined to support not only academic achievement but also student engagement, well-being, civic contribution, and workforce readiness. Achieving this would require multidimensional accountability frameworks that move beyond standardized test scores to reflect the broader aims of 21st-century education. Additionally, the federal government could explore social impact investment models, such as public–private matching funds or innovation bonds, to channel private sector resources toward high-need educational priorities, while ensuring public oversight and ethical governance.

Alongside funding innovations, the federal government must lead the development of modernized national standards. These should be voluntary yet rigorous frameworks addressing ethical AI use, algorithmic transparency, and student data protection. Existing laws such as FERPA and COPPA, while foundational, are insufficient to address emerging issues related to predictive analytics, biometric data, and algorithmic decision-making (U.S. Department of Education, 2021; Federal Trade Commission, 2022).

Interagency collaboration is equally critical. The Department of Education must work closely with the Department of Labor, the Federal Communications Commission, and the National Science Foundation to align AI policy, broadband infrastructure, and workforce development efforts. Without such coordination, federal initiatives risk reinforcing existing silos instead of building integrated systems that meet the evolving needs of learners and communities.

Past federal reforms often sought accountability through standardization. A transformation agenda must instead build the national infrastructure for coherence, adaptability, and ethical innovation. The federal government has a unique opportunity to serve as an equity architect, creating conditions in which diverse local and state systems can thrive, experiment, and continuously improve in service of all learners.

Public–Private Partnerships and Collaborative Governance

Transforming public education at scale requires collaborative governance that reaches beyond the public sector and draws on the expertise, resources, and creativity of diverse partners. Policymakers must recognize that sustainable innovation depends on shared responsibility across government, higher education, nonprofits, and the private sector, working together toward common goals of equity, adaptability, and learner-centered design.

A critical but often underleveraged component of this collaboration is the relationship between higher education and K–12 systems. Universities can play a pivotal role in supporting K–12 transformation by providing design-based research, longitudinal evaluation, and prototype development that inform local innovation efforts. Academic institutions such as MIT, Harvard, and Drexel, along with regional colleges and public universities, can act as research and development partners, offering expertise in emerging technologies, learning sciences, and data ethics. Strengthening these collaborations can help districts access evidence-based practices, develop scalable models, and create stronger pathways between K–12 learning and postsecondary opportunity.

Nonprofit networks add another layer of critical infrastructure. Organizations such as the Consortium for School Networking (CoSN), Project Unicorn, and Education Reimagined offer resources, data standards, and policy models that support alignment across governance levels. These networks help districts and states navigate the complexities of technology integration, interoperability, and ethical innovation, while also advocating for student-centered practices at the national level.

Ethical partnerships with technology providers are also essential to building modern educational systems. Procurement processes must prioritize interoperability, user agency, cultural responsiveness, and protection against commercialization that undermines educational values. Districts and states need to establish clear frameworks for evaluating educational technology tools, ensuring that partnerships support rather than erode public trust, student privacy, and educational integrity.

The governance of public education must shift from command-and-control structures toward a model of networked stewardship, where diverse actors share responsibility for transformative change. When public agencies, higher education institutions, nonprofits, and private-sector partners come together within frameworks of transparency, shared purpose, and ethical commitment, they can help create an educational ecosystem that is adaptive, inclusive, and equipped to meet the demands of a rapidly evolving world.

Toward a System of Sustained Change

This policy blueprint is not a call for incremental adjustment. It is a call for systemic redesign, where each layer of governance holds itself accountable not for enforcing uniformity, but for creating coherence around a learner-centered, adaptive educational paradigm. This paradigm is anchored in reciprocity, adaptability, interoperability, continuous improvement, and ethical stewardship.

Transformation will endure only when innovation is no longer treated as an exception, but established as an expectation. Redesign at the school level must be mirrored by flexibility at the local level, adaptability at the state level, and foresight at the federal level. Ethical responsibility must remain at the core, safeguarding not only access but also privacy, dignity, and human agency within an increasingly AI-integrated system.

What is needed is not the construction of a new bureaucracy, but the forging of a new civic compact. This compact must align authority with innovation, responsibility with responsiveness, and investment with imagination. It must recognize education not simply as a set of institutional functions, but as a public service and civic infrastructure essential to democracy, economic vitality, and social resilience.

The future of public education will depend on the creation of learning systems that evolve, reflect, and regenerate in response to both community needs and technological change. Policy must serve as the infrastructure that enables this evolution, not as the boundary that contains it. Only by embedding innovation as a collective civic responsibility, across schools, municipalities, states, and the nation, can we create an education system capable of meeting the urgent and complex demands of the mid-21st century. Together, these findings capture the paradox at the heart of AI in education. Public concern, marked by distrust of AI labs and gender divides in perception (Seismic, 2025), exists alongside unprecedented global adoption for tutoring and learning (Chatterji et al., 2025). A credible policy blueprint must bridge this divide by ensuring that systemic reform protects against harm while empowering equitable participation in AI-enhanced learning.

References

Chatterji, A., Cunningham, T., Deming, D. J., Hitzig, Z., Ong, C., Shan, C. Y., & Wadman, K. (2025). *How people use ChatGPT* (Working Paper No. 34255). National Bureau of Economic Research. https://doi.org/10.3386/w34255

Connecticut General Statutes. (2024). *Title 10, Chapter 164, Section 10-74h: Innovation schools.* https://www.cga.ct.gov/current/pub/chap_164.htm#sec_10-74h

Federal Trade Commission. (2022). *Children's Online Privacy Protection Rule (COPPA).* https://www.ftc.gov/legal-library/browse/rules/childrens-online-privacy-protection-rule-coppa

Fullan, M. (2016). *The new meaning of educational change* (5th ed.). Teachers College Press.

Massachusetts Department of Elementary and Secondary Education. (2014). *603 CMR 48.00: Innovation schools.* https://www.mass.gov/regulations/603-CMR-4800-innovation-schools

Massachusetts General Laws. (n.d.). *Chapter 71, Section 92: Innovation schools.* https://malegislature.gov/Laws/GeneralLaws/PartI/TitleXII/Chapter71/Section92

New Hampshire Department of Education. (2017). *Performance Assessment of Competency Education (PACE): Overview and outcomes.* https://www.education.nh.gov/who-we-are/division-of-educator-and-analytic-resources/pace

Seismic. (2025). *On the razor's edge: Public attitudes toward AI in 2025.* https://report2025.seismic.org/media/documents/On_the_Razors_Edge_Seismic_Report_2025.pdf

U.S. Department of Education. (2021). *Protecting student privacy while using online educational services: Requirements and best practices.* https://studentprivacy.ed.gov/resources/protecting-student-privacy-while-using-online-educational-services-requirements-and-best

The Vision for the Future

Some may interpret the vision outlined in this book as idealistic or lacking precise implementation detail. That critique misses the central intent. This book is not a prescriptive blueprint for top-down reform. It is a contribution to an ongoing collective dialogue about what public education can become. It draws from decades of research, practitioner experience, policy evolution, and community innovation, integrating insights from scholars, educators, thought leaders, and policymakers. The future of public education will not be built by perfect plans, but by the collective courage to let go of what no longer serves and to design, together, what every learner deserves.

Rather than proposing a rigid series of reforms, this work offers a flexible framework to inform decision-making across varied contexts. It identifies essential conditions, structural shifts, and equity-centered priorities while recognizing that the path forward must reflect local realities, governance structures, and community needs. The argument here is clear: sustainable transformation demands a coherent, adaptive system rather than scattered interventions.

This work is not an endpoint; rather, it is an entry point. It invites education leaders, teachers, policymakers, and families to ask more incisive questions, challenge outdated systems, and align efforts around a shared commitment to student-centered, future-ready learning. Redesign is not a one-time achievement. It is an ongoing, collaborative process that requires courage, adaptability, and sustained commitment across all levels of the system.

If the ideas presented here disrupt conventional thinking, that disruption is intentional. Preserving outdated educational models carries real risks, with costs borne disproportionately by historically marginalized learners. Incremental change is no longer sufficient. The time has come for bold, coordinated action that redefines not only the mechanics of schooling but also its purpose, values, and public mandate.

This vision calls for public education systems that are responsive, inclusive, and oriented toward continuous improvement. It calls for governance models that prioritize local flexibility, state adaptability, and federal foresight. It demands ethical leadership that protects access, privacy, dignity, and agency in an artificial intelligence (AI)-integrated world. The goal is not to construct a new bureaucracy but to forge a renewed civic compact, one that aligns authority with innovation, responsibility with responsiveness, and investment with imagination.

The future of public education depends on creating learning systems that can evolve, reflect, and regenerate in response to societal needs and technological change. Policy must serve as the infrastructure for this adaptive learning, not as a boundary that contains it. This is the work ahead, and anything less limits what students can become.

Circa 2050

Schools in 2050 and beyond are no longer defined by buildings, bells, or geographic boundaries. The familiar image of the schoolhouse has evolved into a distributed and interconnected learning ecosystem. Physical learning hubs coexist with immersive extended reality (XR) campuses, offering students seamless access to education from home, community spaces, libraries, and collaborative digital platforms. Virtual cohorts work across districts, states, and nations, supported by AI-enhanced tutors and educator-designers who coordinate learning across physical and virtual environments. What was once called "remote learning" is no longer a stopgap or substitute. It has become a fully realized model of spatial, adaptive, and interdisciplinary engagement.

This transformation reflects more than the addition of new tools. It marks a deliberate shift away from the industrial-era structures that have constrained public education, including rigid time blocks, age-based cohorts, seat time requirements, and standardized assessments. By 2050, redesign has become not just a policy goal but a systemic necessity. The accelerating pace of technological, environmental, and social change requires schools to be flexible, learner-centered, and resilient.

At the heart of this future is a human-centered design. AI systems amplify, rather than replace, the expertise of educators by providing real-time insights, personalized supports, and adaptive learning pathways. Learning is no longer confined to static curricula but organized around authentic problems, interdisciplinary projects, and the development of durable competencies. Students build agency, creativity, and ethical reasoning instead of focusing solely on compliance or test performance.

Equity serves as the moral foundation of this redesign. By 2050, the notion of access has expanded beyond devices and broadband to include cultural relevance, accessible design, and learner dignity. The public education system has accepted its responsibility to close historical gaps, ensuring that race, geography, language, and disability status no longer determine opportunity. Governance models prioritize local flexibility, professional autonomy, and community voice, moving past bureaucratic control toward anticipatory and adaptive systems. Policy operates as the infrastructure for innovation rather than as a barrier.

Looking ahead, public education stands as a redefined civic institution. It integrates emerging technologies not as novelties but as catalysts for ethical and student-centered transformation. The challenge was never just to adopt new tools. It was to reimagine the purpose, values, and design of schooling itself. The framework for 2050 envisions learning systems that evolve, reflect, and regenerate in response to human needs and global change.

Redesigning the Purpose of School

For more than a century, public education has been anchored to goals of a past era of standardization, compliance, and preparation for predictable employment. These goals, once aligned with the needs of a manufacturing capitalist economy, no longer match the complexity, diversity, and pace of the quickly changing modern world. As we look toward 2050, the very notion of what constitutes a school must be redefined. Education is no longer confined to physical buildings or rigid time structures. It exists as a distributed public institution, both physical and virtual, that serves as a cornerstone of democratic life.

Redesigning the purpose of school requires more than updated curricula or modernized infrastructure. It calls for a fundamental shift in mission. Schools must evolve from credentialing centers and employment pipelines into launchpads for human potential. Their purpose must center on cultivating civic agency, ethical reasoning, emotional intelligence, cultural literacy, and the capacity for lifelong adaptation. In this future, success is no longer defined solely by standardized metrics but by the degree to which learners develop critical thinking, collaborative problem-solving, and a commitment to shaping a more just, inclusive, and sustainable society.

As a public institution, the school of 2050 must continue to serve as one of the few remaining civic spaces where individuals from diverse backgrounds engage in shared learning, deliberation, and problem-solving. Its value is not only instructional but also social and civic. Schools must prepare students to navigate a pluralistic world, contribute to democratic processes, and participate in the stewardship of local and global communities. They must nurture not only the competencies required for work but also those essential for citizenship and personal flourishing.

This redefinition demands the dismantling of outdated structural models. The boundaries between formal and informal learning will dissolve, as schools connect with homes, libraries, cultural centers, workplaces, and digital platforms. Interdisciplinary learning will replace narrow subject silos, and project-based inquiry will supplant fragmented assignments. Adaptive systems supported by AI will personalize learning pathways, while educators will serve as designers, facilitators, and ethical guides.

Technology will play a critical role, but its function must remain anchored in human-centered and equity-focused design. AI, XR, and data-driven systems must support learner agency, safeguard dignity, and amplify human connection rather than automate it. Schools must hold fast to their public mission: to ensure that educational opportunity is not a commodity accessible only to some, but a public good accessible to all.

By 2050, schools will stand as reimagined public institutions, designed not only to prepare individuals for employment but also to equip them for life in a rapidly changing and interconnected world. The purpose of education will be measured by its ability to help learners navigate uncertainty, innovate with responsibility, and contribute to the health of democratic and ecological systems. In this future, education will serve as the connective tissue of society, advancing not just personal success but the collective well-being of communities and the planet.

Learning Ecosystems, Not Institutions

The traditional school building will remain part of public education in 2050, but it will no longer serve as the exclusive or primary site of learning. Education must evolve into a dynamic ecosystem that spans hybrid, immersive, and place-based environments. Students will navigate fluidly between physical classrooms, virtual reality studios, AI-supported platforms, and community-based learning spaces. This shift redefines public education not as a single institution, but as a distributed network of interconnected learning opportunities.

In this emerging ecosystem, learner agency replaces passive compliance. Mastery-based progress replaces age-based grade levels, enabling students to advance according to demonstrated competencies rather than seat time. Holographic simulations and immersive XR environments will allow learners to explore complex systems and scenarios once inaccessible within the walls of a classroom. AI mentors will provide real-time feedback and adaptive guidance, complementing the expertise of human educators. Real-time translation systems will further expand these possibilities, allowing students to collaborate across languages and cultures without interruption. Prototypes of hearable devices already demonstrate the capacity to capture multiple speakers in noisy settings, translate their voices in real time, and preserve spatial cues and tone (Chen et al., 2025). Augmented reality glasses extend these tools to the visual world, instantly translating books, signage, or even graffiti, ensuring that written expression across languages remains accessible (Mucha et al., 2024). Together, these technologies embed multilingual engagement into the fabric of daily learning, transforming classrooms into global commons where communication barriers no longer restrict participation.

Community engaged projects will connect learners to local and global challenges, positioning education as both preparation for the future and active contribution to the present. This vision is not speculative fiction. It is an urgent design imperative. Without systemic transformation, public education will continue to mirror outdated industrial-era models that restrict creativity, agency, and equity. The move toward learning ecosystems reflects a recognition that education is no longer confined to discrete locations or fixed schedules. It is relational, adaptive, and deeply intertwined with the social, technological, and environmental systems that shape human life.

As a public institution, education must ensure that these ecosystems are not exclusive to privileged communities. Access to immersive technologies, translation systems, and interdisciplinary opportunities must be guaranteed as a matter of educational justice. The role of public governance will be to establish frameworks that protect equity, privacy, and dignity while enabling local adaptation and innovation. Educators will serve as designers of learning environments, curators of meaningful experiences, and mentors of ethical and collaborative practice.

By 2050, learning will no longer be organized solely within the walls of a school. It will take place across an ecosystem that bridges formal and informal, physical and digital, local and global contexts. This transformation will require bold leadership, sustained investment, and a shared societal commitment to reimagining education as a public good that prepares every learner to thrive in complexity and contribute to the collective future.

Human-Centered Technology and Equity by Design

Technology will not replace educators. Instead, it will amplify human connection and individualized learning. AI can support real-time feedback, enable multilingual access, and provide adaptive tools for neurodivergent learners. Yet, without intentional safeguards, technology can reinforce inequities. Therefore, digital equity must be embedded in every policy and platform from the outset. This includes universal broadband, device accessibility, multilingual support, and transparent, student-centered data ethics. Educational transformation that fails to close the opportunity gap is not true transformation. Equity must be the blueprint, not the retrofit.

Empowering Educators, Students, and Families

Artificial intelligence reshapes how educators extend their expertise rather than replacing it. In practice, AI can deliver real-time feedback, support multilingual communication, provide adaptive tools for neurodivergent learners, and enable personalized learning pathways aligned with individual strengths. These capabilities expand access for students historically underserved by conventional systems. At the same time, impact depends on design and governance. Without explicit safeguards, AI can reproduce bias, obscure decision-making, and intensify inequities rather than reduce them.

Digital equity must be embedded into every policy, platform, and practice from the start. It cannot be a retrofit or secondary consideration. Universal broadband access, device availability, adaptive interfaces, multilingual supports, and transparent, student-centered data governance are not enhancements. They are foundational infrastructure for any learning ecosystem that claims to serve all students. Equally critical is the commitment to cultural relevance, linguistic diversity, and universal design, ensuring that digital tools reflect the identities, histories, and needs of the communities they serve.

Educational transformation that fails to close the opportunity gap is not true transformation. It is replication under a new banner. Equity must function as the blueprint guiding every layer of educational design, from procurement decisions to platform development, from algorithmic auditing to classroom practice. This requires moving beyond narrow definitions of access or compliance toward a holistic commitment to justice, dignity, and inclusion.

The ethical integration of technology requires a fundamental reorientation of purpose. It is not about efficiency, automation, or productivity alone. It is about strengthening human potential, deepening learner agency, and fostering relational and intellectual growth. Every technological tool must be evaluated against the standard of whether it advances inclusion, cultivates curiosity, and supports meaningful human connection. AI is not an endpoint but a relational tool, amplifying educator judgment and learner voice. Data is not a commodity but a responsibility, demanding governance models that protect privacy, ensure transparency, and uphold student rights.

To achieve this, educational leaders must reject the false binary between innovation and ethics. Transformation and responsibility are not competing priorities; they are inseparable. Technology in education is only as transformative as the commitments, guardrails, and shared values that guide its design and use. Without these, the system risks accelerating existing hierarchies and exclusions under the guise of progress. With them, it holds the potential to become a powerful engine of equity, inclusion, and democratic renewal.

Empowering Educators, Students, and Families

At the center of this redesign is the human infrastructure of education. Educational transformation is not a product to deliver but a process to co-create. Educators, students, and families must be positioned not as passive recipients of change but as co-designers and stewards of the system's future. Their collective agency, expertise, and lived experience form the foundation on which meaningful and sustainable transformation must be built.

Educators will serve as architects of learning ecosystems, using AI-supported systems to deepen relationships, personalize instruction, and design authentic, interdisciplinary learning experiences. Their expertise will be amplified, not diminished, by technology. They will move beyond the role of content deliverers to become mentors, designers, and ethical guides, supporting students in developing critical thinking, creativity, and adaptive capacity. Professional learning will center not on compliance with external mandates but on collaboration, inquiry, and continuous improvement, supported by tools that expand teacher judgment and leadership.

Students will take on leadership roles not only in their own learning but in the governance and evolution of their schools. They will co-create learning pathways tailored to their interests and aspirations, engage in interdisciplinary capstone projects addressing real-world challenges, and participate as full partners in shaping school priorities and policies. Students will no longer be positioned as consumers of curriculum but as contributors to knowledge, civic life, and innovation. Their voices will carry weight in decision-making processes, and their insights will shape how learning environments evolve.

Families will serve as informed and empowered partners in this ecosystem. Equipped with real-time, accessible tools, they will monitor progress, engage in dialogue with educators, and help co-design educational priorities that reflect the needs and values of their communities. Families will be welcomed not as compliance monitors or occasional volunteers but as essential collaborators, contributing cultural knowledge, local expertise, and intergenerational perspective.

This collaborative redesign is not a departure from the original purpose of public education; it is a return to it. At its best, public education has always been a civic institution intended to foster human development, social cohesion, and shared opportunity. Its foundational promise was to serve as a public good, ensuring that all individuals, regardless of background, identity, or geography, have access to the knowledge, skills, and relationships needed to participate fully in democratic life and human flourishing. By re-centering public education as human-centered, equity-driven, and universally guaranteed, we reclaim its original purpose while preparing it for the demands of an interconnected and rapidly changing world.

This redesign moves beyond top-down compliance models and institutional silos, building a system rooted in distributed agency, shared accountability, and civic partnership. It recognizes that educational transformation cannot be achieved through institutional mandates or technological fixes alone. Lasting change requires co-creation with those most directly engaged in the work of learning and teaching, grounded in relationships of trust, mutual respect, and shared purpose.

By 2050, public education has the opportunity to stand as a global model of human-centered, equity-driven, and ethically guided transformation. It can serve not only as a system for delivering instruction but also as a civic platform for developing the capacities, commitments, and connections needed to sustain democracy, advance justice, and foster human flourishing. Anything less would fall short of the public mission it is called to fulfill.

The Power Is Yours!

This future cannot be realized through marginal adjustments or isolated pilots. It requires bold, coordinated action across every level of the education ecosystem. Policymakers must reimagine funding models to prioritize equity instead of inertia. District leaders must embed interoperability, student privacy, and innovation into long-term strategies. State and federal agencies must replace outdated accountability structures with measures that reflect student agency, well-being, and meaningful contribution. Every delay perpetuates a system built for a world that no longer exists.

This book is a roadmap, not a script. It does not claim to offer every answer, but it provides a coherent, research-grounded framework for those ready to lead. The future will not be shaped by those who fear change. It will be shaped by those who are willing to challenge assumptions, dismantle obsolete structures, and lead with vision, courage, and purpose.

Your actions, whether local or incremental, are the first stone cast into still water. The ripples will extend outward, shaping classrooms, schools, communities, and public systems for years to come. The challenge is not only to make an impact but also to ensure that impact evolves with time, adapting to new needs and possibilities rather than hardening into new forms of rigidity. We must not redesign public education only to freeze it in place for another century.

The future of public education will not be built by perfect plans, but by the collective courage to let go of what no longer serves and to design, together, what every learner deserves. As the late 1990s superhero Captain Planet says, "The power is yours." Let this be the moment we choose possibility over preservation, purpose over hesitation, and transformation over accommodation. Take that first step.

The future belongs to the learners we serve today and will be shaped by those willing to take responsibility for building what comes next.

References

Chen, T., Wang, Q., He, R., & Gollakota, S. (2025). *Spatial speech translation: Translating across space with binaural hearables*. Proceedings of the 2025 CHI Conference on Human Factors in Computing Systems. https://doi.org/10.1145/3706598.3713745

Mucha, W., Cuconasu, F., Etori, N. A., Kalokyri, V., & Trappolini, G. (2024). TEXT2TASTE: A versatile egocentric vision system for intelligent reading assistance using large language models. In *Computers helping people with special needs* (Lecture Notes in Computer Science, pp. 285–291). Springer. https://doi.org/10.1007/978-3-031-62849-8_35

Appendix

Vocabulary and Terms

Adaptive Learning Systems (Chapter 1: Legacy without Progress)
Educational technologies that adjust the content, pace, and instructional approach based on individual student performance data, providing personalized pathways to mastery.

Adaptive Physical and Digital Infrastructure (Chapters 8 and 18: Modernizing Infrastructure and Governance; Embedding Innovation)
Flexible and responsive learning spaces, both physical and virtual, designed to accommodate diverse student needs, emerging technologies, and evolving pedagogical practices.

Artificial Intelligence (AI) (Chapters 5 and 9: Beyond Smart; Advancing Equity in the Age of AI)
AI supports personalized learning, automates administrative tasks, and enables predictive analytics, raising important ethical and equity considerations.

Civic Compact (Chapter 10: The Institutional Anchor)
An agreement among educators, families, policymakers, and communities to uphold shared responsibilities for advancing equity and innovation.

Cross-Sector Collaboration (Chapters 12 and 18: Reimagining Support Systems through Innovation and Partnership; Embedding Innovation)
Partnerships between education and other sectors to address complex challenges and expand opportunities.

Human–AI Collaboration (Chapters 5 and 6: Beyond Smart; From Instructor to Architect)

Blending human judgment, creativity, and empathy with AI's analytical power to enhance teaching and learning.

Shared Governance (Chapter 12: Reimagining Support Systems through Innovation and Partnership)
Decision-making distributed among educators, families, students, and policymakers to build trust and sustainability.

Student Agency (Chapters 1, 3, 4, 5, and 16: Legacy without Progress; The Great Pivot; Defining Personalized Learning; Beyond Smart; Beyond Readiness)
The capacity of students to set goals, make choices, and own their learning.

Universal Design for Learning (UDL) (Chapters 4 and 5: Defining Personalized Learning; Beyond Smart)
An instructional framework providing flexible goals, methods, and assessments to meet diverse learner needs.

Systemic Alignment (Chapter 16: Beyond Readiness)
Coordination of policies, practices, and resources to create coherence in advancing shared educational goals.

Illustrative/Emerging Models

Extended Reality (XR) Learning Ecosystems (Chapters 5 and 17: Beyond Smart; Transformation by Design)
Learning environments that integrate virtual reality (VR), augmented reality (AR), and mixed reality (MR) to create immersive, adaptive, and place-independent experiences.

Innovation Zones (Chapter 17: Transformation by Design)
Policy-enabled spaces where schools or districts can pilot innovative practices with regulatory flexibility.

Intergenerational Learning Pods (Chapter 17: Transformation by Design)

Small, mixed-age groups designed to exchange knowledge and build community through learning.

Micro-School Networks (Chapter 17: Transformation by Design)
Independent, small-scale schools linked for shared resources and personalized learning.

Neurodiversity-Centered Learning Labs (Chapter 17: Transformation by Design)
Inclusive spaces designed to leverage the strengths of neurodiverse learners with individualized supports.

Schools Without Buildings (Chapter 17: Transformation by Design)
Education models operating outside fixed physical locations, often virtual or community-based.

Transformation Labs (Chapter 17: Transformation by Design)
Small-scale, local pilots designed to test and refine new models before scaling systemwide.

For Product Safety Concerns and Information please contact our EU representative GPSR@taylorandfrancis.com
Taylor & Francis Verlag GmbH, Kaufingerstraße 24, 80331 München, Germany

www.ingramcontent.com/pod-product-compliance
Lightning Source LLC
Chambersburg PA
CBHW061426300426
44114CB00014B/1558